NINJA Foodi
The pressure cooker that crisps.

ONE-POT COOKBOOK

NINJA Foodi

The pressure cooker that crisps.

ONE-POT
COOKBOOK

100 Fast and Flavorful Meals
to Maximize Your Foodi™

Janet A. Zimmerman

Foreword by Elizabeth Karmel
Photography by Hélène Dujardin

ROCKRIDGE
PRESS

To Dave, as always.

CONTENTS

Foreword x

Say Good-bye to Your Stovetop
and Oven xii

1 Revolutionizing the One-Pot Meal 1

2 Breakfast 19

Monkey Bread 20

Tex-Mex Breakfast Casserole 22

Scotch Eggs 24

French Cinnamon Toast 26

Savory Custards with Bacon
and Cheese 28

Egg Muffin Breakfast Sandwich 30

Artichoke and Red Pepper
Frittata 32

Sausage-Mushroom Strata 34

Apple Turnovers 36

Shakshuka 38

Creamy Steel-Cut Oats with
Toasted Almonds 40

Breakfast Clafoutis 42

3 Meatless Mains 45

Penne with Mushrooms
and Gruyère 46

Easy Eggplant Parmesan 48

Mediterranean White
Bean Salad 50

Cajun Twice-Baked Potatoes 52

"Spanish" Rice and Beans 54

Minestrone with Garlic Cheese
Toasts and Pesto 56

Vegetable Korma 58

Masoor Dal (Indian
Red Lentils) 60

Creamy Pasta Primavera 62

Kung Pao Tofu and Peppers 64

Risotto with Chard, Caramelized
Onions, and Mushrooms 66

Mushroom Lasagna 68

Roasted Red Pepper Soup and
Grilled Cheese 70

Tunisian Chickpea Soup 72

4 Poultry 75

Sesame-Garlic Chicken Wings 76

Quick Cassoulet 78

Spicy Air-Crisped Chicken
and Potatoes 80

Chicken Fajitas with Refritos 82

Braised Chicken Thighs with
Mushrooms and Artichokes 84

Chicken and Spinach
Quesadillas 86

Cajun Chicken and Dumplings 88

Chicken Caesar Salad 90

Chicken Tikka Masala
with Rice 93

Tandoori Chicken and
Coconut Rice 96

Chicken Shawarma with
Garlic-Yogurt Sauce 98

Cajun Roasted Turkey Breast with
Sweet Potatoes 100

Easy Chicken Cordon Bleu with
    Green Beans 102
Chicken Chili Verde
    with Nachos 104
Coq au Vin 106
Italian Wedding Soup with
    Turkey Sausage 108
Chicken Stroganoff 110
Turkey and Wild Rice Salad 112

5 Meat 115

Honey-Mustard Spare Ribs 116
Carnitas 118
Sunday Pot Roast and
    Biscuits 120
Beefy Onion Soup with
    Cheese Croutons 122
Kielbasa with Braised Cabbage
    and Noodles 124
Pork Ragu with Penne 126
Chorizo-Stuffed Peppers 128
Southwestern Shepherd's Pie 130
Sausage and Pepper Calzones 132
Simple Potato Gratin with
    Ham and Peas 135
Pork Lo Mein with Vegetables 137
Meatloaf and Mashed
    Potatoes 139
Jerk Pork 141
Japanese Pork Cutlets (Tonkatsu)
    with Ramen 143
Beef Satay with Peanut Sauce 145
Italian Beef Sandwiches 148
Deviled Short Ribs
    with Noodles 150
Carbonnade Flamande 152
Pork Tenderloin with Peppers and
    Roasted Potatoes 154
Sloppy Joes 156

6 Seafood 159

Bow Tie Pasta with Shrimp
    and Arugula 160
Lax Pudding 162
Warm Potato and Green Bean
    Salad with Tuna 164
Teriyaki Salmon and
    Vegetables 166
Shrimp and Vegetable
    Egg Rolls 168
Clam Chowder with
    Parmesan Crackers 171
Crab and Roasted
    Asparagus Risotto 173
Thai Fish Curry 175
Blackened Salmon with
    Creamy Grits 177
Salmon Cakes 179
Shrimp and Sausage Gumbo 182
Tilapia Veracruz 184
Cheesy Tuna Noodle
    Casserole 186
Potato-Crusted Cod with
    Succotash 188
Quinoa Pilaf with Smoked Trout
    and Corn 190
Trout Florentine 192

7 **Desserts** 195

Mixed Berry Crisp **196**
Peach Cobbler **198**
Chocolate Marble
  Cheesecake **200**
Crème Brûlée **202**
Lemon Bars **204**
Tarte Tatin **207**
Blueberry Cream Tart **208**
Caramel-Pecan Brownies **211**
Mocha Pots de Crème **213**
Spiced Poached Pears **214**

8 **Kitchen Staples** 217

Chicken Stock **218**
Roasted Vegetable Stock **219**
Sautéed Mushrooms **220**
Caramelized Onions **222**
Cajun Seasoning Mix **223**
Mexican/Southwestern
  Seasoning Mix **224**
Teriyaki Sauce **225**
Barbecue Sauce **226**
Mustard Sauce **227**
Marinara Sauce **228**

Ninja® Foodi™ Cooking Time
  Charts **231**
Measurement Conversions **244**
The Dirty Dozen™ and
  The Clean Fifteen™ **246**
Index **247**

FOREWORD

One thing you need to know about me is that besides being a chef and cookbook author, I am a housewares junkie and I love new kitchen appliances and gadgets.

But let's face it, everyone is busy, and fitting meal prep into our daily routine can be a challenge, especially if you want fresh, wholesome and satisfying meals. So if something comes along that can make the job easier and deliver high-quality home-cooked meals, why not try it?

The Ninja® Foodi™ is one such appliance and it is going to change the way you cook at home. The combination of pressure cooking and crisping, a.k.a. TenderCrisp™ Technology builds flavor and texture in your one-pot meals. And, one-pot meals mean less clean up, less prep, and fewer tools.

The electric pressure cooker is a staple in many kitchens, but personally speaking, I never used one before because I knew that all the food that came out of it was going to be the same texture. This is where the Ninja® Foodi™ makes all the difference. Not only does it cut down on time spent on making a meal and cleaning it up, but the Crisping Lid takes meals to the next level.

On my first test drive, I made a simple yet immensely satisfying dish: chicken and rice. Pressure cooking works by building super-heated steam that cooks food at a super high temperature. As a chef, I knew I needed to add extra flavor so that I wouldn't end up with bland chicken so I used chicken stock, white wine and a homemade spice rub to up the flavor ante. There was very little prep to do and I threw everything into the pot at once. After I pressure cooked the chicken and rice together, I used the Crisping Lid to add the finishing touch.

I could not believe the results. Not only was the rice silky and perfect, but even more, the chicken was crispy on the outside and tender and succulent in the inside. With the Crisping Lid, the Foodi™ has re-written the definition of a one-pot meal by adding the possibility of crispy textures to our favorite tender flavor-filled dishes.

One of my favorite ways to use the Foodi™ is to make pasta, and this book features crowd-pleasing, restaurant-worthy options like Mushroom Lasagna (page 68). This pasta dish exemplifies the benefits of the Foodi™ After throwing everything into the appliance, you can simultaneously make the homemade sauce and cook the lasagna noodles al dente. Once done, the dish is topped with cheese and the Crisper Lid works its magic! It melts the cheese and browns it, leaving the cheese ooeey and gooey and crisping around the edges just like my favorite wood-fired oven.

The other recipes in this book also focus on delivering exceptional one-pot experiences. And, they were developed using everyday ingredients to make extraordinary everyday meals. Simple ingredients are transformed in the Foodi™ and deliver dishes that are as impressive as they are quick and easy.

We crave flavor and texture equally. And, it's the combination of flavors and textures that make your favorite dishes so irresistible. Take cream brûlée for example. That creamy sweet custard topped with a crisp burnt caramelized sugar. If it was only custard, you would get bored eating it after a bite or two. The crunchy texture is what keeps you coming back for more. Lucky for you, you can now make Crème Brûlée (page 202) and so many other tender, crispy recipes at home with your Foodi.™

That is why the Ninja® Foodi™ is a meal-making gamechanger. It has the capacity to infuse your food with flavor and finish the dish with a caramelized, roasty toasty crispy crust…giving you the kinds of flavors and textures we crave—all in one pot.

If you are like me, the more you use your Foodi,™ the more you will love it! All the flavor, all the texture in less time that it takes to go to a restaurant. And, the beauty of the Foodi™ is that you don't have to be a chef to use it. It does all the work for you. The Foodi™ gives you the power of a restaurant kitchen in your own home.

Have fun with your Foodi!

ELIZABETH KARMEL
Chef, Author, Media Personality & Entrepreneur

SAY GOOD-BYE TO YOUR STOVETOP AND OVEN

Even though I love to cook, I haven't always had the luxury of indulging my passion. For much of my working life, the daily routine of getting dinner on the table felt like a lengthy, laborious chore. After eight hours at work and a long, grueling commute, the last thing I wanted to do was stand in the kitchen and cook, not eat dinner until 10 p.m., and then wake up to a kitchen full of dirty dishes. So, most evenings, I found myself picking up something from the deli or the taqueria, or ordering Indian or Chinese delivery—not always the healthiest or most budget-friendly choices.

Even with the best intentions for homemade family meals, very few of us have the time, desire, creativity, or energy to cook dinner from scratch every night. Sure, every so often a kitchen innovation comes along that claims to make dinner a breeze—but seldom really does. Microwaves are great, but who actually cooks meals with one? And yes, those meal kits are a boon for some, but they're expensive, and you still eat at 10 p.m. and end up with a sink full of dirty dishes.

Slow cookers, electric pressure cookers, and "multi-cookers" that do both have proven to be an answer for many of today's harried cooks. Most of the cooking process is hands-off, which allows a busy parent to help kids with homework, or finish folding laundry, or do the million other things that need doing around the house. Meals are ready to be eaten at or near "real" dinner times, either because the food cooks while you're at work (slow cooker) or because it cooks much faster than traditional methods (pressure cooker). And, happily, these appliances produce mostly "one-pot" dinners, so cleanup is minimal.

Another thing about these appliances—and it's not trivial—is that for many people, they've kindled a love of cooking (or at least a new non-hatred of it), and a spirit of experimentation. When an indifferent cook can make beef stew from scratch in one hour, and it's edible—even delicious—it can turn what used to be a loathed chore into something pleasurable.

The one big drawback to these wonder appliances, though, is they're limited in the types of meals they can produce in just one pot. They cook with steam, or pressure and steam, which means lots of soups and stews and braises. And that's fine as far as it goes, unless you also want to fire up the oven or stovetop to start or finish the meal. But for most people, the fewer dishes and fewer appliances used, the better.

Frankly speaking, man and woman do not live by soup alone. We also crave foods with crispy and crunchy textures but without all that oil and mess. That's where the Ninja® Foodi™ comes in. It's an air crisper *and* pressure cooker in just one appliance. Using the Ninja Foodi, you can quickly and with very little mess turn out an almost limitless variety of tasty, tender, and crispy meals in one pot. No need to turn on the oven or stove, or fill up that sink with dirty dishes.

In this book, you'll find recipes that vary not only in flavors, textures, and cuisines, but also in the amount of time and energy they take to complete—all in one pot. Most make full meals with no side dishes required. Some recipes are easy, taking around 30 minutes or so, and make perfect weeknight dinners, while others are more elaborate and probably better suited to the weekend. Whatever your occasion, cooking skills, time, and energy level, you'll find something that brings out your inner chef, making cooking less of a chore and more an activity to be enjoyed.

You'll save money cooking at home, and you'll eat healthier as a result. Also, less time in the kitchen means more time for doing the things you actually want to do. You'll be able to connect with friends, family, and loved ones; read a book; catch up on your favorite series; or whatever you like to do when you have some precious extra minutes.

I hope that with a little time and the information and recipes in this book, you'll come to love cooking as much as I do.

1

Revolutionizing the One-Pot Meal

For busy cooks, getting delicious and nutritious meals on the table easily, with a variety of flavors and textures but a minimum of fuss and mess, might seem an impossible task—the Holy Grail of the kitchen, as it were. But with the Ninja® Foodi,™ it's possible to do just that.

Left: Southwestern Shepherd's Pie, page 130

TENDERCRISP™ TECHNOLOGY

The beauty of the Ninja® Foodi™ is you can use it to prepare foods with a variety of textures—steamed, crisped, baked, braised—in one pot. Sure, you can make great soups and braises with a pressure cooker, and you can use an air fryer to get crisp foods. But if you want meals and dishes that combine the two, you need counter space to store more than one appliance, and a multitude of pots and pans. *That is, until now.* The Ninja Foodi is unique in today's kitchen: *It's the pressure cooker that also crisps.*

USING YOUR FOODI'S FUNCTIONS

This TenderCrisp effect is possible with one appliance because of the Foodi's unique design: two lids that cook with different functions.

The Pressure Lid and Its Functions

The **Pressure Lid** is separate and detachable from the appliance base and turns your Foodi into a *pressure cooker, steamer,* or *slow cooker!* The lid must be locked into place, which is easy to do: Just align the arrow on the base with the arrow on the lid and turn the lid clockwise.

A valve on the top of the lid seals the unit for *pressure cooking* (Seal) with two levels (7.25 psi on Low, 11.6 psi on High). The valve can be opened for *steaming* (such as for vegetables) or *slow cooking* (soups and stews, for example), and also for releasing pressure after pressure cooking (Vent).

Pressure Cooking

For pressure cooking, the Foodi allows you to choose the pressure level (High or Low) and the time. The screen on the Foodi indicates when the pressure is building and when it's reached the proper level, at which point the timer automatically starts. After the Foodi reaches the selected pressure level, the heat is regulated to maintain that pressure until cooking is complete. At that point, you can leave it alone so the pressure drops naturally, or move the valve to Vent to quickly release the pressure, or use a combination. You do, however, have to wait for the pressure pin to drop before you can open the lid.

Steaming

You can also steam foods without pressure using the Pressure Lid. Simply add water to the inner pot, insert a steaming rack and your food, and lock the lid

Under Pressure

In the simplest terms, pressure cookers work because the boiling point of liquid depends on the atmospheric pressure. In a conventional pot, water-based cooking liquids will never reach temperatures above 212°F. Water boils and turns to steam, and the steam dissipates, even if the pot has a lid. But in the sealed chamber of a pressure cooker, the water that turns to steam can't escape, which increases the pressure in the pot. With the higher pressure, more energy is necessary for the water to boil, so the boiling temperature rises as the steam builds up.

In the Ninja° Foodi,™ low pressure equals 7.25 psi, and high pressure equals 11.6 psi. That raises the working temperature (at sea level) to between 233°F/112°C (low pressure) and 243°F/117°C (high pressure). Once the pot comes to pressure, the liquid inside is *not* boiling. However, as the pressure reduces, either naturally or quickly through the steam vent, the still-hot liquid will begin to boil.

Because cooking under pressure requires boiling liquid, it's important to make sure you have enough. Since virtually no evaporation occurs once the lid is locked into place, you don't need a lot; generally, 1 cup or so is sufficient. And keep in mind that foods give off liquid while they cook, so with many dishes, beginning with around ¼ cup is fine.

into place with the valve set to Vent. The temperature is set automatically, so you simply have to set the time. You should not open the lid while steaming.

Slow Cooking

To slow cook, use the Pressure Lid with the valve set to Vent. Select the Slow Cook function, which has two levels, and set the time, which is adjustable for up to 12 hours.

Sear/Sauté

The final function on the Pressure section of the Foodi's panel is Sear/Sauté. Although you can use this function with the Pressure Lid in place, you'll likely want to leave it off so you can see and stir the food that is browning and sautéing before pressure cooking.

You can choose from five heat levels (Low, Medium-Low, Medium, Medium-High, and High) when you select the Sear/Sauté function, but you cannot set the time; the function stays on until you cancel it. You can, however, change from one heat level to another without turning the function off and starting over.

The Crisping Lid and Its Functions

With the innovative **Crisping Lid**, the Foodi™ becomes an *air crisper, broiler,* or *baking/roasting oven*. Adjustable temperatures (from 250°F to 450°F) and a built-in timer give you lots of flexibility in the types of dishes you can prepare and finish, and you don't need a ton of oil (and those added calories) to do it.

The Crisping Lid is permanently attached to the unit by a hinge. It opens and closes without locking and can be opened during any convection cooking function (as opposed to the pressure cooking functions), so you can turn, toss, or check on your ingredients. When the lid is opened, the cooking element turns off and the timer will pause. As soon as the lid is closed again, cooking and the timer resume.

Each Crisping Lid cooking function cooks with the same mechanics but has different temperature levels to choose from, meaning you can crisp food for the great crunchy texture we all love, bake or roast it, broil it, and, on some models, even dehydrate it.

Air Crisp

This setting is generally used with the included Cook & Crisp™ Basket, which allows for easy tossing of ingredients, but it can also be used with the Reversible Rack (also included). The temperature for this function range from 300°F to 400°F, and is adjustable as needed. Air Crisp works best with no liquid in the pot.

Bake/Roast

As its name suggests, this setting is used for baking or roasting. The temperature can be adjusted from 250°F to 400°F, and the setting can be used with the Reversible Rack in either the upper or lower position. It is generally the best cooking option for baking desserts or casseroles in heat-proof dishes.

Broil

The Broil function automatically sets to 450°F and is not adjustable, as this type of cooking requires the high heat. You can use this setting to brown and crisp food in the bottom of the inner pot, or with the Reversible Rack in either the upper or lower position.

OTHER ACCESSORIES AND EQUIPMENT

The Foodi™ comes with two accessories to use with its particular cooking functions. There are also several optional accessories available for purchase that might be of real value once you master the appliance and become more adventurous in your cooking.

The Reversible Rack

With its two levels, the Reversible Rack can be used for broiling (in the upper position) and for pressure cooking, steaming, and baking/roasting (in the lower position).

The Cook & Crisp™ Basket

This basket is specially designed for air crisping. The bottom is removable for easier cleaning.

Additional Accessories and Equipment

The following are available for purchase and will make cooking with your Foodi more fun and versatile:

Cook & Crisp™ Layered Insert. This increases the capacity of the Cook & Crisp Basket, enabling you to create layered meals and also crisp more food at once.

Roasting Rack Insert. This rack, which fits in the Cook & Crisp Basket, is handy if you like to roast or glaze ribs.

The Multi-Purpose Pan or a metal or ceramic 1- to 1.5-quart bowl. You'll want one of these for cooking "pot-in-pot" dishes such as quiches, cakes, brownies, or casseroles. Make sure it's no more than about 8½ inches across. The Multi-Purpose Pan, sold by Ninja, is perfect for this purpose, but you may already have a suitable bowl.

An extra sealing ring or two. Not only can the silicone ring pick up odors (see FAQ, page 13, for advice on how to minimize this), but despite its durability, it can become stretched or nicked from frequent use. If your sealing ring is compromised, you can't use your pot. Make sure you buy the ones designed for the Foodi, as other brands' rings will not fit correctly.

THE NINJA® FOODI™

Pressure Release Valve
Easily release pressure.

Pressure Lid
Quickly tenderize and cook ingredients.

Reversible Rack
Use to steam, or reverse to broil.

Cook & Crisp™ Basket
4-quart nonstick, ceramic-coated basket fits 3 lbs of French fries.

Crisping Lid
Use to finish off pressure cooked recipes or to air fry your food.

Cooking Pot
6.5-quart nonstick, ceramic-coated cooking pot, fits a 6-lb roast.

14 Levels of Safety
Passed rigorous testing to earn UL safety certification, giving you peace of mind.

Safety First

Today's pressure cookers, including the Foodi," are equipped with multiple safety features, but you should always exercise caution when cooking under pressure.

- *Always*, and carefully, open the lid *away from you* when removing it.

- *Never* force the lid open.

- *Always* keep your hands away from the steam escaping from the vent.

- *Never* fill the pot more than two-thirds full (and only half full if you're cooking anything that expands or foams, like pasta, rice, oatmeal, or beans).

An extra Reversible Rack, or a round 8-inch wire cooling rack. Some recipes call for using the rack twice in one recipe (once for steaming and once for broiling). An extra rack makes this easier. While a cooling rack is good only for the lower position, it's still quite handy to have.

Aside from the included accessories, I find that just a few common pieces of kitchen equipment are all that are needed when using this versatile appliance. While the Reversible Rack that comes with the Foodi can be used for steaming small amounts of food, you'll be able to fit a lot more food in a silicone steamer basket. If you plan to make desserts such as cheesecake, a small (7-inch) springform pan or deep cake pan with a removable bottom is indispensable. Other kitchen tools that will be very useful include sturdy tongs, an immersion blender, a fat separator, a meat thermometer, and an extra timer. You will also want nonslip potholders or finger mitts. Nonstick aluminum foil and parchment paper will also come in handy for many recipes.

ONE-POT CONVENIENCE

The Ninja® Foodi™ offers home cooks the advantage of cooking an entire meal in one pot, whether your tastes run to meat and potatoes with a vegetable on the side, or stews and soups, or main dish casseroles. Unlike stand-alone pressure cookers, the unique TenderCrisp™ technology of the Foodi can finish a dish that would otherwise require browning in the oven or frying in oil for a crispy, crunchy texture. And unlike a dedicated air fryer, the Foodi produces tender, juicy meat or saucy pasta. It's the best of both worlds.

Frozen to Crispy

For a true one-pot experience, use the Foodi™ to defrost frozen foods under pressure, and then crisp them with the Crisping Lid.

A few foods, such as thin fish fillets or shrimp, can be cooked in minutes under pressure along with a sauce (for instance, Tilapia Veracruz, page 184), or even steamed alone. The Air Crisp function is a natural for frozen foods like French fries or breaded chicken nuggets.

In general, the smaller and more evenly shaped the frozen food, the better it will cook, either under pressure or with the Air Crisp function. Frozen chicken wing segments are a better choice than a whole frozen chicken or a block of frozen chicken breasts. And always use the timing suggested for your frozen food of choice.

360 Meals

When you want a homemade meal with multiple components, made quickly and without using multiple pots and pans, look no further than your new Foodi. Pressure cook part of the meal, then finish it by roasting or broiling, for a main dish and sides in less time than it takes to wait for takeout. Create fabulous meals like these:

- Pork Lo Mein with Vegetables in 30 minutes (page 137)

- Easy Chicken Cordon Bleu with Green Beans in 35 minutes (page 102)

- Potato-Crusted Cod with Succotash in 35 minutes (page 188)

- Kielbasa with Braised Cabbage and Noodles in 35 minutes (page 124)

One-Pot Wonders

One-pot dishes can be lifesavers to the busy home cook, but let's face it, they can get monotonous. Now, though, with your Ninja® Foodi™ you can enhance your favorite stews, pasta dishes, or soups—even desserts—with a finishing touch that elevates them from simple to spectacular.

- Turn savory beef chili into an impressive Southwestern Shepherd's Pie (page 130).

- Top delicious chicken and vegetables with crusty herb dumplings in Cajun Chicken and Dumplings (page 88).

Mix-and-Match Cooking

Most recipes in this book make full meals, either one-pot dishes or the components for a whole dinner. (Okay, maybe you'll need a salad every now and then). But as you become familiar with the Foodi™ and these recipes, you'll quickly see just how easy it is to combine components from various recipes for almost endless variety. Here's just a sample of some possible combinations:

SIDE DISHES	PROTEIN
Succotash (page 188)	Meatloaf (page 139)
Mashed Potatoes (page 139)	Cajun Roasted Turkey Breast (page 100)
Sweet Potatoes (page 100)	Japanese Pork Cutlets (page 143)
Lo Mein (page 137)	Broiled Shrimp (see Bow Tie Pasta with Shrimp and Arugula, page 160)
Green Beans (page 102)	Blackened Salmon (page 177)
Coconut Rice (page 96)	Chicken Shawarma (page 98)

Some recipes lend themselves to almost endless variation, too. For instance, once you learn how to make risotto (page 66), or quesadillas (page 86), you can add or substitute ingredients or fillings to your liking. Such recipes also include customization tips for ideas on improvising.

In addition, pair the sauces and spice rubs from Kitchen Staples (page 217) with pretty much any protein. Try them on chicken wings, chicken thighs, pork tenderloin, salmon, flank steak—even some vegetables such as potatoes, broccoli, cauliflower, sweet potatoes, or green beans—to easily tailor meals to your family's tastes.

- Boost hearty minestrone (page 56) with crunchy garlic cheese toasts that cook while the soup finishes.

- Layer eggy chilaquiles with crispy nachos for an easy but showy Tex-Mex Breakfast Casserole (page 22).

CHOOSING YOUR MEAT AND SEAFOOD FOR THE NINJA® FOODI™

One of the great things about the Foodi is that, with its dual cooking methods of pressure cooking *and* crisping, it can handle all kinds of proteins, from quick-cooking tender shrimp to tough cuts of meat like pork shoulder. Just pick the right cut for the recipe, and you're ready to go.

Pantry Staples

Most cooks have a pantry (either an actual pantry or a few shelves in a cabinet) that contains the ingredients they turn to regularly. Your pantry will depend on the types of cuisine you like to cook as well as your personal tastes. The recipes in this book cross geographical boundaries and call upon various flavor profiles. Following is a partial list of the staples the recipes call for.

SHELF STAPLES

- Beans: various types, dried and canned
- Broth:
    - Low-sodium or unsalted beef broth
    - Low-sodium or unsalted chicken broth (or make your own Chicken Stock, page 218)
    - Low-sodium or unsalted vegetable broth (or make your own Roasted Vegetable Stock, page 219)
- Canned diced tomatoes (I like fire roasted, but any type will work.)
- Canned whole tomatoes (Italian are nice but not absolutely necessary.)
- Cooking oil spray or your own oil in a mister
- Extra-virgin olive oil

- Hot sauce, such as Tabasco or Sriracha
- Jarred roasted red peppers
- Panko bread crumbs (Try to find a Japanese brand; I like Kikkoman.)
- Pasta: farfalle, penne, shells, linguine
- Potato flakes
- Rice: primarily long-grain white rice but also basmati and wild rice
- Strained tomatoes (I recommend Pomi brand) or tomato sauce
- Vinegar: red wine, rice, sherry, and white wine
- Wine: dry red and white wines (if you're not a wine drinker, 4-packs of small bottles are a great option), and dry sherry

ASIAN COOKING STAPLES

- Asian chile-garlic sauce (I like Lee Kum Kee brand)
- Hoisin sauce
- Oyster sauce

- Soy sauce
- Thai curry paste (I prefer Mae Ploy brand)

MEXICAN/SOUTHWEST COOKING STAPLES

- Canned chipotles (I usually purée the whole can; it lasts for weeks and I can use exactly what I need.)

- Salsa: red and green (I like Frontera brand.)

SPICES (BEYOND THE USUAL)

- Black peppercorns for freshly ground pepper

- Cajun Seasoning Mix (page 223) or a store-bought mix

- Kosher salt (My recipes are developed using Diamond brand kosher salt, which is coarser than table salt. If you don't use it, use the quantity of fine salt given in the recipes.)

- Mexican/Southwestern Seasoning Mix (page 224), or a store-bought mix

- Smoked paprika (sweet rather than hot)

REFRIGERATOR STAPLES

- Butter, unsalted (I use unsalted butter; if you prefer salted butter, you may want to slightly reduce the amount of salt used in the recipe.)

- Heavy (whipping) cream

- Parmesan or similar cheese (It isn't necessary to use Parmigiano-Reggiano, the official Italian cheese, as there are good domestic versions available, but try to avoid bags of grated cheese, and definitely avoid the green can. A bonus to grating your own is that you can save the rinds in the freezer—they're great for soups.)

- Sour cream

- Whole milk

- Whole-milk yogurt or Greek yogurt

FREEZER STAPLES

- IQF (individually quick frozen) raw shrimp

- Orange juice concentrate

- Parmesan rinds (see Refrigerator Staples, above)

- Tilapia or cod fillets (frozen)

FREEZER OR REFRIGERATOR STAPLES

Once made, both of these can be refrigerated for up to 1 week or frozen for up to 6 weeks.

- Caramelized Onions (page 222)

- Sautéed Mushrooms (page 220)

Meats

Pressure cookers excel at cooking tougher cuts of meat such as beef or pork shoulder, ribs, lamb shanks, or oxtails. The two most popular cuts for pressure cooking are beef shoulder (called chuck roast or steak) and pork shoulder (also called pork butt and, when cut into strips, country-style ribs). These are the meats that cook to delicious tenderness and can be shredded for carnitas, pulled pork, or barbecue beef sandwiches. They can also be cubed and cooked in stews and chilis, or left whole and cooked as roasts. The bonus when cooking in the Foodi™ is that after pressure cooking, you can brown and crisp up carnitas, or glaze and broil ribs to get that crispy, gooey exterior.

The leaner, more tender cuts such as pork tenderloin or sirloin steak are excellent candidates for roasting or broiling, which the Foodi also does! These cuts can also be cooked under pressure, if you prefer; they just take more attention and much less time.

Poultry

Like meat, poultry cuts, whether chicken, turkey, or duck, fall into two general categories: lean, tender breast cuts, and the more resilient thighs and wings. Despite the fact that they come from the same bird, they should not be substituted for each other.

First, let's look at chicken breasts. When selecting, it's best to go with thick cuts or frozen pieces (any cut), as either will work well for 360 Meals. If you have only thin cutlets or tenders, they are best cooked with the Air Crisp or Broil function and cook better if they are sliced or cut into pieces (see Chicken Fajitas with Refritos, page 82). Whole turkey breasts can be cooked to perfection with a combination cooking method: starting them under pressure and finishing with roasting to crisp the skin.

Chicken thighs, either bone-in or boneless, are extremely versatile. They can be pressure cooked without overcooking, but when boned and flattened, they can also be marinated and broiled. Options abound.

Seafood

Most seafood cooks so quickly that it's usually best to skip pressure cooking, but there are a couple of exceptions. For ultimate convenience, frozen fish fillets can be cooked very quickly under pressure—just add a sauce and you'll have dinner in a flash. Try the Tilapia Veracruz (page 184) and see how easy it is. Mussels and clams can be steamed beautifully, either under pressure or without. However, in most cases, you'll want to cook seafood using the Air Crisp, Bake/Roast, or Broil settings. They can be served just as they are or used in a dish like Bow Tie Pasta with Shrimp and Arugula (page 160).

NINJA® FOODI™ FAQ

Q Can I double the recipes?

Doubling a recipe can often be done, but it will almost always change the length of time a recipe takes to cook, either because of increased time to reach pressure, or because of needing multiple batches of air-crisped or broiled ingredients. For safety and functionality, remember to never exceed the PRESSURE MAX fill level when pressure cooking.

Q Can I use recipes designed for other pressure cookers?

Most well-written pressure cooker recipes will work in the Foodi as long as they are written for a unit with a capacity of less than 6 quarts. For recipes with very short cooking times, you may find it necessary to adjust the cook time.

Q Is it okay to roast or broil foods with nothing in the bottom of the inner pot?

Yes. In fact, the Air Crisp function works best with no liquid in the pot. It's fine to broil or roast food on the rack with or without food or liquid below. For some tasks, like cooking cakes or breads, a little water in the bottom helps ensure a better texture.

Q Are the Foodi's parts dishwasher safe?

All the accessories are dishwasher safe, as is the inner pot. The sealing ring in the Pressure Lid can be removed and cleaned in the dishwasher, *but the lid itself is not dishwasher safe*. The base, Pressure Lid, and Crisping Lid should be cleaned with a sponge or dishcloth and wiped dry.

Q My sealing ring smells like curry/garlic/chile. How can I get the smell out?

Ideally, remove the sealing ring after every time you use your pot and wash and dry it, either by hand or in the dishwasher. Then leave it out of the lid to air. Some cooks swear by leaving it in the sun, or in the freezer, or storing it in a bag of ground coffee. I don't find that these help much, but then I don't notice any transfer of flavors from my ring. Some people may be more sensitive to smells, so if that's the case with you, consider buying an extra ring (or two).

Q The Seal valve seems loose. Is it supposed to be?

Yes, the valve easily moves from Seal to Vent without an audible click or other sign that it's in place. When doing a quick pressure release, you may find that you need to jiggle it a bit to get the steam to release in a steady stream. Just take care to keep your hand and face away from the steam.

Q Can I open the lid while cooking?

If you are using any of the convection settings—Air Crisp, Broil, or Bake/Roast—you can open the lid at any time. The cooking and timer will pause and only restart when you close the lid.

While pressure cooking or steaming, you should never open the lid until cooking is complete; when pressure cooking, you will not be able to. While sautéing, you generally don't use a lid, but if you do, it's fine to open it whenever you need to.

Q Do I need to preheat the Foodi™ when using the crisping/roasting functions?

While not necessary, you will have better results if you let the unit preheat for 5 minutes before cooking. If you are using the Cook & Crisp™ Basket, place that inside the unit so it can preheat as well.

Q Can I adjust the temperature when sautéing or searing?

Yes, just press the Temperature up and down arrows twice, and the unit will continue at the new setting.

Q Why do some foods (vegetables and rice, for instance) seem to call for different cook times in different recipes?

With vegetables, this may have to do with how they are cut—a whole head of cauliflower will take longer than florets, and cubed potatoes will cook much more quickly than whole potatoes. Sometimes the difference is due to how the food is being prepared—potatoes for mashing can cook much longer than potatoes for a salad, for instance. With rice, the timing has to do with how it's cooked. Rice that's pressure cooked directly in the pot will cook faster than rice that's in a bowl set on the rack.

THE RECIPES

The recipes in this book are mostly organized by main ingredient, except for two course-driven chapters—Breakfast and Desserts—and one chapter on Kitchen Staples. When you first look at the recipes, they may seem long, but don't worry. I've tried to be as explicit and complete as possible in explaining which settings, times, and lids to use at each step along the way. Once you get the hang of using your Ninja® Foodi,™ most recipes are easy and pretty fast.

The recipes also contain nutritional information. Most of the recipes in this book make four servings, while some make six. For main dishes, the serving sizes are generous, so if you have smaller appetites, they might yield more than the specified number of servings.

Times

At the beginning of each recipe, there's an "at a glance" section that indicates prep time, pressure time and level, pressure release method, searing time, roasting/broiling/air crisp time, and total time.

Prep time includes tasks like chopping and mixing, and sometimes finishing dishes. I've tried to indicate when prep tasks can be done while part of the dish is cooking, and the times listed take that into consideration.

Total time includes all the other times listed, plus an average of the time it takes a dish to come to pressure, when that is applicable. I aim to be as precise as possible, but variable ingredients, equipment, and kitchen skills can affect these times. I always try to provide guidelines on how a given food is supposed to look (or with meats, temperature guidelines); use those cues for doneness rather than simply relying on cook times.

Labels

The recipes are flagged with four dietary labels, **Dairy-Free** (or Dairy-Free Option), **Gluten-Free** (or **Gluten-Free Option**), **Vegan** (or **Vegan Option**), and **Vegetarian**. When an option is listed in the labels, that means an easy substitution or omission in ingredients will make the dish comply with the label (like leaving out yogurt as a garnish). If avoiding gluten is important for you, always check packaging labels carefully to ensure foods are processed in a completely gluten-free facility. There are also two time labels: **Around 30 minutes** and **Under 60 minutes**.

Tips

The recipes are followed by one or more tips, which may include substitute ingredients, make-ahead information, timesaving steps, ways to customize the recipe, or optional steps to improve flavor or texture.

Make from Scratch

Some recipes include a sidebar on making one of the ingredients from scratch, such as biscuits or salad dressing. It's optional, but if you have extra time or like to keep track of what's in your food, you have all the information you need.

LET'S GET COOKING!

I've tried to provide a variety of recipes in the chapters that follow so all readers can find dishes that match their tastes. They range from standard American fare like Sunday Pot Roast and Biscuits (page 120) to more exotic dishes such as Tunisian Chickpea Soup (page 72). Some are quick, while some require a bit more work. Some are lower in fat than others and some lower in carbohydrates, and many can be altered to fit various dietary requirements. Armed with your Foodi™ and these recipes, any day is a great day in the kitchen!

2

Breakfast

Left: French Cinnamon Toast, page 26

Monkey Bread

SERVES 4

The first two times I made monkey bread, I made my own dough. Then I promised some friends I'd make it for brunch, but I didn't have the time to start from scratch. Desperate, I bought a bag of pizza dough from the grocery store instead. You know the end of the story—it was just as good as my from-scratch dough. I guess butter and cinnamon sugar make up for a lot.

3 tablespoons unsalted butter, melted

⅓ cup firmly packed light or dark brown sugar

1 teaspoon ground cinnamon, or more to taste

8 ounces pizza dough or frozen bread dough, thawed

1. Pour the melted butter into a small bowl. Using a pastry brush, lightly coat the bottom and sides of a small (3- to 4-cup capacity) Bundt pan, or a 6-inch cake pan or baking dish, with a little of the butter.

2. In a shallow bowl, stir together the brown sugar and cinnamon.

3. Divide the dough into about 15 small balls, each about 1 inch in diameter. I use a small ice cream scoop for this, but you can also just pinch off pieces of dough—just be sure to get them fairly even.

4. A few at a time, place the dough pieces in the melted butter and roll to coat thoroughly. Transfer to the cinnamon–brown sugar mixture and roll to coat. Place the sugarcoated dough balls in the prepared pan. They should be touching but not crowded. Repeat with the remaining dough balls, spacing them evenly in two or three layers if using a Bundt pan or one layer if using a baking dish. Drizzle with the remaining butter and sprinkle with a little additional cinnamon sugar to coat evenly.

5. Let the dough rest for about 45 minutes.

6. Pour 1 cup of water into the Foodi's™ inner pot. Place the Reversible Rack in the pot in the lower position and place the pan on top. Cover loosely with aluminum foil.

PREP TIME
15 MINUTES

REST
45 MINUTES

STEAM
12 MINUTES

BAKE/ROAST
20 MINUTES

TOTAL TIME
1 HOUR 35 MINUTES

VEGETARIAN

CUSTOMIZATION TIP: Make a savory version of this bread by substituting grated Parmesan or similar cheese for the brown sugar–cinnamon mixture.

MAKE-AHEAD TIP: The bread can be baked and frozen for up to 1 month. Wrap in aluminum foil and then in plastic wrap or a freezer bag.

7. Lock the Pressure Lid into place, making sure the valve is set to Vent. Select Steam and set the time to 12 minutes. Press Start.

8. When steaming is complete, carefully unlock and remove the Pressure Lid.

9. Close the Crisping Lid. Select Bake/Roast and set the temperature to 325ºF and the cook time to 15 minutes. Press Start.

10. When baking is complete, open the lid and remove the foil. Close the Crisping Lid. Select Bake/Roast and adjust the temperature to 350ºF and the cook time to 5 minutes. Press Start.

11. The bread should be browned on top, with syrup bubbling up throughout. Let cool for 20 to 30 minutes, then unmold. Serve warm.

Per Serving Calories: 406; Total fat: 13g; Saturated fat: 5g; Cholesterol: 23mg; Sodium: 466mg; Carbohydrates: 68g; Fiber: 2g; Protein: 8g

Tex-Mex Breakfast Casserole

Think of this dish as chilaquiles with a side of scrambled eggs, but all mixed together and with a bonus layer of nachos on top. The bottom layer is rich and eggy and dense, and the top layer provides the crunch.

8 ounces corn tortilla chips, divided

1 cup green salsa (I like Frontera brand), plus more for serving

2 cups shredded pepper Jack cheese, divided

3 large eggs

¼ cup whole milk

¼ cup heavy (whipping) cream

1 teaspoon Mexican/ Southwestern Seasoning Mix (page 224), or a store-bought mix

½ teaspoon kosher salt (or ¼ teaspoon fine salt)

PREP TIME
10 MINUTES

PRESSURE COOK
10 MINUTES, HIGH PRESSURE

RELEASE
NATURAL FOR 5 MINUTES, THEN QUICK

BROIL
7 MINUTES

TOTAL TIME
40 MINUTES

GLUTEN-FREE, VEGETARIAN, UNDER 60 MINUTES

SUBSTITUTION TIP: While chilaquiles are usually made with green salsa, substitute red salsa if you prefer.

1. Place about half the chips in a 1- to 1.5-quart heat-proof dish. Pour the salsa over the chips and toss gently to distribute the salsa. Sprinkle about half the cheese over the top.

2. In a medium bowl, whisk the eggs, milk, heavy cream, seasoning, and salt. Pour the egg mixture over the chips and cheese. Cover the dish with aluminum foil.

3. Pour 1 cup of water into the inner pot. Place the Reversible Rack in the pot in the lower position and place the dish on top.

4. Lock the Pressure Lid into place, making sure the valve is set to Seal. Select Pressure and set the pressure to High and the cook time to 10 minutes. Press Start.

5. After cooking, let the pressure release naturally for 5 minutes, then quick release any remaining pressure. Carefully unlock and remove the Pressure Lid.

6. Remove the foil from the casserole. Arrange about half the remaining chips over the top and sprinkle with half the remaining cheese. Repeat the layers with the remaining chips and cheese.

7. Close the Crisping Lid. Select Broil and adjust the time to 7 minutes. Press Start. Broil until the cheese is melted and the chips are browned in spots.

8. Remove the dish from the pot and let cool for several minutes. Serve with additional salsa.

Per Serving Calories: 648; Total fat: 42g; Saturated fat: 18g; Cholesterol: 240mg; Sodium: 1345mg; Carbohydrates: 44g; Fiber: 3g; Protein: 24g

Scotch Eggs

SERVES 4

Scotch eggs—soft-cooked eggs wrapped in sausage, then coated in bread crumbs and fried—are often eaten as a snack, but they make a hearty breakfast or brunch. They can also be cut into quarters and served as an appetizer. Pressure cooking the eggs makes them a breeze to peel, even when soft.

4 large eggs

Nonstick cooking spray, for preparing the rack

12 ounces bulk breakfast sausage

1 cup panko bread crumbs (or gluten-free bread crumbs for a gluten-free dish)

2 tablespoons melted unsalted butter

PREP TIME
10 MINUTES

PRESSURE COOK
3 MINUTES, HIGH PRESSURE

RELEASE
QUICK

AIR CRISP
15 MINUTES

TOTAL TIME
40 MINUTES

GLUTEN-FREE OPTION, UNDER 60 MINUTES

SUBSTITUTION TIP: For spicier eggs, try hot Italian sausage instead of breakfast sausage.

1. Pour 1 cup of water into the Foodi's™ inner pot. Place the Reversible Rack in the pot in the lower position and place the eggs on top.

2. Lock the Pressure Lid into place, making sure the valve is set to Seal. Select Pressure and set the pressure to High and the cook time to 3 minutes. Press Start.

3. While the eggs cook, prepare an ice bath by half filling a medium bowl with cold water and adding a handful of ice cubes.

4. After cooking, use a quick pressure release. Carefully unlock and remove the Pressure Lid.

5. Using tongs, transfer the eggs to the ice bath. Let cool for 3 to 4 minutes or until cool enough to handle. Carefully peel the eggs and blot them dry.

6. Empty the water out of the inner pot and return it to the base. Spray the Reversible Rack with cooking spray or oil. Make sure the rack is in the upper position and place it in the pot.

7. Close the Crisping Lid. Select Air Crisp and set the temperature to 360ºF and the time to 4 minutes to preheat. Press Start.

8. While the pot preheats, divide the sausage into four pieces and flatten each piece into an oval. One at a time, place an egg on a sausage oval and carefully pull the sausage around the egg, sealing the edges.

9. In a small bowl, combine the panko and melted butter. One at a time, roll the sausage-covered eggs in the crumbs, pressing the panko firmly into the sausage.

10. Open the Crisping Lid and carefully transfer the coated eggs to the rack. Close the Crisping Lid. Select Air Crisp and adjust the temperature to 360°F and the cook time to 15 minutes. Press Start.

11. When cooking is complete, the crumbs should be crisp and a deep golden brown. Carefully remove the eggs and let cool for several minutes. Cut them in half and serve.

Per Serving Calories: 460; Total fat: 33g; Saturated fat: 13g; Cholesterol: 287mg; Sodium: 642mg; Carbohydrates: 18g; Fiber: 1g; Protein: 22g

French Cinnamon Toast

I rarely eat French toast, since it almost always seems to get soggy before it gets to my plate. One day, I wondered what would happen if I turned French toast into cinnamon toast (which I love, incidentally). Turned out to be a great idea, if I do say so myself. The beauty of this recipe is that the double cooking method keeps the French toast from getting soggy, even if you have to cook it in batches.

⅔ cup whole milk

⅔ cup heavy (whipping) cream

3 large eggs

1 large egg yolk

1 teaspoon maple syrup or honey

¼ teaspoon vanilla extract

Pinch kosher salt (or small pinch fine salt)

Nonstick cooking spray, as needed

8 small slices dense bread, ½ to ⅝ inch thick, somewhat dry or stale

6 tablespoons unsalted butter, at room temperature, divided

½ cup sugar

1 teaspoon ground cinnamon, or more to taste

PREP TIME
15 MINUTES

SEAR/SAUTÉ
5 MINUTES

BROIL
5 MINUTES

TOTAL TIME
25 MINUTES

VEGETARIAN, AROUND 30 MINUTES

INGREDIENT TIP: My favorite bread for this recipe is Italian or French baguette-style bread. This recipe is a great way to use stale bread, but if you don't have any, leave the slices of bread out overnight to dry.

MAKE-AHEAD TIP: Sautéing the French toast can be done a couple of hours before the final stint under the broiler, making the recipe mostly do-ahead.

1. Pour the milk and heavy cream into a small deep bowl. Add the eggs, egg yolk, maple syrup, vanilla, and salt. Using an immersion blender or handheld electric mixer, blend the ingredients thoroughly. Pour the custard into a shallow dish wide enough to fit a slice of bread.

2. Place a wire rack on top of a rimmed baking sheet (if the rack is not nonstick, spray it with cooking spray).

3. Place 1 slice of bread in the custard and let it soak for 20 seconds. Turn it over and let it soak for 20 seconds more. Using a large slotted spatula, carefully lift it out of the custard and place it on the prepared rack. Repeat with the remaining slices of bread and custard. If you have custard left over, drizzle it evenly over the bread.

4. On your Foodi,™ select Sear/Sauté and adjust to Medium to preheat the inner pot. Press Start. Allow the pot to preheat for 5 minutes.

5. Put 2 tablespoons of butter into the pot and heat until foaming. Add the slices of bread. If they will not fit in one layer, cook the toast in batches, using more butter as necessary. Cook for 2 to 3 minutes or until the surface is a deep golden brown with some darker spots. Flip the slices and cook on the second side for about 2 minutes or until that side is deep golden brown. Transfer the cooked slices to the wire rack.

6. Wipe out the inner pot and return it to the base. Place the Reversible Rack in the pot in the upper position.

7. Close the Crisping Lid. Select Broil and adjust the time to 2 minutes to preheat. Press Start.

8. While the broiler heats, in a small bowl, stir together the sugar and cinnamon. Spread a thin layer of butter on one side of each French toast slice and sprinkle the cinnamon sugar evenly over the slices.

9. Carefully transfer the bread slices to the rack. (If they will not fit in one layer, broil in two batches.) Close the Crisping Lid. Select Broil again and adjust the cook time to 4 minutes. Press Start. Serve immediately.

Per Serving Calories: 665; Total fat: 39g; Saturated fat: 22g; Cholesterol: 314mg; Sodium: 504mg; Carbohydrates: 66g; Fiber: 2g; Protein: 15g

Savory Custards with Bacon and Cheese

Here's something you might not know. Those Starbucks sous vide egg bites that every-one's so crazy about? They're really just little crustless quiches, cooked in a sous vide bath. Granted, they do have a delectably smooth texture, but you can get almost the same results for a fraction of the cost by pressure cooking.

2 bacon slices, halved widthwise

4 large eggs

1 ounce cream cheese, at room temperature

¼ cup heavy (whipping) cream

¼ teaspoon kosher salt (or ⅛ teaspoon fine salt)

Freshly ground black or white pepper

¼ cup grated Gruyère or other Swiss-style cheese

¼ cup Caramelized Onions (page 222)

PREP TIME
10 MINUTES

SEAR/SAUTÉ
5 MINUTES

PRESSURE COOK
7 MINUTES, HIGH PRESSURE

RELEASE
QUICK

TOTAL TIME
30 MINUTES

GLUTEN-FREE, AROUND 30 MINUTES

INGREDIENT TIP: Once you have the technique down, you can add any fillings you like. Aim for 2 to 3 tablespoons total of vegetables, cheese, or meat. Any vegetables should be cooked before they are added; raw vegetables will exude water and ruin the texture of the quiche.

1. On your Foodi™ select Sear/Sauté and adjust to Medium to preheat the inner pot. Press Start. Allow the pot to preheat for 5 minutes.

2. Add the bacon. Cook for 3 to 4 minutes, turning occasion-ally, or until browned. Using a slotted spoon, transfer the bacon to a paper towel–lined plate to drain, leaving the fat in the pot. Using a basting or pastry brush, coat the inside of four custard cups or 1-cup ramekins with the bacon fat. Set the cups aside. Wipe out the inner pot and replace it in the base.

3. Crack the eggs into a small bowl. Add the cream cheese, heavy cream, salt, and several grinds of pepper. Using a hand-held electric mixer, beat the mixture until it is homogeneous with no clumps of cream cheese remaining.

4. Stir in the grated cheese and mix again to incorporate the cheese.

5. Place a piece of bacon in the bottom of each custard cup. Evenly divide the onions among the cups and pour the egg mixture over, dividing it as evenly as possible. Cover each cup with a square of aluminum foil.

6. Pour 1 cup of water into the inner pot. Place the Reversible Rack in the pot in the lower position and place the ramekins on top. Depending on the size of the cups, you may need to stack one of them on top of the others.

7. Lock the Pressure Lid into place, making sure the valve is set to Seal. Select Pressure and adjust the pressure to High and the cook time to 7 minutes. Press Start.

8. After cooking, use a quick pressure release. Carefully unlock and remove the Pressure Lid.

9. Using tongs, carefully remove the custard cups from the pressure cooker. Let cool for 1 to 2 minutes before serving.

Per Serving Calories: 204; Total fat: 17g; Saturated fat: 8g; Cholesterol: 251mg; Sodium: 359mg; Carbohydrates: 3g; Fiber: 0g; Protein: 11g

OPTIONAL PREPARATION TIP: If you want a browned top, unmold the quiches by running the tip of a thin knife around the inside edge of the cups. One at a time, place a small plate over the top of the cup and invert the quiche onto the plate. Cover the Reversible Rack with a round of parchment paper or nonstick foil (or regular foil coated with cooking spray). Place the quiches bacon-side up on the rack and place the rack back into the Foodi. Close the Crisping Lid, select Broil, press Start, and broil for 3 to 4 minutes or until the bacon is browned.

Egg Muffin Breakfast Sandwich

SERVES 2

In not much more time than it takes to toast and butter an English muffin, you can have a tasty to-go breakfast: an egg, ham, and cheese sandwich. For the best results, use a ramekin that's close to the diameter of the English muffins, but really, any small cup will work. Note that eggs can be temperamental; if you like your eggs more done than the cook time here produces, cook them for 2 minutes.

2 tablespoons unsalted butter, at room temperature, divided

2 tablespoons diced ham or Canadian bacon

2 large eggs

¼ teaspoon kosher salt (or ⅛ teaspoon fine salt)

Freshly ground black pepper

2 tablespoons grated Cheddar cheese

2 English muffins, split

PREP TIME
5 MINUTES

PRESSURE COOK
1 MINUTE, HIGH PRESSURE

RELEASE
QUICK

BROIL
6 MINUTES

TOTAL TIME
15 MINUTES

AROUND 30 MINUTES

CUSTOMIZATION TIP: Use any breakfast meat you prefer (or none) in place of the ham. If you like, bake biscuits (see Sunday Pot Roast and Biscuits, page 120) instead of toasting English muffins—just bake them before you start the eggs; by the time the eggs are done, the biscuits will be cool enough to slice

1. Coat the insides of two heat-proof custard cups or small ramekins using 1 tablespoon of butter. Divide the ham between the two cups. Crack one egg into each cup and carefully pierce the yolks in several places. You don't want to scramble the egg; you just want the yolk to cook through evenly. Sprinkle with the salt and pepper, then divide the cheese between the two cups, covering the eggs. Cover the cups with aluminum foil, crimping it down to seal.

2. Pour 1 cup of water into the Foodi's™ inner pot. Place the Reversible Rack in the pot in the lower position and place the cups on top.

3. Lock the Pressure Lid into place, making sure the valve is set to Seal. Select Pressure and adjust the pressure to High and the cook time to 1 minute. Press Start.

4. After cooking, use a quick pressure release. Carefully unlock and remove the Pressure Lid. Remove the rack and set the cups aside but do not remove the foil.

5. Empty the water out of the inner pot and return the pot to the base. Using tongs, place the cups in the bottom of the pot. Place the Reversible Rack in the pot in the upper position.

6. Close the Crisping Lid. Select Broil and adjust the time to 2 minutes to preheat. Press Start.

7. While the Foodi™ heats, spread the remaining 1 tablespoon of butter over the English muffin halves.

8. Open the Crisping Lid and arrange the English muffin halves on the rack, buttered-side up. Close the lid. Select Broil again and adjust the cook time to 4 minutes. Press Start.

9. When the muffins are toasted, transfer them to a cutting board. Using tongs, remove the cups. To serve, use a small offset spatula or knife to loosen the eggs. Tip each one out onto the bottom half of one of the English muffins. Top with the other half.

Per Serving Calories: 359; Total fat: 21g; Saturated fat: 11g; Cholesterol: 257mg; Sodium: 880mg; Carbohydrates: 27g; Fiber: 2g; Protein: 16g

Artichoke and Red Pepper Frittata

SERVES 4

A frittata is an Italian egg dish, rather like a flat omelet. It's not filled, as a French omelet would be; instead, vegetables and cheese are cooked as a part of the eggs. It's easy and fast and absolutely delicious. In this version, artichoke hearts play the lead role. You can use either canned (not marinated) or frozen hearts, each chopped into three or four pieces so they're easier to distribute evenly in the eggs.

2 tablespoons unsalted butter

½ small onion, chopped (about ¼ cup)

¼ large red bell pepper, chopped (about ¼ cup)

1 cup coarsely chopped artichoke hearts (drained if canned, or thawed if frozen)

8 large eggs

½ teaspoon kosher salt (or ¼ teaspoon fine salt)

¼ cup whole milk

¾ cup shredded mozzarella cheese, divided

¼ cup grated Parmesan or similar cheese

¼ teaspoon freshly ground black pepper

PREP TIME
10 MINUTES

SEAR/SAUTÉ
12 MINUTES

BAKE/ROAST
3 MINUTES

TOTAL TIME
30 MINUTES

GLUTEN-FREE, AROUND 30 MINUTES

CUSTOMIZATION TIP: Frittatas are wonderfully adaptable—use any cheese or vegetables you like. Make sure the vegetables are cooked and dry before adding the eggs, and use about 1½ cups total for 8 eggs.

MAKE-AHEAD TIP: Frittatas are good hot, warm, or at room temperature, so you can make this up to an hour before serving.

1. On your Foodi™ select Sear/Sauté and adjust to Medium-High to preheat the inner pot. Press Start. Allow the pot to preheat for 5 minutes. Put the butter in the pot and heat until it just stops foaming. Add the onion, bell pepper, and artichoke hearts. Cook for about 5 minutes, stirring occasionally, or until the onion and pepper are soft.

2. While the vegetables cook, in a medium bowl, whisk the eggs with the salt. Let sit for a minute or two. Add the milk and whisk again. The eggs should be thoroughly mixed, with no streaks of white remaining but not foamy. Stir in ½ cup of mozzarella cheese.

3. When the vegetables are soft, pour the egg and cheese mixture into the pot. Stir gently just to distribute the vegetables evenly. Turn the heat down to Medium and let the eggs cook, undisturbed, for 7 to 9 minutes or until the edges are set. The center will still be quite liquid. (If the frittata begins to form large bubbles on the bottom, use a silicone spatula to pierce the bubbles and let the air out so the frittata flattens out again.)

4. Press Stop to cancel the Sear/Sauté function. Run a silicone spatula around the edges of the frittata to dislodge it from the sides of the pot.

5. Close the Crisping Lid. Select Bake/Roast and adjust the temperature to 375ºF and the cook time to 3 minutes. Press Start. After 1 minute, open the lid and sprinkle the remaining ¼ cup of mozzarella and the Parmesan over the frittata. Close the lid and cook for the remaining 2 minutes. Open the lid. The cheese should be melted, with the top completely set but not browned. Sprinkle the pepper over the frittata.

6. Let the frittata rest for 1 to 2 minutes. You can divide the frittata into four wedges in the pot, using a silicone spatula to avoid scratching the pot's lining. Or if you prefer, remove the pot from the base, run the spatula around the edges again, and slide the whole frittata out onto a plate or cutting board before cutting into wedges.

Per Serving Calories: 326; Total fat: 25g; Saturated fat: 11g; Cholesterol: 462mg; Sodium: 771mg; Carbohydrates: 7g; Fiber: 1g; Protein: 21g

Sausage-Mushroom Strata

SERVES 4

Breakfast casseroles (strata, if you want to get fancy) make impressive, delicious weekend breakfast or brunch dishes. Once you get the technique down, it's easy to change the ingredients for endless variations. Other than this version, bacon, onions, and Swiss cheese, or Italian sausage and peppers with mozzarella are two of my favorite combinations.

8 ounces breakfast sausage

3 large eggs

1 cup whole milk

½ teaspoon kosher salt (or ¼ teaspoon fine salt)

¼ teaspoon freshly ground black pepper

3 cups stale 1-inch bread cubes (from 3 or 4 slices)

1 teaspoon unsalted butter

½ cup Sautéed Mushrooms (page 220)

1 cup grated Cheddar cheese, divided

PREP TIME
10 MINUTES

SEAR/SAUTÉ
3 MINUTES

PRESSURE COOK
10 MINUTES, HIGH PRESSURE

RELEASE
NATURAL FOR 5 MINUTES, THEN QUICK

BROIL
5 MINUTES

TOTAL TIME
40 MINUTES

UNDER 60 MINUTES

MAKE-AHEAD TIP: You can assemble the strata the night before cooking. Follow the directions through step 3. Cover and refrigerate, then the next day, continue with the recipe as written.

1. On your Foodi,™ select Sear/Sauté and adjust to Medium to preheat the inner pot. Press Start. Allow the pot to preheat for 5 minutes. Add the sausage, breaking it up with a spatula into small bite-size pieces. Cook for 2 to 3 minutes, stirring, until the sausage pieces are browned. Don't worry if the sausage isn't cooked all the way through, as it will cook again. Transfer the sausage to a paper towel–lined plate to drain. Rinse out the inner pot, scraping off any browned bits, then return the inner pot to the base.

2. In a medium bowl, whisk the eggs until the yolks and whites are completely mixed. Add the milk, salt, and pepper. Whisk to combine. Add the bread cubes and gently stir to coat with the egg mixture. Let sit for 2 to 3 minutes so the bread absorbs some of the custard. Gently stir again.

3. While the bread cubes soak, coat the bottom and sides of a 1-quart baking dish with the butter. Pour about one-third of the bread mixture into the bottom of the dish. Top with half the sausage. Top the sausage with half the mushrooms and sprinkle about half of the cheese over the top. Add another third of the bread cubes. Repeat the layers of sausage and mushrooms, and top with the final third of the bread. Pour any custard remaining in the bowl over the top. Place a square of aluminum foil over the top. Do not crimp it down, as the casserole will expand; you just want to keep moisture off the top.

4. Pour 1 cup of water into the inner pot. Place the Reversible Rack in the pot in the lower position and place the baking dish on top.

5. Lock the Pressure Lid into place, making sure the valve is set to Seal. Select Pressure and adjust the pressure to High and the cook time to 10 minutes. Press Start.

6. After cooking, let the pressure release naturally for 5 minutes, then quick release any remaining pressure. Carefully open and remove the Pressure Lid.

7. Remove the rack and baking dish from the inner pot and empty the water out of the pot. Return the inner pot to the base and place the rack back into the pot in the lower position. Close the Crisping Lid and select Broil. Adjust the time to 2 minutes to preheat. Press Start.

8. While the Foodi™ preheats, sprinkle the remaining cheese over the strata. Open the Crisping Lid and place the dish on the rack. Close the lid, select Broil, and set the cook time to 5 minutes. Press Start. When broiling is complete, open the lid and carefully remove the strata. Let cool for a few minutes before serving.

Per Serving Calories: 525; Total fat: 32g; Saturated fat: 14g; Cholesterol: 237mg; Sodium: 922mg; Carbohydrates: 32g; Fiber: 1g; Protein: 28g

Apple Turnovers

When I was a kid, Pillsbury apple turnovers were a favorite treat reserved by my budget-conscious mother for special occasions. With the Foodi,™ you can easily make these from scratch for a fraction of the cost of the frozen kind—and they're much more delicious.

5 Granny Smith apples, peeled and cut into small chunks

2 teaspoons ground cinnamon

¼ cup sugar

½ cup apple juice

Nonstick cooking spray, for preparing the rack

½ package frozen puff pastry (1 sheet), thawed

½ cup confectioners' sugar

PREP TIME
10 MINUTES

PRESSURE COOK
4 MINUTES, HIGH PRESSURE

RELEASE
NATURAL FOR 5 MINUTES, THEN QUICK

BAKE/ROAST
20 MINUTES

TOTAL TIME
55 MINUTES

VEGETARIAN, UNDER 60 MINUTES

MAKE-AHEAD TIP: Make the filling up to 3 days in advance. Refrigerate until ready to use.

SUBSTITUTION TIP: Use refrigerated pie dough instead of puff pastry. Cut out circles about 6 inches in diameter. Fill, fold, and crimp. Bake as directed.

1. Place the apples in the Foodi's inner pot. Sprinkle the cinnamon and sugar over. Pour in the apple juice. Stir to coat the apples.

2. Lock the Pressure Lid into place, making sure the valve is set to Seal. Select Pressure and adjust the pressure to High and the cook time to 4 minutes. Press Start.

3. After cooking, let the pressure release naturally for 5 minutes, then quick release any remaining pressure. Carefully unlock and remove the Pressure Lid.

4. Place a strainer or colander over a bowl. Pour the apples into the strainer. Reserve the strained cooking liquid. Wipe out the inner pot and return it to the base.

5. Spray the Reversible Rack with cooking spray or oil and place it in the pot in the upper position.

6. Close the Crisping Lid. Select Bake/Roast and adjust the temperature to 350ºF and the time to 4 minutes to preheat. Press Start.

7. On a cutting board, roll out the puff pastry into a rectangle that's about 12 inches by 18 inches. Cut the dough in half and cut the halves in half. Spoon about ¼ cup of apples onto one side of one of the dough pieces. Fold the other side over the filling and crimp the edges to seal. Repeat with the other three pieces of dough and remaining apples.

8. Once the pot is preheated, open the lid and transfer the turnovers to the rack. Close the lid again. Select Bake/Roast again and adjust the temperature to 350ºF and the cook time to 20 minutes. Press Start. After 10 minutes, open the lid and flip the turnovers so the bottom side can brown. Close the lid and continue cooking.

9. While the turnovers cook, make the glaze. In a small bowl, combine the confectioners' sugar and the reserved apple cooking liquid by teaspoons, stirring, until the consistency is thin enough to drizzle.

10. When the turnovers are done, remove them from the pot. Let cool for a few minutes and drizzle with the glaze. Let cool for 10 to 15 minutes before serving.

Per Serving Calories: 674; Total fat: 32g; Saturated fat: 8g; Cholesterol: 0mg; Sodium: 211mg; Carbohydrates: 93g; Fiber: 5g; Protein: 7g

Shakshuka

If you're not familiar with shakshuka, the North African dish of spicy tomato sauce with eggs, prepare to fall in love. Long prepared in various forms throughout the Middle East, it's become wildly popular in the United States over the past couple of years. I like mine on the spicy side, but if you prefer a milder dish, leave out the red pepper flakes.

3 tablespoons olive oil

1 small onion, chopped (about ¾ cup)

½ medium red or green bell pepper, seeded and chopped (about ⅓ cup)

1 medium jalapeño pepper, seeded and minced

2 garlic cloves, chopped

1 teaspoon kosher salt (or ½ teaspoon fine salt)

2 (14.5-ounce) cans diced tomatoes with their juice

½ teaspoon ground cumin

½ teaspoon smoked paprika

½ teaspoon red pepper flakes

¼ teaspoon freshly ground black pepper

4 large eggs

⅓ cup crumbled feta cheese (optional)

2 tablespoons chopped fresh parsley

PREP TIME
10 MINUTES

SEAR/SAUTÉ
3 MINUTES

PRESSURE COOK
4 MINUTES, HIGH PRESSURE

RELEASE
QUICK

STEAM
3 MINUTES

TOTAL TIME
30 MINUTES

DAIRY-FREE OPTION, GLUTEN-FREE, VEGETARIAN, AROUND 30 MINUTES

MAKE-AHEAD TIP: Make the sauce ahead of time and refrigerate for a couple of days or freeze for up to 1 month. Bring to a simmer and proceed, starting with step 4.

1. On your Foodi™ select Sear/Sauté and adjust to Medium to preheat the inner pot. Press Start. Allow the pot to preheat for 5 minutes. Pour in the olive oil and heat until shimmering. Add the onion, bell pepper, jalapeño, and garlic. Sprinkle lightly with salt. Cook for about 2 minutes, stirring occasionally, or until the vegetables are fragrant and beginning to soften. Add the tomatoes, cumin, paprika, red pepper flakes, and black pepper.

2. Lock the Pressure Lid into place, making sure the valve is set to Seal. Select Pressure and adjust the pressure to High and the cook time to 4 minutes. Press Start.

3. After cooking, use a quick pressure release. Carefully unlock and remove the Pressure Lid.

4. Gently crack the eggs onto the surface of the tomato sauce.

5. Lock the Pressure Lid back into place, but leave the valve set to Vent. Select Steam and adjust the cook time to 3 minutes. Press Start.

6. When cooking is complete, carefully unlock and remove the Pressure Lid. If the eggs are not done to your liking, baste the tops with some of the sauce and cook until they are. Sprinkle with the feta cheese (if using; omit for a dairy-free dish) and parsley before serving.

Per Serving Calories: 209; Total fat: 16g; Saturated fat: 3g; Cholesterol: 211mg; Sodium: 663mg; Carbohydrates: 11g; Fiber: 3g; Protein: 8g

Creamy Steel-Cut Oats with Toasted Almonds

SERVES 4

I have to admit, after a couple of bad experiences at summer camp, I was not a fan of oat-meal. These steel-cut oats with their crunchy almond topping changed my mind—creamy and rich, with a hint of cinnamon, they're worlds away from the oatmeal of my youth.

½ cup blanched slivered almonds

2 tablespoons unsalted butter

1 cup gluten-free steel-cut oats

¼ teaspoon kosher salt (or ⅛ teaspoon fine salt)

2 tablespoons sugar, plus more for serving

½ teaspoon vanilla extract

¼ teaspoon ground cinnamon

2 cups water

1 cup whole milk, plus more for serving

PREP TIME
5 MINUTES

AIR CRISP
5 MINUTES

SEAR/SAUTÉ
2 MINUTES

PRESSURE COOK
10 MINUTES, HIGH PRESSURE

RELEASE
NATURAL FOR 10 MINUTES, THEN QUICK

TOTAL TIME
35 MINUTES

GLUTEN-FREE, VEGETARIAN, AROUND 30 MINUTES

CUSTOMIZATION TIP:
These oats are the perfect background for any of your favorite fruit add-ins— apples, raisins, peaches, and cranberries are all delicious.

1. Pour the almonds into a heat-proof bowl that fits in the Cook & Crisp™ Basket. Place the basket in the inner pot and place the bowl into the basket. Close the Crisping Lid. Select Air Crisp and adjust the temperature to 375ºF and the cook time to 5 minutes. Press Start. When the almonds are toasted, remove the bowl and basket from the pot and set aside.

2. On your Foodi™ select Sear/Sauté and adjust to Medium to preheat the inner pot. Press Start. Allow the pot to preheat for 5 minutes. Put the butter into the pot. When the butter stops foaming, add the oats and stir to coat with the butter. Continue cooking for 2 to 3 minutes or until the oats smell nutty.

3. Add the salt, sugar, vanilla, cinnamon, water, and milk. Stir to combine.

4. Lock the Pressure Lid into place, making sure the valve is set to Seal. Select Pressure and adjust the pressure to High and the cook time to 10 minutes. Press Start.

5. After cooking, let the pressure release naturally for 10 minutes, then quick release any remaining pressure. Carefully unlock and remove the Pressure Lid.

6. Spoon the oatmeal into four bowls. Top with the toasted almonds. Adjust to your taste, adding extra milk or sugar if you like.

Per Serving Calories: 387; Total fat: 20g; Saturated fat: 6g; Cholesterol: 21mg; Sodium: 126mg; Carbohydrates: 42g; Fiber: 7g; Protein: 13g

Breakfast Clafoutis

SERVES 4

Clafouti is a classic French dessert, but I first tasted it at breakfast. Individual clafoutis—light and eggy and filled with cherries—were served alongside muffins and, in my mind, completely outshone their American cousins.

2 teaspoons unsalted butter, softened

1 cup frozen sweet cherries, thawed, drained, and blotted dry

⅔ cup whole milk

⅓ cup heavy cream

⅓ cup sugar

½ cup all-purpose flour

2 large eggs

½ teaspoon vanilla extract

¼ teaspoon cinnamon

1 pinch fine salt

1 to 2 tablespoons confectioner's sugar

PREP
10 MINUTES

PRESSURE COOK
11 MINUTES, HIGH PRESSURE

RELEASE
QUICK

BAKE/ROAST
6 MINUTES

TOTAL TIME
40 MINUTES

VEGETARIAN, UNDER 60 MINUTES

SUBSTITUTION TIP:
Blueberries or raspberries are excellent in place of the cherries.

1. Coat the insides of four 1-cup custard cups or ramekins with the softened butter. Divide the cherries evenly among the cups.

2. In a bowl, combine the milk, cream, sugar, flour, eggs, vanilla, and salt. Using a hand mixer, beat the ingredients on medium speed until the batter is smooth, about 2 minutes. Pour the batter over the berries. The cups should be filled about ¾ of the way with batter.

3. Add 1 cup of water to the inner pot. Place the Reversible Rack in the low position in the pot and place the ramekins on top, stacking if necessary. Place a square of aluminum foil over the ramekins but don't crimp it down (it's just to keep steam from condensing on the surface of the cakes). Lock the Pressure Lid into place, making sure the valve is set to Seal. Select Pressure; adjust the pressure to High and the cook time to 11 minutes. Press Start.

4. After cooking, quick release the pressure. Carefully unlock and remove the Pressure Lid.

5. Carefully remove the foil from the custards. If you have stacked the ramekins, remove the second layer and do the next stage in batches.

6. Close the Crisping lid and select Bake/Roast. Adjust the temperature to 400ºF and the time to 6 minutes to preheat. Press Start. Check after about 4 minutes; the tops of the clafoutis should be lightly browned. Continue cooking if necessary, and repeat for the second batch if necessary.

7. Let cool for about 5 minutes, then dust with the confectioner's sugar. Serve warm.

Per serving: Calories: 298; Total fat: 10g; Saturated fat: 5g; Cholesterol: 116g; Sodium: 108mg; Carbohydrates 48g; Fiber 2g; Protein 7g

3

Meatless Mains

Left: Minestrone with Garlic Cheese Toasts and Pesto, page 56

Penne with Mushrooms and Gruyère

If you're a fan of macaroni and cheese, this dish will make you very happy. Even if you're not, you may find this grown-up version, with nutty-tasting Gruyère cheese and savory mushrooms, is enough to change your mind.

8 ounces penne pasta

1 (12–fluid ounce) can evaporated milk, divided

1¼ cups water or Roasted Vegetable Stock (page 219)

1½ teaspoons kosher salt (or ¾ teaspoon fine salt)

1 large egg

1½ teaspoons cornstarch

8 ounces Gruyère cheese, shredded

1 recipe Sautéed Mushrooms (page 220)

2 tablespoons chopped fresh parsley

3 tablespoons sour cream

1½ cups panko bread crumbs

3 tablespoons melted unsalted butter

3 tablespoons grated Parmesan or similar cheese

PREP TIME
10 MINUTES

PRESSURE COOK
4 MINUTES, HIGH PRESSURE

RELEASE
NATURAL FOR 3 MINUTES, THEN QUICK

BROIL
5 MINUTES

TOTAL TIME
30 MINUTES

VEGETARIAN, AROUND 30 MINUTES

SUBSTITUTION TIP: If you can't find Gruyère cheese, Emmental is a close substitute, and any Swiss-style cheese will work in a pinch, although the flavor won't be quite as complex.

1. Pour the penne into the Foodi's™ inner pot. Add 6 fluid ounces (¾ cup) of evaporated milk, the water, and salt.

2. Lock the Pressure Lid into place, making sure the valve is set to Seal. Select Pressure and adjust the pressure to High and the cook time to 4 minutes. Press Start.

3. While the pasta cooks, in a small bowl, thoroughly whisk the remaining 6 fluid ounces (¾ cup) of evaporated milk with the egg. In another small bowl, sprinkle the cornstarch over the Gruyère cheese and toss to coat.

4. After cooking, let the pressure release naturally for 3 minutes, then quick release any remaining pressure. Carefully unlock and remove the Pressure Lid.

5. Add the milk-egg mixture and a large handful of the Gruyère cheese and stir to melt the cheese. Add the rest of the Gruyère cheese in 3 or 4 batches, stirring to melt after each addition. Stir in the mushrooms, parsley, and sour cream.

6. In a medium bowl, stir together the panko, melted butter, and Parmesan cheese. Sprinkle the panko over the pasta.

7. Close the Crisping Lid. Select Broil and adjust the time to 5 minutes. Press Start. When done, the topping should be brown and crisp; if not, broil for 1 to 2 minutes more. Serve immediately.

Per Serving Calories: 804; Total fat: 39g; Saturated fat: 22g; Cholesterol: 169mg; Sodium: 1437mg; Carbohydrates: 74g; Fiber: 3g; Protein: 38g

Easy Eggplant Parmesan

SERVES 4

The combination of pressure cooking and then roasting in the Foodi™ means making eggplant Parmesan—usually messy, fussy, and time consuming—is easy enough for a weeknight. This delicious version comes together in about half an hour and won't dirty all the dishes in your kitchen.

1 large eggplant, cut into ¾-inch-thick rounds

2 teaspoons kosher salt (or 1 teaspoon fine salt)

3 tablespoons melted unsalted butter

1½ cups panko bread crumbs

⅓ cup grated Parmesan or similar cheese

2 cups Marinara Sauce (page 228)

1 cup shredded mozzarella cheese

PREP TIME
15 MINUTES

PRESSURE COOK
5 MINUTES, HIGH PRESSURE

RELEASE
QUICK

BAKE/ROAST
10 MINUTES

TOTAL TIME
40 MINUTES

VEGETARIAN, UNDER 60 MINUTES

SUBSTITUTION TIP: If you don't have homemade marinara on hand, many good commercial versions are available. I like Classico Riserva.

1. Sprinkle the eggplant slices on both sides with the salt and place on a wire rack over a rimmed baking sheet to drain for 5 to 10 minutes.

2. While the eggplant drains, in a medium bowl, stir together the melted butter, panko, and Parmesan cheese. Set aside.

3. Rinse the eggplant slices and blot them dry. Place them in a single layer (as much as possible) in the Foodi's inner pot and cover with the marinara sauce.

4. Lock the Pressure Lid into place, making sure the valve is set to Seal. Select Pressure and adjust the pressure to High and the cook time to 5 minutes. Press Start.

5. After cooking, use a quick pressure release. Carefully unlock and remove the Pressure Lid.

6. Cover the eggplant slices with the mozzarella cheese.

7. Close the Crisping Lid. Select Bake/Roast and adjust the temperature to 375°F and the cook time to 2 minutes. Press Start.

8. When cooking is complete, open the lid and sprinkle the eggplant and cheese with the panko mixture. Close the Crisping Lid again. Select Bake/Roast and adjust the temperature to 375°F and the cook time to 8 minutes. Press Start. When done, the topping should be brown and crisp; if not, broil for 1 to 2 minutes more. Serve immediately.

Per Serving Calories: 434; Total fat: 20g; Saturated fat: 11g; Cholesterol: 52mg; Sodium: 906mg; Carbohydrates: 47g; Fiber: 8g; Protein: 18g

Mediterranean White Bean Salad

SERVES 4

I have nothing against canned beans. In fact, I think they're one of the best things ever to happen to the kitchen pantry. But when beans are the star of the show, there's nothing like cooking them from scratch. With a pressure cooker, they'll cook up perfectly in just minutes. In this dish, the warm beans marinate in a simple dressing before being tossed with herbs and vegetables for a great brunch or light dinner.

1 tablespoon plus 1 teaspoon kosher salt (or 2 teaspoons fine salt), divided

14 ounces dried cannellini beans

4 tablespoons plus 1 teaspoon extra-virgin olive oil, divided

1 quart water

3 tablespoons freshly squeezed lemon juice

1 teaspoon ground cumin

¼ teaspoon freshly ground black pepper

1 medium red or green bell pepper, chopped (about 1 cup)

1 large celery stalk, chopped (about ½ cup)

3 or 4 scallions, chopped (about ⅓ cup)

1 large tomato, seeded and chopped (about ½ cup)

½ cucumber, peeled, seeded, and chopped (about ¾ cup)

1 cup crumbled feta cheese (optional)

2 tablespoons minced fresh mint

¼ cup minced fresh parsley

PREP TIME
10 MINUTES

PRESSURE COOK
5 MINUTES, HIGH PRESSURE

RELEASE
NATURAL FOR 10 MINUTES, THEN QUICK

TOTAL TIME
30 MINUTES, PLUS SOAKING TIME

DAIRY-FREE OPTION, GLUTEN-FREE, VEGAN OPTION, VEGETARIAN, AROUND 30 MINUTES

MAKE-AHEAD TIP: Although the salad is best served at room temperature, it can be made up to a day ahead and refrigerated. Bring to room temperature and add the herbs right before serving.

1. In a large bowl, dissolve 1 tablespoon of kosher salt (or 1½ teaspoons of fine salt) in 1 quart of water. Add the beans and soak at room temperature for 8 to 24 hours.

2. Drain and rinse the beans. Place them in the Foodi's™ inner pot. Add 1 teaspoon of olive oil and stir to coat the beans. Add the 1 quart of water and ½ teaspoon of kosher salt (or ¼ teaspoon of fine salt).

3. Lock the Pressure Lid into place, making sure the valve is set to Seal. Select Pressure and adjust the pressure to High and the cook time to 5 minutes. Press Start.

4. While the beans cook and the pressure releases, in a small jar with a tight-fitting lid, combine the lemon juice and 3 tablespoons of olive oil. Add the cumin, the remaining ½ teaspoon of kosher salt (or ¼ teaspoon of fine salt), and the pepper. Cover the jar and shake the dressing until thoroughly combined. (Alternatively, whisk the dressing in a small bowl, but it's easier to make it in a jar.)

5. After cooking, let the pressure release naturally for 10 minutes, then quick release any remaining pressure. Carefully unlock and remove the Pressure Lid.

6. Drain the beans and pour them into a bowl. Immediately pour the dressing over the beans and toss to coat. Let cool to room temperature, stirring occasionally.

7. Add the bell pepper, celery, scallions, tomato, cucumber, and feta cheese (if using; omit for a dairy-free and vegan dish) to the beans. Toss gently. Right before serving, add the mint and parsley and toss to combine.

Per Serving Calories: 489; Total fat: 16g; Saturated fat: 2g; Cholesterol: 0mg; Sodium: 622mg; Carbohydrates: 66g; Fiber: 27g; Protein: 25g

Cajun Twice-Baked Potatoes

SERVES 4

A little cheese, a few vegetables, and spicy seasoning elevate plain baked potatoes into a delicious entrée. I like to serve these with a salad on the side, which I make while the potatoes cook.

4 small russet potatoes, scrubbed clean

¼ cup heavy (whipping) cream

¼ cup sour cream

½ cup chopped roasted red pepper

1 teaspoon Cajun Seasoning Mix (page 223) or a store-bought mix

1½ cups shredded white Cheddar cheese

4 scallions, white and green parts, chopped, divided

⅓ cup grated Parmesan or similar cheese

PREP TIME
10 MINUTES

PRESSURE COOK
10 MINUTES, HIGH PRESSURE

RELEASE
NATURAL FOR 5 MINUTES, THEN QUICK

AIR CRISP
15 MINUTES

TOTAL TIME
45 MINUTES

GLUTEN-FREE, VEGETARIAN, UNDER 60 MINUTES

CUSTOMIZATION TIP:
These potatoes are perfect for customizing with any of your favorite vegetables and cheeses. Swiss cheese, Caramelized Onions (page 222), and Sautéed Mushrooms (page 220) make a good combination, or top them with Marinara Sauce (page 228) and shredded mozzarella.

1. Pour 1 cup of water into the Foodi's™ inner pot. Place the Reversible Rack in the pot in the lower position and place the potatoes on top.

2. Lock the Pressure Lid into place, making sure the valve is set to Seal. Select Pressure and adjust the pressure to High and the cook time to 10 minutes. Press Start.

3. After cooking, let the pressure release naturally for 5 minutes, then quick release any remaining pressure. Carefully unlock and remove the Pressure Lid.

4. Using tongs, transfer the potatoes to a cutting board. When cool enough to handle, slice off a ½-inch strip from the top, long side of each potato. Scoop the flesh into a large bowl, including the flesh from the tops. Add the heavy cream and sour cream. Using a potato masher, mash until fairly smooth. Stir in the roasted red pepper, seasoning, and Cheddar cheese. Set aside about 2 tablespoons of the green part of the scallions, and stir the rest into the potatoes. Spoon the mashed potato mixture into the potato skins, mounding it slightly. Sprinkle the Parmesan evenly over the tops.

5. Empty the water out of the inner pot and return it to the base.

6. Place the Cook & Crisp™ Basket into the pot. Close the Crisping Lid. Select Air Crisp and adjust the temperature to 375ºF and the time to 2 minutes to preheat. Press Start.

7. When the Foodi™ is heated, open the lid and place the potatoes in the basket. Close the Crisping Lid. Select Air Crisp and adjust the temperature to 375ºF and the cook time to 15 minutes. Press Start.

8. When done, the potatoes should be lightly browned and crisp on top. Let cool for a few minutes and serve garnished with the reserved scallions.

Per Serving Calories: 429; Total fat: 25g; Saturated fat: 15g; Cholesterol: 80mg; Sodium: 418mg; Carbohydrates: 35g; Fiber: 3g; Protein: 18g

"Spanish" Rice and Beans

SERVES 4

Chances are pretty good that if you've been to a Mexican restaurant anywhere in the United States, you've had "Spanish" rice. Chances are almost as good that it was mediocre. But it turns out that red rice is a great dish if you make it yourself. With a pressure cooker, it's fast, too. Add beans, and you have a delicious meatless dinner.

3 tablespoons olive oil

1 small onion, chopped (about ⅔ cup)

2 large garlic cloves, minced

1 jalapeño pepper, seeded and chopped (about 2 tablespoons)

1 cup long-grain white rice, thoroughly rinsed

⅓ cup red salsa

¼ cup tomato sauce

½ cup Roasted Vegetable Stock (page 219), low-sodium vegetable broth, or water

1 teaspoon Mexican/ Southwestern Seasoning Mix (page 224), or store-bought mix

1 (16-ounce) can pinto beans, drained and rinsed

1 teaspoon kosher salt (or ½ teaspoon fine salt)

1 tablespoon chopped fresh cilantro (optional)

PREP TIME
5 MINUTES

SEAR/SAUTÉ
2 MINUTES

PRESSURE COOK
6 MINUTES, HIGH PRESSURE

RELEASE
NATURAL FOR 10 MINUTES, THEN QUICK

TOTAL TIME
30 MINUTES

DAIRY-FREE, GLUTEN-FREE, VEGAN, VEGETARIAN, AROUND 30 MINUTES

SUBSTITUTION TIP: Substitute other canned beans for the pintos; black beans are a great choice.

1. On your Foodi,™ select Sear/Sauté and adjust to Medium to preheat the inner pot. Press Start. Allow the pot to preheat for 5 minutes. Pour in the olive oil and heat until shimmering. Add the onion, garlic, and jalapeño. Cook for 2 minutes, stirring occasionally, or until fragrant and beginning to soften. Stir in the rice, salsa, tomato sauce, vegetable stock, seasoning, pinto beans, and salt. (If using water, add another ½ teaspoon of kosher salt or ¼ teaspoon of fine salt).

2. Lock the Pressure Lid into place, making sure the valve is set to Seal. Select Pressure and adjust the pressure to High and the cook time to 6 minutes. Press Start.

3. After cooking, let the pressure release naturally for 10 minutes, then quick release any remaining pressure. Carefully unlock and remove the Pressure Lid. Stir in the cilantro (if using) and serve.

Per Serving Calories: 384; Total fat: 12g; Saturated fat: 2g; Cholesterol: 0mg; Sodium: 1089mg; Carbohydrates: 60g; Fiber: 7g; Protein: 10g

Minestrone with Garlic Cheese Toasts and Pesto

SERVES 4

Homemade minestrone is worlds away from any versions you can get out of a can, and with a pressure cooker, it's almost as fast. A few extra minutes gets you crunchy, cheesy, garlicky toasts to go along with this savory vegetable soup.

3 tablespoons olive oil

1 medium onion, diced

1 large carrot, peeled and diced

1 celery stalk, diced

1 small zucchini, diced

1 (14-ounce) can diced tomatoes

1 large (27-ounce) can cannellini beans, rinsed and drained

3 cups Roasted Vegetable Stock (page 219) or water

1 cup macaroni

1 bay leaf

1 teaspoon Italian seasoning (or ½ teaspoon dried oregano and ½ teaspoon dried basil)

¼ teaspoon red pepper flakes

½ teaspoon kosher salt (or ¼ teaspoon fine salt)

1 Parmesan rind (optional)

3 tablespoons unsalted butter, at room temperature

1 small garlic clove, pressed or finely minced

¼ cup shredded Parmesan or similar cheese

4 slices Italian or French bread

⅓ cup pesto

PREP TIME
10 MINUTES

SEAR/SAUTÉ
3 MINUTES

PRESSURE COOK
4 MINUTES, HIGH PRESSURE

RELEASE
NATURAL FOR 2 MINUTES, THEN QUICK

BROIL
5 MINUTES

TOTAL TIME
35 MINUTES

VEGETARIAN, AROUND 30 MINUTES

1. On your Foodi,™ select Sear/Sauté and adjust to Medium to preheat the inner pot. Press Start. Allow the pot to preheat for 5 minutes. Pour in the olive oil and heat until shimmering. Add the onion, carrot, and celery. Cook for 3 minutes, stirring occasionally, or until the vegetables start to soften.

2. Add the zucchini, tomatoes, cannellini beans, vegetable stock, macaroni, bay leaf, Italian seasoning, red pepper flakes, salt, and Parmesan rind (if using).

3. Lock the Pressure Lid into place, making sure the valve is set to Seal. Select Pressure and adjust the pressure to High and the cook time to 4 minutes. Press Start.

4. While the soup cooks, in a small bowl, stir together the butter, garlic, and shredded cheese. Spread the mixture evenly on the slices of bread.

5. After cooking, let the pressure release naturally for 2 minutes, then quick release any remaining pressure. Carefully unlock and remove the Pressure Lid. Taste the soup and adjust the seasoning. Remove and discard the bay leaf.

6. Place the Reversible Rack in the pot in the upper position and place the slices of bread on it, buttered-side up.

7. Close the Crisping Lid. Select Broil and adjust the cook time to 5 minutes. Press Start.

8. When the bread is crisp, carefully remove the rack and set aside. Ladle the soup into bowls and drizzle the pesto over. Serve with the garlic toasts.

FROM SCRATCH

If you have an immersion blender or small food processor, it's quick and easy to make your own pesto.

1½ cups packed basil leaves (about ¾ ounce)

¼ cup extra-virgin olive oil, plus more as needed

¼ cup grated Parmesan or similar cheese (about 1 ounce)

1 garlic clove, minced

1 tablespoon toasted pine nuts

In a small food processor, combine the basil, olive oil, cheese, garlic, and pine nuts. If using an immersion blender, combine the ingredients in a deep narrow container. Pulse until a coarse paste forms, adding 1 to 2 tablespoons of water (or more olive oil) if necessary to get a loose enough consistency.

Per Serving Calories: 723; Total fat: 29g; Saturated fat: 9g; Cholesterol: 28mg; Sodium: 1539mg; Carbohydrates: 93g; Fiber: 3g; Protein: 24g

Vegetable Korma

When I lived in San Francisco, I loved to order vegetable korma from a neighborhood Indian restaurant. I'm not a vegetarian, but that dish was so fabulous I could never resist it. When I moved and couldn't get my weekly fix, I looked for a recipe so I could make my own. Turned out to be a rather long and complicated recipe when made the traditional way. My cheater's version in the Foodi™ takes a fraction of the time and tastes almost as good as my old neighborhood takeout.

1 (14-ounce) can diced tomatoes, drained

1 cup coconut milk

5 garlic cloves, peeled and smashed

1 small onion, chopped

1 jalapeño pepper, seeded and sliced

1½ teaspoons garam masala

1 teaspoon ground turmeric

1 teaspoon kosher salt (or ½ teaspoon fine salt)

½ teaspoon ground cumin

½ teaspoon red pepper flakes, or more to taste

1 tablespoon cashew or almond butter (optional)

2 medium carrots, peeled, cut into 1-inch chunks

1 large russet potato, peeled, cut into 1-inch cubes

2 cups large cauliflower florets

½ cup frozen green peas

¼ cup chopped fresh cilantro

¼ cup roasted unsalted cashews or almonds

PREP TIME
10 MINUTES

PRESSURE COOK
5 MINUTES, HIGH PRESSURE, PLUS 2 MINUTES, LOW PRESSURE

RELEASE
QUICK

TOTAL TIME
30 MINUTES

DAIRY-FREE, GLUTEN-FREE, VEGAN, VEGETARIAN, AROUND 30 MINUTES

INGREDIENT TIP: The nut butter is there mostly to thicken the sauce, so if you don't have it, just leave it out (don't substitute peanut butter—that has too distinct a flavor). It does add some flavor, but the nut garnish on top helps make up for that.

1. In the Foodi's inner pot, combine the tomatoes and coconut milk. Add the garlic, onion, jalapeño, garam masala, turmeric, salt, cumin, red pepper flakes, and nut butter (if using).

2. In a shallow, heat-proof bowl or steamer basket, combine the carrots and potato. Place the Reversible Rack in the po in the lower position and place the bowl on top.

3. Lock the Pressure Lid into place, making sure the valve is set to Seal. Select Pressure and adjust the pressure to High and the cook time to 5 minutes. Press Start.

4. After cooking, use a quick pressure release. Carefully unlock and remove the Pressure Lid. Remove the rack and bowl (or steamer basket) and set aside.

5. Using an immersion blender, purée the sauce until mostly smooth. Taste and adjust the seasoning.

6. Add the potatoes and carrots to the pot, along with the cauliflower and peas. Stir to coat the vegetables with the sauce.

7. Lock the Pressure Lid into place again, making sure the valve is set to Seal. Select Pressure; adjust the pressure to Low and the cook time to 2 minutes. Press Start.

8. After cooking, use a quick pressure release. Carefully unlock and remove the Pressure Lid. Serve the korma over rice, if you like, and garnish with the cilantro and nuts.

Per Serving Calories: 308; Total fat: 17g; Saturated fat: 12g; Cholesterol: 0mg; Sodium: 418mg; Carbohydrates: 37g; Fiber: 6g; Protein: 8g

Masoor Dal (Indian Red Lentils)

SERVES 4

Lentils are a great choice when you don't want to soak beans or other pulses before cooking—they cook so quickly they don't need the soak. Indian cooks are masters at cooking lentils, and masoor dal is, I think, one of the best the cuisine offers.

¼ cup vegetable or olive oil

¼ teaspoon cumin seeds

¼ teaspoon mustard seeds

1 large onion, sliced (about 1½ cups), divided

4 garlic cloves, sliced, divided

16 ounces dried red lentils, rinsed

1 teaspoon ground turmeric

½ teaspoon ground cumin

1 bay leaf

4 cups water

1 (14-ounce) can diced tomatoes with their juice

1 serrano chile or jalapeño pepper, seeded and minced

1 teaspoon kosher salt (or ½ teaspoon fine salt)

2 tablespoons coarsely chopped fresh cilantro

PREP TIME
5 MINUTES

SEAR/SAUTÉ
6 MINUTES

PRESSURE COOK
10 MINUTES, HIGH PRESSURE

RELEASE
QUICK

TOTAL TIME
30 MINUTES

DAIRY-FREE, GLUTEN-FREE, VEGAN, VEGETARIAN, AROUND 30 MINUTES

MAKE-AHEAD TIP: The dal (minus the onion garnish) can be made ahead and refrigerated for up to 2 days. To serve, sauté the onions and garlic in steps 1 and 2, then add the dal to heat through.

1. On your Foodi,™ select Sear/Sauté and adjust to Medium to preheat the inner pot. Press Start. Allow the pot to preheat for 5 minutes. Pour in the oil and heat until shimmering. Add the cumin seeds and mustard seeds. Cook, stirring, until the seeds begin to pop. Add 1 cup of the onion and half the garlic. Stir to coat the onion and garlic with the oil, then let them cook in a single layer until browned, about 4 minutes. Resist the urge to stir until you can see them browning.

2. Stir to expose the other side to the heat and repeat the cooking. The onion should be quite browned but still slightly firm. Remove the onion, garlic, and oil from the pan and set aside.

3. Add the remaining (about ½ cup) onion and garlic to the pot along with the lentils, turmeric, ground cumin, bay leaf, water, tomatoes, chile pepper, and salt. Stir to combine and dissolve the salt.

4. Lock the Pressure Lid into place, making sure the vent is set to Seal. Adjust the pressure to High and the cook time to 10 minutes. Press Start.

5. After cooking, use a quick pressure release.

6. Carefully unlock and remove the Pressure Lid. Remove and discard the bay leaf. Add the reserved browned onions and garlic with the oil and stir. Let the dal sit for 2 to 3 minutes to heat the onions. Taste and adjust the seasoning. Serve alone or over rice, garnished with the cilantro.

Per Serving Calories: 544; Total fat: 16g; Saturated fat: 2g; Cholesterol: 0mg; Sodium: 596mg; Carbohydrates: 75g; Fiber: 14g; Protein: 29g

Creamy Pasta Primavera

SERVES 4

Sirio Maccioni from New York's famed Le Cirque restaurant is supposed to have "invented" this dish, but it's kind of hard to believe he was the first to think of pairing fresh spring vegetables with pasta and a light sauce. But he probably did make it fashionable, and most versions, including mine, are based on his famous dish.

1 bunch asparagus, trimmed, cut into 1-inch pieces

2 cups small broccoli florets (about 1 medium crown)

3 tablespoons olive oil, divided

3 teaspoons kosher salt (or 1½ teaspoons fine salt), divided

10 ounces fettucine, broken in half

3 garlic cloves, minced

2½ cups water

½ cup heavy (whipping) cream

1 cup cherry tomatoes, halved

½ cup grated Parmesan or similar cheese

¼ cup chopped fresh parsley or basil

PREP TIME
10 MINUTES

AIR CRISP
10 MINUTES

PRESSURE COOK
5 MINUTES, HIGH PRESSURE

RELEASE
QUICK

TOTAL TIME
35 MINUTES

VEGETARIAN, AROUND 30 MINUTES

SUBSTITUTION TIP: Pasta primavera is traditionally made with long pasta, but without care, fettucine and linguine can clump under pressure cooking. Feel free to substitute penne, rotini, or farfalle.

1. Place the Cook & Crisp™ Basket in the Foodi.™ Close the Crisping Lid and select Air Crisp; adjust the temperature to 375ºF and the time to 2 minutes to preheat. Press Start.

2. Place the asparagus and broccoli in a large bowl and drizzle with 1 tablespoon of olive oil. Sprinkle with ½ teaspoon of kosher salt (or ¼ teaspoon of fine salt) and toss. Open the cooker and transfer the vegetables to the basket.

3. Close the Crisping Lid and select Air Crisp; adjust the temperature to 375ºF and the cook time to 10 minutes. Press Start. After 5 minutes, open the lid and stir the vegetables. Close the lid and continue cooking.

4. When cooking is complete, remove the basket and cover it with aluminum foil. Set aside.

5. Place the fettucine into the inner pot and pour the remaining 2 tablespoons of olive oil over it. Using tongs, toss the pasta to coat and fan it out as much as possible (this helps keep it from clumping). Add the remaining 2½ teaspoons of kosher salt (or 1¼ teaspoons of fine salt), the garlic, and water.

6. Lock the Pressure Lid into place, making sure the valve is set to Seal. Select Pressure; adjust the pressure to High and the cook time to 5 minutes. Press Start.

7. After cooking, use a quick pressure release. Carefully unlock and remove the Pressure Lid.

8. Add the heavy cream and tomatoes to the pasta. Toss well to separate the fettucine. Select Sear/Sauté and adjust to Medium. Press Start. Bring the cream to a simmer and cook until the sauce is the consistency you prefer. Gently stir in the asparagus and broccoli and let them warm through. Serve garnished with the cheese and fresh herbs.

Per Serving Calories: 538; Total fat: 26g; Saturated fat: 11g; Cholesterol: 52mg; Sodium: 518mg; Carbohydrates: 62g; Fiber: 5g; Protein: 18g

Kung Pao Tofu and Peppers

I probably never would have thought to cook tofu in a pressure cooker if I hadn't read a recipe by cookbook author Jill Nussinow for Mediterranean tofu with bell peppers. Her assertion that the texture gets firmer and the tofu absorbs the flavors of the sauce is absolutely true. Plus, it cooks at the same rate as many vegetables, so it makes a perfect pairing, as in this spicy kung pao dish.

2 tablespoons vegetable oil

2 garlic cloves, minced

1 (1-inch) piece fresh ginger, peeled, minced or grated (about 1 tablespoon)

3 tablespoons soy sauce

1 teaspoon hoisin sauce

½ teaspoon red pepper flakes, or more to taste

1 tablespoon cornstarch

1 teaspoon sugar

1 tablespoon rice vinegar

¼ cup water or Roasted Vegetable Stock (page 219)

1 pound firm tofu or extra-firm tofu, cut into 1-inch cubes

1 small green bell pepper, cut into bite-size pieces

1 small red bell pepper, cut into bite-size pieces

2 tablespoons roasted unsalted peanuts

2 scallions, sliced

PREP TIME
10 MINUTES

SEAR/SAUTÉ
3 MINUTES

PRESSURE COOK
4 MINUTES, HIGH PRESSURE

RELEASE
QUICK

TOTAL TIME
25 MINUTES

DAIRY-FREE, VEGAN, AROUND 30 MINUTES

SUBSTITUTION TIP: You can substitute or add any vegetables you like, as long as they cook relatively quickly. Snow peas, small broccoli florets, or thin green beans are great options.

1. On your Foodi™ select Sear/Sauté and adjust to Medium to preheat the inner pot. Press Start. Allow the pot to preheat for 5 minutes. Pour in the vegetable oil and heat until shimmering. Add the garlic and ginger. Cook for 2 minutes, stirring occasionally, or until fragrant. Add the soy sauce, hoisin, red pepper flakes, cornstarch, sugar, vinegar, and water. Stir to combine and dissolve the cornstarch.

2. Add the tofu and green and red bell peppers. Stir to coat in the sauce.

3. Lock the Pressure Lid into place, making sure the valve is set to Seal. Select Pressure; adjust the pressure to High and the cook time to 4 minutes. Press Start.

4. After cooking, use a quick pressure release. Carefully unlock and remove the Pressure Lid.

5. Stir in the peanuts. Taste and adjust the seasoning. Garnish with the scallions and serve.

Per Serving Calories: 180; Total fat: 11g; Saturated fat: 2g; Cholesterol: 0mg; Sodium: 850mg; Carbohydrates: 9g; Fiber: 2g; Protein: 12g

Risotto with Chard, Caramelized Onions, and Mushrooms

SERVES 4

Watching a risotto cooking demonstration many years ago was what convinced me to get my very first pressure cooker. I actually love making risotto the traditional way; I find the rhythm of adding the stock and stirring to be soothing. But it's very labor intensive and time consuming, and I often want risotto when I don't have an hour or more to devote to cooking it. That's when I turn to this method, which produces risotto almost as good as the long-cooked version, in about half the time and with virtually no effort.

3 tablespoons unsalted butter, divided

1 small bunch chard, stemmed, chopped (about 2 cups)

1 cup arborio rice

⅓ cup white wine

2½ to 3 cups Roasted Vegetable Stock (page 219) or low-sodium vegetable broth

½ teaspoon kosher salt (or ¼ teaspoon fine salt)

½ cup Caramelized Onions (page 222)

½ cup Sautéed Mushrooms (page 220)

⅓ cup grated Parmesan or similar cheese

PREP TIME
10 MINUTES

SEAR/SAUTÉ
8 MINUTES PLUS 3 MINUTES

PRESSURE COOK
8 MINUTES, HIGH PRESSURE

RELEASE
QUICK

TOTAL TIME
35 MINUTES

GLUTEN-FREE, VEGETARIAN, AROUND 30 MINUTES

CUSTOMIZATION TIP: Risotto is a dish that lends itself to variation. Almost any cooked vegetables can be used in place of the chard and mushrooms. Asparagus and peas are among my favorites. Butternut squash is another popular choice.

1. On your Foodi™ select Sear/Sauté and adjust to Medium to preheat the inner pot. Press Start. Allow the pot to preheat for 5 minutes. Add 2 tablespoons of butter to melt. When it stops foaming, add the chard. Cook for about 5 minutes, stirring, until the chard is wilted and softened. Transfer the chard to a bowl and set aside. Wipe out any liquid left in the pot. Add the remaining 1 tablespoon of butter. When it's foaming, add the rice and stir to coat, cooking for about 1 minute. Add the wine and cook for 2 to 3 minutes, stirring, until it's almost evaporated.

2. Add 2½ cups of stock and the salt. Stir to combine everything.

3. Lock the Pressure Lid into place, making sure the valve is set to Seal. Select Pressure; adjust the pressure to High and the cook time to 8 minutes. Press Start.

4. After cooking, use a quick pressure release. Carefully unlock and remove the Pressure Lid.

5. Test the risotto. The rice should be soft with a slightly firm center and the sauce should be creamy, but it may not be quite done. If not, add another ¼ to ½ cup of stock. Select Sear/Sauté and adjust to Medium-Low. Press Start. Bring the mixture to a simmer. Cook for 2 to 3 minutes more until done. If the rice is done but too dry, add enough stock to loosen it up.

6. Stir in the reserved chard, the mushrooms, and the onions and let the risotto heat for a minute or so. Stir in the cheese. Taste and adjust the seasoning. Serve immediately.

Per Serving Calories: 349; Total fat: 12g; Saturated fat: 7g; Cholesterol: 30mg; Sodium: 526mg; Carbohydrates: 50g; Fiber: 3g; Protein: 10g

Mushroom Lasagna

SERVES 4

Lasagna is an ideal candidate for starting in the pressure cooker and finishing in the oven. But with the Foodi,™ there's no need for two appliances, and you still get gooey pasta with a browned cheesy top in less than an hour. I personally have never been a fan of dried lasagna noodles—either the regular or the "no-boil" kind; they're too thick and chewy for my taste. Try fresh pasta and you'll never go back. I promise.

2 cups ricotta cheese

1 large egg

½ teaspoon freshly ground black pepper

1 recipe Sautéed Mushrooms (page 220)

1 teaspoon fennel seeds

½ teaspoon pressed garlic (1 very small clove)

½ teaspoon red pepper flakes

1 teaspoon unsalted butter

2 cups Marinara Sauce (page 228)

5 or 6 fresh pasta sheets or egg roll wrappers, or more as needed depending on the size of your dish

3 ounces Parmesan or similar cheese, coarsely grated

½ cup shredded whole-milk mozzarella or provolone cheese

PREP TIME
15 MINUTES

PRESSURE COOK
10 MINUTES, HIGH PRESSURE

RELEASE
NATURAL FOR 5 MINUTES, THEN QUICK

BAKE/ROAST
15 MINUTES

TOTAL TIME
55 MINUTES

VEGETARIAN, UNDER 60 MINUTES

INGREDIENT TIP: If you're making the mushrooms just for this recipe, season them as they cook. As soon as the water evaporates, add the garlic, fennel seeds, and red pepper flakes. Sauté them, along with the mushrooms. Add ¼ cup of red wine to deglaze the pan, scraping up any browned bits from the bottom, cooking until the wine is mostly gone.

SUBSTITUTION TIP: Some grocery stores sell sheets of pasta in the refrigerated section; if you can't find them, eggroll wrappers make a pretty good substitute.

1. In a small bowl, stir together the ricotta, egg, and black pepper. In a medium bowl, stir together the mushrooms, fennel seeds, garlic, and red pepper flakes.

2. Begin assembling the lasagna by lightly coating the bottom of a 1-quart baking dish with the butter and spreading a spoonful of marinara sauce over the bottom. Add a layer of pasta, overlapping as little as possible, and trimming the edges to fit.

3. Spoon some marinara sauce over the noodles, spreading it out. The sauce should cover the noodles in a very thin layer; it's okay if you can see the noodles through the sauce in places.

4. Sprinkle ½ cup of the mushroom mixture over the sauce. Dot with dollops of the ricotta mixture (a small ice-cream scoop is useful here), and dust with grated Parmesan.

5. Repeat as many more times as you have room and ingredients for, pressing each layer of noodles onto the fillings below—this will even out the ricotta. Be sure to reserve enough tomato sauce to spread on top of the final pasta layer. Top the last layer with the mozzarella cheese. Place a square of aluminum foil over the top and crimp lightly.

6. Pour 1 cup of water into the inner pot. Place the Reversible Rack in the pot in the lower position and place the baking dish on top.

7. Lock the Pressure Lid into place, making sure the valve is set to Seal. Select Pressure; adjust the pressure to High and the cook time to 10 minutes. Press Start.

8. After cooking, let the pressure release naturally for 5 minutes, then quick release any remaining pressure. Carefully unlock and remove the Pressure Lid.

9. Remove the foil from the dish. Close the Crisping Lid and select Bake/Roast; adjust the temperature to 375°F and the cook time to 15 minutes. Press Start.

10. After cooking, the lasagna should be browned and bubbling; if not, cook for a few minutes more. Before serving, let the lasagna cool and set up for 10 to 15 minutes.

Per Serving Calories: 572; Total fat: 28g; Saturated fat: 17g; Cholesterol: 152mg; Sodium: 820mg; Carbohydrates: 45g; Fiber: 3g; Protein: 34g.

Roasted Red Pepper Soup and Grilled Cheese

Some years back, I was trying to duplicate a roasted red pepper soup I'd had at a restaurant. I couldn't get the taste right until the day I had some leftover caramelized onions and thought I'd add them. Turned out to be a good instinct, as was adding a touch of sherry. I've ended up with one of my most popular recipes. Despite its lack of tomatoes, everyone who tastes it says it's like the best tomato soup ever, so the grilled cheese sandwiches are a natural accompaniment.

⅔ cup dry or medium-dry sherry

1 recipe Caramelized Onions (page 222)

3 large roasted red peppers (about 16 ounces jarred peppers), cut into chunks, blotted dry if using jarred

2 cups Roasted Vegetable Stock (page 219) or low-sodium vegetable broth

8 Italian or French bread slices

8 ounces grated aged Cheddar or Gouda cheese

4 tablespoons (½ stick) unsalted butter, at room temperature

¼ cup heavy (whipping) cream

PREP TIME
10 MINUTES

SEAR/SAUTÉ
5 MINUTES

PRESSURE COOK
6 MINUTES, HIGH PRESSURE

RELEASE
QUICK

BAKE/ROAST
6 MINUTES

TOTAL TIME
35 MINUTES

VEGETARIAN, AROUND 30 MINUTES

INGREDIENT TIP: One of my favorite cheese pairings is aged Gouda with roasted red peppers. If you are near a Trader Joe's, their Unexpected Cheddar is a very close match to aged Gouda. But if you aren't, or if you can't find Gouda, aged Cheddar is a good substitute.

1. On your Foodi™ select Sear/Sauté and adjust to High to preheat the inner pot. Press Start. Allow the pot to preheat for 5 minutes. Pour in the sherry and add the caramelized onions and roasted peppers. Bring to a boil. Cook for about 5 minutes until the sherry has mostly evaporated. Add the vegetable stock.

2. Lock the Pressure Lid into place, making sure the valve is set to Seal. Select Pressure; adjust the pressure to High and the cook time to 6 minutes. Press Start.

3. While the soup cooks, lay out 4 slices of bread on a cutting board and evenly divide the cheese among them. Top with the remaining bread slices. Butter one side of each sandwich, then carefully turn them over and butter the other side.

4. After the soup is cooked, use a quick pressure release. Carefully unlock and remove the Pressure Lid. Stir in the cream.

5. Place the Reversible Rack in the pot in the upper position. Transfer the sandwiches to the rack.

6. Close the Crisping Lid and select Bake/Roast; adjust the temperature to 390ºF and the cook time to 6 minutes. Press Start. After 3 minutes, open the lid and check the sandwiches. The tops should be crisp and golden brown. If not, continue cooking for another minute. When the tops are browned, flip the sandwiches. Close the lid and continue cooking until the other side is browned. Remove the rack.

7. Ladle the soup into bowls and serve with the sandwiches.

Per Serving Calories: 656; Total fat: 37g; Saturated fat: 23g; Cholesterol: 109mg; Sodium: 1055mg; Carbohydrates: 56g; Fiber: 5g; Protein: 24g

Tunisian Chickpea Soup

SERVES 4

It's probably no surprise that I get pretty much every food and cooking newsletter in the known world, or that my Facebook feed is filled with recipe videos and links. While it can get monotonous, every once in a while I discover a completely new-to-me dish, and it's all worth it. Lablabi, a spicy Tunisian chickpea soup, is one of the latest. It's often served over stale bread and is sometimes served with a garnish of browned onions, garlic, and cumin, so I decided to combine those and serve it over toasted garlic-cumin bread. Not traditional, but delicious nonetheless.

1 tablespoon plus 1 teaspoon kosher salt (or 2 teaspoons fine salt), divided

1 pound dried chickpeas

5 garlic cloves

1 small onion, chopped

1 teaspoon cumin seeds

3 tablespoons olive oil, divided

6 cups water

¼ teaspoon ground cumin

4 Italian or French bread slices

Juice of 1 lemon (about 2 tablespoons)

2 tablespoons harissa (optional)

¼ cup Greek yogurt (optional)

PREP TIME
10 MINUTES

PRESSURE COOK
6 MINUTES, HIGH PRESSURE

RELEASE
NATURAL FOR 8 MINUTES, THEN QUICK

BROIL
7 MINUTES

TOTAL TIME
40 MINUTES, NOT INCLUDING SOAKING TIME

DAIRY-FREE OPTION, VEGAN OPTION, VEGETARIAN, UNDER 60 MINUTES

INGREDIENT TIP: Harissa is a spicy North African condiment made from a variety of hot chiles, roasted red peppers, Baklouti pepper, and spices. If you like spicy food but don't have harissa, try a little Sriracha, Asian chile-garlic paste, or Tabasco instead.

1. In a large bowl, dissolve 1 tablespoon of kosher salt (or 1½ teaspoons of fine salt) in 1 quart of water. Add the chickpeas and soak at room temperature for 8 to 24 hours.

2. Smash and peel 4 garlic cloves. Peel and mince the remaining clove and set aside.

3. Drain and rinse the chickpeas. Place them in the Foodi's™ inner pot. Add the 4 smashed garlic cloves, the onion, cumin seeds, 1 tablespoon of olive oil, the remaining 1 teaspoon of kosher salt (or ½ teaspoon of fine salt), and the water.

4. Lock the Pressure Lid into place, making sure the valve is set to Seal. Select Pressure; adjust the pressure to High and the cook time to 6 minutes. Press Start.

5. While the soup cooks, in a small bowl, stir together the remaining 2 tablespoons of olive oil, the minced garlic, and the ground cumin. Spread over the bread slices.

6. After cooking, let the pressure release naturally for 8 minutes, then quick release any remaining pressure. Carefully unlock and remove the Pressure Lid.

7. Taste the soup and adjust the seasoning. There should be plenty of broth; if the texture is too thick, add more water. Stir in the lemon juice and harissa (if using).

8. Place the Reversible Rack in the pot in the upper position. Place the bread slices on the rack.

9. Close the Crisping Lid and select Broil. Adjust the cook time to 7 minutes. Press Start.

10. When the bread is crisp, remove the rack. Place a slice of bread in each of four bowls. Ladle the soup over and garnish with a spoonful of yogurt (if using; omit for a dairy-free or vegan version).

Per Serving Calories: 607; Total fat: 18g; Saturated fat: 2g; Cholesterol: 0mg; Sodium: 818mg; Carbohydrates: 90g; Fiber: 21g; Protein: 26g

4

Poultry

Left: Spicy Air-Crisped Chicken and Potatoes, page 80

Sesame-Garlic Chicken Wings

SERVES 4

These sticky, spicy wings are so much better than boring old Buffalo wings that once you try them, you'll never go back. Starting them under pressure and finishing with the Air Crisp setting is not only quick and easy, it also results in both tender meat and crisp skin. Serve with a tossed salad or perhaps a potato salad or coleslaw.

24 chicken wing segments

2 tablespoons toasted sesame oil

2 tablespoons Asian chile-garlic sauce

2 tablespoons honey

2 garlic cloves, minced

1 tablespoon toasted sesame seeds

PREP TIME
5 MINUTES

PRESSURE COOK
10 MINUTES, HIGH PRESSURE

RELEASE
QUICK

AIR CRISP
15 MINUTES

TOTAL TIME
35 MINUTES

DAIRY-FREE, GLUTEN-FREE, AROUND 30 MINUTES

1. Pour 1 cup of water into the Foodi's™ inner pot and place the Reversible Rack in the pot in the lower position. Place the chicken wings on the rack.

2. Lock the Pressure Lid into place, making sure the valve is set to Seal. Select Pressure; adjust the pressure to High and the cook time to 10 minutes. Press Start.

3. While the wings cook, make the glaze. In a large bowl, whisk the sesame oil, chile-garlic sauce, honey, and garlic.

4. After cooking, use a quick pressure release. Carefully unlock and remove the Pressure Lid. Remove the rack from the pot and empty out the remaining water. Return the inner pot to the base.

5. Close the Crisping Lid and select Air Crisp; adjust the temperature to 375ºF and the time to 3 minutes to preheat the inner pot. Press Start.

CUSTOMIZATION TIP: Substitute your favorite sauce—Teriyaki Sauce (page 225) and Barbecue Sauce (page 226) are both good in place of the sesame-garlic sauce used here.

INGREDIENT TIP: Whole wings are much less expensive than wing segments, so if you're up for a little more work, you can save money and hone your butchery skills. Cut off the tips of the wings and save for Chicken Stock (page 218) or discard. Cut each wing at the joint into two pieces, the "drumette" and the "flat."

6. While the Foodi™ preheats, add the wings to the sauce and gently toss to coat. Transfer the wings to the Cook & Crisp™ Basket, leaving behind any excess sauce. Place the basket in the Foodi and close the Crisping Lid. Select Air Crisp and adjust the cook time to 15 minutes. Press Start.

7. After 8 minutes, open the lid and gently toss the wings. Close the lid to continue cooking. Check the wings; they should be crisp and the glaze set. Before serving, drizzle with any extra sauce and sprinkle with the sesame seeds.

Per Serving Calories: 440; Total fat: 32g; Saturated fat: 8g; Cholesterol: 113mg; Sodium: 258mg; Carbohydrates: 12g; Fiber: 1g; Protein: 28g

Quick Cassoulet

SERVES 4

Cassoulet is a labor of love. The traditional French casserole takes a couple of days to make, and even modern-day so-called streamlined recipes take several hours. I've taken some shortcuts, substituted chicken thighs for duck confit, and used canned beans, but I believe my version produces a damn fine dish in about an hour.

4 small bone-in skin-on chicken thighs

1½ teaspoons kosher salt (or ¾ teaspoon fine salt), divided

¼ teaspoon freshly ground black pepper, plus more as needed

2 bacon slices, cut into thirds

4 small garlic sausages (chicken or pork)

½ small onion, diced (about ½ cup)

1 medium carrot, peeled and diced (about ½ cup)

½ cup dry red wine

2 (14-ounce) cans navy beans, drained

½ cup Chicken Stock (page 218), or store-bought low-sodium chicken broth

1 cup panko bread crumbs

Olive oil, as needed

PREP TIME
10 MINUTES

SEAR/SAUTÉ
20 MINUTES

PRESSURE COOK
5 MINUTES, HIGH PRESSURE

RELEASE
NATURAL FOR 5 MINUTES, THEN QUICK

BROIL
7 MINUTES

TOTAL TIME
60 MINUTES

DAIRY-FREE, UNDER 60 MINUTES

SUBSTITUTION TIP: If you can find duck quarters or thighs at your local market, try this dish with them instead of the chicken thighs. They'll take a few more minutes to cook under pressure, but they're absolutely delicious.

1. Sprinkle the chicken thighs on both sides with 1 teaspoon of kosher salt (or ½ teaspoon of fine salt) and the pepper. Set aside on a wire rack.

2. On your Foodi,™ select Sear/Sauté and adjust to Medium to preheat the inner pot. Press Start. Allow the pot to preheat for 5 minutes. Place the bacon slices in the pot in a single layer and let cook for 3 to 4 minutes or until browned on the first side. Turn and brown the other side. With a slotted spoon, transfer the bacon to a paper towel–lined plate to drain, leaving the fat in the pot.

3. Add the chicken thighs to the pot, skin-side down, and let them cook, undisturbed, for about 5 minutes or until the skin is golden brown and some of the fat under the skin has rendered out. Turn the chicken to the other side and cook for about 2 minutes more or until that side is a light golden brown. Transfer the chicken to a plate.

4. Add the sausages to the pot and cook for 1 to 2 minutes per side or until lightly browned. Transfer to the plate with the chicken.

5. Carefully pour almost all the fat from the pot into a small bowl and reserve, leaving just enough in the pot to cover the bottom with a thick coat (about 1 tablespoon).

6. Add the onion and carrot to the pot. Cook for about 3 minutes, stirring, until the onion begins to brown. Add the wine and scrape the bottom of the pot to release any browned bits. Boil until the wine reduces by about one-third in volume, about 2 minutes. Add the navy beans and chicken stock, and stir to combine. Return the chicken (skin-side up) and sausages to the pot.

7. Lock the Pressure Lid into place, making sure the valve is set to Seal. Select Pressure; adjust the pressure to High and the cook time to 5 minutes. Press Start.

8. While the cassoulet cooks, in a small bowl, stir together 2 tablespoons of the reserved fat with the panko. If you don't have 2 tablespoons, add some olive oil to make up the difference.

9. After cooking, let the pressure release naturally for 5 minutes, then quick release any remaining pressure. Carefully unlock and remove the Pressure Lid.

10. Crumble the bacon over the top of the cassoulet. Spoon the panko over the top of the beans and sausages, avoiding the chicken thighs.

11. Close the Crisping Lid and select Broil. Adjust the cook time to 7 minutes. Press Start.

12. When cooking is complete, let the cassoulet rest for a few minutes before serving.

Per Serving Calories: 788; Total fat: 32g; Saturated fat: 10g; Cholesterol: 110mg; Sodium: 1876mg; Carbohydrates: 77g; Fiber: 17g; Protein: 46g

Spicy Air-Crisped Chicken and Potatoes

SERVES 4

One of the first cookbooks I ever got was from the Sunset *magazine series* Cooking with Spices and Herbs. *I've forgotten most of the recipes, but a few have become part of my repertoire. This is one of them. It might seem like an odd assortment of spices, but it works. Along the way, I've added potatoes and switched from a whole cut-up chicken to thighs, but the original has stood the test of time.*

4 bone-in skin-on chicken thighs

½ teaspoon kosher salt (or ¼ teaspoon fine salt)

2 tablespoons melted unsalted butter

2 teaspoons Worcestershire sauce

2 teaspoons curry powder

1 teaspoon dried oregano leaves

½ teaspoon dry mustard

½ teaspoon granulated garlic

¼ teaspoon paprika

2 dashes hot pepper sauce, such as Tabasco

¼ cup Chicken Stock (page 218), or store-bought low-sodium chicken broth

1 tablespoon olive oil

1½ pounds medium Yukon gold potatoes (about 4), quartered

PREP TIME
5 MINUTES

SEAR/SAUTÉ
5 MINUTES

PRESSURE COOK
3 MINUTES, HIGH PRESSURE

RELEASE
QUICK

BAKE/ROAST
16 MINUTES

TOTAL TIME
35 MINUTES

GLUTEN-FREE, AROUND 30 MINUTES

CUSTOMIZATION TIP: This cooking method can be used with any seasoning mix you like. It's good with either the Cajun Seasoning Mix (page 223) or Mexican/Southwestern Seasoning Mix (page 224). Simply stir about 2 tablespoons of the seasoning mix into ¼ cup of stock with 2 teaspoons of melted butter.

1. Sprinkle the chicken thighs on both sides with the salt.

2. In a small bowl, stir together the melted butter, Worcestershire sauce, curry powder, oregano, dry mustard, granulated garlic, paprika, and hot pepper sauce. Stir in the chicken stock.

3. On your Foodi™ select Sear/Sauté and adjust to Medium-High to preheat the inner pot. Press Start. Allow the pot to preheat for 5 minutes. Pour in the olive oil and heat until shimmering. Add the chicken thighs, skin-side down, and cook for 4 to 5 minutes or until browned. Turn and briefly sear the other side, about 1 minute. Remove from the pot.

4. Add the potatoes to the pot and stir to coat with the fat. Add about half the sauce and stir to coat. Place the chicken thighs on top and drizzle with the remaining sauce.

5. Lock the Pressure Lid into place, making sure the valve is set to Seal. Select Pressure; adjust the pressure to High and the cook time to 3 minutes. Press Start.

6. After cooking, use a quick pressure release. Carefully unlock and remove the Pressure Lid.

7. Using tongs, transfer the chicken to the Reversible Rack in the upper position. Gently move the potatoes aside and spoon some of the sauce over the chicken. Stir the potatoes back into the sauce. Carefully set the rack into the pot.

8. Close the Crisping Lid and select Bake/Roast; adjust the temperature to 375ºF and the cook time to 16 minutes. Press Start.

9. When cooking is complete, open the lid and transfer the chicken and potatoes to a platter, drizzling with any remaining sauce.

Per Serving Calories: 575; Total fat: 24g; Saturated fat: 8g; Cholesterol: 95mg; Sodium: 409mg; Carbohydrates: 68g; Fiber: 5g; Protein: 24g

Chicken Fajitas with Refritos

I've seen recipes for chicken fajitas made in a pressure cooker or slow cooker, and it makes me sad. That way produces dried-out chicken and mushy peppers. Using the Air Crisp setting, you can cook seasoned chicken and peppers the way they're meant to be, and still have time to make your own refritos. If you're really in a hurry, skip the beans and you'll have a delicious dinner in even less time.

1 large (27-ounce) can pinto beans

1 bacon slice, halved widthwise

1 garlic clove, smashed

¼ cup Chicken Stock (page 218), or store-bought low-sodium chicken broth

4 tablespoons vegetable or olive oil, divided

1 pound chicken tenders or boneless skinless chicken breast cut into ½-inch slices

1 red bell pepper, seeded and sliced

1 green bell pepper, seeded and sliced

1 jalapeño pepper, seeded and sliced (optional)

1 small onion, cut into 8 wedges

1 teaspoon kosher salt (or ½ teaspoon fine salt)

1 tablespoon Mexican/ Southwestern Seasoning Mix (page 224), or store-bought mix

Warm corn or flour tortillas, for serving

Avocado slices, for serving

Salsa, for serving

PREP TIME
15 MINUTES

PRESSURE COOK
5 MINUTES, HIGH PRESSURE

RELEASE
QUICK

AIR CRISP
10 MINUTES

TOTAL TIME
40 MINUTES

DAIRY-FREE, GLUTEN-FREE (WITH CORN TORTILLAS), UNDER 60 MINUTES

SUBSTITUTION TIP: Substitute large shrimp (26 to 30 count) for the chicken. Keep the cook time the same.

1. To make the refritos, pour the pinto beans with their liquid into the Foodi's™ inner pot. Add the bacon, garlic, chicken stock, and 2 tablespoons of vegetable oil.

2. Lock the Pressure Lid into place, making sure the valve is set to Seal. Select Pressure; adjust the pressure to High and the cook time to 5 minutes. Press Start.

3. While the beans cook, in a large bowl, combine the chicken, red and green bell peppers, jalapeño, and onion. Drizzle with the remaining 2 tablespoons of oil. Sprinkle with the salt and seasoning and toss to coat. Set aside.

4. Once the beans are cooked, use a quick pressure release. Carefully unlock and remove the Pressure Lid. Pour the beans and liquid into a large bowl and cover them with aluminum foil to keep warm. Set aside.

5. Place the Cook & Crisp™ Basket into the inner pot. Close the Crisping Lid and select Air Crisp; adjust the temperature to 375ºF and the time to 4 minutes to preheat. Press Start.

6. While the Foodi™ preheats, uncover the beans. Remove and discard the bacon pieces and garlic clove. Spoon off about ¼ cup of the liquid and reserve it. Using a potato masher, smash the beans into the remaining liquid until mostly smooth, adding more liquid if necessary. If you prefer smoother beans, use an immersion blender to purée. Re-cover the bowl with the foil.

7. When the pot has preheated, open the lid and add the chicken and vegetables to the basket. Close the Crisping Lid. Select Air Crisp; adjust the temperature to 375ºF and the cook time to 10 minutes. Press Start. After 5 minutes, open the lid and use tongs to toss the chicken and vegetables. Continue cooking until the chicken is done and the vegetables are browned. Serve the fajitas and beans in warm tortillas or serve the beans separately. Garnish with the avocado and salsa.

Per Serving Calories: 631; Total fat: 25g; Saturated fat: 5g; Cholesterol: 70mg; Sodium: 1614mg; Carbohydrates: 59g; Fiber: 15g; Protein: 42g

Braised Chicken Thighs with Mushrooms and Artichokes

SERVES 4

Chicken thighs are truly delicious when braised; the meat turns silky and tender and gets infused with the braising sauce. The only problem with braised thighs is that the skin gets soggy, and I really like crisp chicken skin. The answer? Braising, then roasting to crisp the skin. Best of both worlds.

4 bone-in skin-on chicken thighs

1 teaspoon kosher salt (or ½ teaspoon fine salt), plus more for seasoning, divided

1 tablespoon olive oil

½ small onion, sliced (about ½ cup)

½ cup dry white wine

⅓ cup Chicken Stock (page 218), or store-bought low-sodium chicken broth

1 cup frozen artichoke hearts, thawed, or canned artichoke hearts, drained

1 bay leaf

¼ teaspoon dried thyme leaves

Freshly ground black pepper

1 cup Sautéed Mushrooms (page 220)

¼ cup heavy (whipping) cream (optional)

PREP TIME
10 MINUTES

SEAR/SAUTÉ
10 MINUTES

PRESSURE COOK
5 MINUTES, HIGH PRESSURE

RELEASE
QUICK

BAKE/ROAST
12 MINUTES

TOTAL TIME
40 MINUTES

DAIRY-FREE OPTION, GLUTEN-FREE, UNDER 60 MINUTES

CUSTOMIZATION TIP: Once you get the technique down of pressure braising then roasting chicken thighs, you can easily make this recipe your own. Try a sauce with balsamic vinegar and a touch of honey and add carrots instead of the artichokes and mushrooms. Or use marinara sauce with mushrooms for a version of chicken cacciatore.

1. Sprinkle the chicken thighs on both sides with half the salt.

2. On your Foodi,™ select Sear/Sauté and adjust to Medium-High to preheat the inner pot. Press Start. Allow the pot to preheat for 5 minutes. Pour in the olive oil and heat until shimmering. Add the chicken thighs, skin-side down, and cook for 4 to 5 minutes or until browned. Turn and briefly sear the other side, about 1 minute. Remove from the pot. If there is more than a thick coating of fat in the pot, pour it off.

3. Add the onion and sprinkle with the remaining salt. Cook for about 2 minutes, stirring, or until softened and just beginning to brown. Add the wine and bring to a boil. Cook for 2 to 3 minutes or until reduced by about half.

4. Add the chicken stock, artichoke hearts, bay leaf, thyme, and several grinds of pepper, and stir. Place the chicken thighs on top, skin-side up.

5. Lock the Pressure Lid into place, making sure the valve is set to Seal. Select Pressure; adjust the pressure to High and the cook time to 5 minutes. Press Start.

6. After cooking, use a quick pressure release. Carefully unlock and remove the Pressure Lid. Carefully remove the bay leaf.

7. Using tongs, transfer the chicken to the Reversible Rack in the upper position. Add the mushrooms to the sauce and stir to combine. Carefully set the rack in the pot.

8. Close the Crisping Lid and select Bake/Roast; adjust the temperature to 375ºF and the cook time to 12 minutes. Press Start.

9. When cooking is complete, open the lid and transfer the chicken to a platter. Add the heavy cream (if using; omit for a dairy-free version) and stir it into the sauce. Season to taste with additional salt and pepper. Pour the sauce and vegetables around the chicken and serve.

Per Serving Calories: 286; Total fat: 20g; Saturated fat: 5g; Cholesterol: 79mg; Sodium: 792mg; Carbohydrates: 7g; Fiber: 2g; Protein: 19g

Chicken and Spinach Quesadillas

SERVES 4

Adding meat and vegetables to quesadillas turns a tasty snack into a light meal. These creamy chicken and spinach quesadillas are coated with a dusting of Parmesan, which gives them an extra-delicious crisp exterior.

¼ cup vegetable or olive oil, divided

1 (10- to 12-ounce) bag fresh baby spinach

1 jalapeño pepper, seeded and minced

¼ cup minced onion

3 ounces cream cheese, at room temperature

2 teaspoons Mexican/Southwestern Seasoning Mix (page 224), or store-bought mix

1 cup shredded cooked chicken

6 ounces shredded Monterey Jack, pepper Jack, or Mexican cheese blend

Nonstick cooking spray, for preparing the rack

4 medium (8-inch) flour tortillas

⅓ cup grated Parmesan or similar cheese

PREP TIME
15 MINUTES

SEAR/SAUTÉ
5 MINUTES

AIR CRISP
12 MINUTES

TOTAL TIME
40 MINUTES

UNDER 60 MINUTES

CUSTOMIZATION TIP:
Quesadillas are one of the "universal donors" of the food world. That is, you can add just about any cooked meat, seafood, or vegetables to the cheese mixture and end up with a tasty result. Leftover steak or shrimp is particularly good.

1. On your Foodi,™ select Sear/Sauté and adjust to Medium to preheat the inner pot. Press Start. Allow the pot to preheat for 5 minutes. Pour in 1 tablespoon of olive oil and heat until shimmering. Add the spinach. Cook for 1 to 2 minutes, stirring occasionally, or until wilted. Add the jalapeño and onion. Continue cooking for 3 to 4 minutes more, stirring occasionally, until the vegetables have softened and most of the liquid from the spinach has evaporated. Add the cream cheese and stir until melted. Add the seasoning and the chicken and stir to combine. Spoon the filling into a large bowl and stir in the shredded cheese. Set aside.

2. Wipe out the inner pot and return it to the base. Spray the Reversible Rack with cooking spray or oil, making sure the rack is in the upper position. Place the rack in the pot.

3. Close the Crisping Lid and select Air Crisp; adjust the temperature to 375ºF and the time to 5 minutes to preheat. Press Start.

4. While the pot preheats, assemble the quesadillas. Place a tortilla on your work surface (a silicone mat or sheet of parchment paper will be helpful). Brush the top with olive oil and sprinkle a scant 1 teaspoon of Parmesan over. Press the cheese down with the palm of your hand to help it adhere. Gently flip the tortilla over. Spread about ⅓ cup of filling over half the tortilla, leaving a ¼-inch border. Fold the other half over the filling and press gently. Repeat with the remaining tortillas, Parmesan, and filling.

5. Carefully transfer two quesadillas to the prepared rack. Close the Crisping Lid and select Air Crisp; adjust the temperature to 375ºF and the cook time to 6 minutes. Press Start. After 3 minutes, or when they are browned on top, flip the quesadillas. Continue cooking until browned on both sides.

6. Once cooked, carefully remove the rack from the pot. Using a large spatula, transfer the quesadillas to the bottom of the pot (this will keep them warm while you finish the last two) and return the now-empty rack to the pot in the upper position. Place the two remaining uncooked quesadillas on the rack and repeat the cooking process. Serve with salsa or guacamole, if desired.

Per Serving Calories: 624; Total fat: 42g; Saturated fat: 17g; Cholesterol: 104mg; Sodium: 946mg; Carbohydrates: 30g; Fiber: 4g; Protein: 32g

Cajun Chicken and Dumplings

SERVES 4

I grew up thinking that my mother made the best chicken and dumplings in the world. Her version was undeniably delicious, and for years I followed her recipe. Then I read about a New Orleans version from Chef Donald Link that called for Cajun spices and browning the dumplings. I was intrigued. This recipe combines the best of both versions.

FOR THE DUMPLINGS

¾ cup heavy (whipping) cream

1 large egg

6 ounces self-rising flour (about 1½ cups)

FOR THE CHICKEN

3 tablespoons unsalted butter

3 tablespoons all-purpose flour

1 teaspoon Cajun Seasoning Mix (page 223) or store-bought mix (optional)

3 cups Chicken Stock (page 218), or store-bought low-sodium chicken broth, plus more as needed

1¼ pounds boneless skinless chicken thighs (about 4 thighs), cut into bite-size pieces

1 bay leaf

3 large carrots, peeled and cut into ½-inch coins

2 large celery stalks, cut into ½-inch chunks

1 cup frozen pearl onions

⅔ cup frozen peas

PREP TIME
10 MINUTES

SEAR/SAUTÉ
5 MINUTES

PRESSURE COOK
6 MINUTES PLUS 2 MINUTES, HIGH PRESSURE

RELEASE
QUICK

BROIL
7 MINUTES

TOTAL TIME
40 MINUTES

UNDER 60 MINUTES

CUSTOMIZATION TIP: If you like the chicken and vegetable mixture, try it in empanadas. Or just top the chicken mixture with a round of commercial refrigerated pie dough for chicken pot pie.

To make the dumplings

In a medium bowl, whisk the heavy cream and egg. Add the flour and stir to make a stiff dough. Refrigerate the dough while you start the chicken.

To make the chicken

1. On your Foodi,™ select Sear/Sauté and adjust to Medium to preheat the inner pot. Press Start. Allow the pot to preheat for 5 minutes. Add the butter to melt, and heat until the foaming stops. Add the flour and seasoning (if using). Cook for 3 to 4 minutes, stirring occasionally, or until golden brown. Add 1 cup of chicken stock, whisking until combined with the roux. Add the remaining 2 cups of stock

and stir, scraping up any browned bits from the bottom of the pot, until the sauce has thickened slightly. If the sauce is very thick, add more chicken stock until the sauce is the consistency of a light gravy.

2. Add the cut-up chicken, bay leaf, carrots, and celery to the inner pot.

3. Lock the Pressure Lid into place, making sure the valve is set to Seal. Select Pressure; adjust the pressure to High and the cook time to 6 minutes. Press Start.

4. After cooking, use a quick pressure release. Carefully unlock and remove the Pressure Lid. Carefully remove the bay leaf. Stir in the onions and peas.

5. Remove the dumpling dough from the refrigerator. Drop it by small spoonfuls on top of the chicken and vegetables.

6. Lock the Pressure Lid back into place, making sure the valve is set to Seal. Select Pressure; adjust the pressure to High and the cook time to 2 minutes. Press Start.

7. After cooking, use a quick pressure release. Carefully unlock and remove the Pressure Lid. The dumplings will be cooked through but pale.

8. Close the Crisping Lid and select Broil. Adjust the cook time to 7 minutes. Press Start. When cooking is complete, the dumplings should be golden brown on top. Ladle into bowls and serve.

Per Serving Calories: 642; Total fat: 32g; Saturated fat: 17g; Cholesterol: 199mg; Sodium: 1120mg; Carbohydrates: 60g; Fiber: 5g; Protein: 28g

Chicken Caesar Salad

SERVES 4

I know what you're thinking: "Chicken Caesar Salad, really? How boring is that?" But the thing about Caesar salads is that most of them aren't very good. This one is different. First, you make your own croutons. Second, since you're in charge of the chicken, it won't be dried out and tasteless. And if you want to take a bit of extra time, making your own dressing will show you exactly why this salad is such a classic.

2 (14- to 16-ounce) boneless skinless chicken breasts

¾ teaspoon kosher salt (or a scant ½ teaspoon fine salt), plus more for sprinkling the croutons

1 large garlic clove, minced

1½ tablespoons extra-virgin olive oil

1 tablespoon unsalted butter

½ small baguette or Italian bread loaf, cut into ¾-inch cubes (about 2 cups)

⅓ cup Caesar dressing, divided

1 romaine lettuce heart, torn into bite-size pieces or 1 (10-ounce) bag torn romaine

1 ounce Parmesan or similar cheese, coarsely grated (about ⅓ cup), plus more for serving

Freshly ground black pepper

PREP TIME
15 MINUTES

PRESSURE COOK
5 MINUTES, LOW PRESSURE

RELEASE
NATURAL FOR 8 MINUTES, THEN QUICK

AIR CRISP
2 MINUTES PLUS 10 MINUTES

TOTAL TIME
45 MINUTES

UNDER 60 MINUTES

INGREDIENT TIP: Cooked shrimp are delicious in this salad in place of the chicken. Follow the directions in the Bow Tie Pasta with Shrimp and Arugula recipe (page 160).

1. Prepare an ice bath by filling a medium bowl half full with cold water and adding a handful of ice cubes. Set aside.

2. Season the chicken on both sides with salt.

3. Pour 1 cup of water into the Foodi's™ inner pot. Place the Reversible Rack in the pot in the lower position and place the chicken on top of the rack.

4. Lock the Pressure Lid into place, making sure the valve is set to Seal. Select Pressure; adjust the pressure to Low and the cook time to 5 minutes. Press Start.

5. After cooking, let the pressure release naturally for 8 minutes, then quick release any remaining pressure. Carefully unlock and remove the Pressure Lid. Use a thermometer to test the temperature of the breasts, which should register at least 150ºF in the center. If not, put the Pressure Lid back on the pot and let the chicken sit for a few minutes more. When done, place the chicken breasts in a resealable plastic bag and seal, squeezing as much air out as possible. Place the bag in the ice bath for 5 minutes to stop the cooking, weighing it down with a small plate if necessary. Pour the liquid out of the inner pot and return it to the base.

6. In a 1-quart heat-proof bowl, combine the garlic, olive oil, and butter. Place the bowl in the Cook & Crisp™ Basket and place the basket in the pot.

7. Close the Crisping Lid and select Air Crisp; adjust the temperature to 375ºF and the cook time to 2 minutes to preheat the Foodi™ and melt the butter. Press Start.

8. When preheating is finished, remove the basket from the pot and the bowl from the basket.

9. Add the bread cubes to the bowl and toss to coat evenly with the oil and butter. Transfer them to the Cook & Crisp Basket and place the basket back into the pot.

10. Close the Crisping Lid and select Air Crisp; adjust the temperature to 375ºF and the cook time to 10 minutes. Press Start. After 5 minutes, open the lid and toss the croutons. Close the lid and continue cooking until the croutons are golden brown on the outside but still slightly soft inside. Remove the basket from the pot and sprinkle the croutons lightly with salt. Let cool. ➤

11. While the croutons cook, remove the chicken from the bag and cut it into bite-size chunks. In a small bowl, toss the chicken with 2 to 3 tablespoons of Caesar dressing, just to coat. Set aside.

12. To assemble, carefully pour about one-third of the remaining dressing around the sides of a serving bowl. Add the lettuce and gently toss to coat, adding more dressing if needed. Add the cheese and pepper to taste and toss to distribute. Divide the salad among four bowls and top with the chicken and croutons, sprinkling extra cheese over, if desired.

FROM SCRATCH

If you have an immersion blender, it's quick and easy to make your own Caesar dressing.

1 teaspoon anchovy paste

¼ teaspoon minced or pressed garlic

¼ teaspoon kosher salt (or ⅛ teaspoon fine salt)

1 large egg

2 tablespoons freshly squeezed lemon juice

½ cup extra-virgin olive oil

In a tall narrow container, combine the anchovy paste, garlic, salt, egg, lemon juice, and olive oil in that order. Place the blade of the immersion blender in the bottom of the container. Turn the blender on and slowly bring it up to the top of the ingredients, repeating if necessary to emulsify the dressing thoroughly.

Per Serving Calories: 433; Total fat: 23g; Saturated fat: 6g; Cholesterol: 78mg; Sodium: 1037mg; Carbohydrates: 24g; Fiber: 4g; Protein: 32g

Chicken Tikka Masala with Rice

Like many Indian dishes, chicken tikka masala has become a British favorite. In fact, it's probably fair to say that most versions are more British than Indian. Also like many Indian dishes, the traditional preparation takes a long time and requires a lot of ingredients. I've tried to streamline the recipe without losing too much of the original flavor, and I like to think I've done a pretty good job. What do you think?

4 teaspoons ground turmeric

2 teaspoons garam masala

2 teaspoons ground coriander

2 teaspoons ground cumin

2½ teaspoons kosher salt (or 1¼ teaspoons fine salt), divided

¾ cup whole-milk yogurt

6 garlic cloves, minced, divided

4 teaspoons grated peeled fresh ginger, divided

1½ pounds boneless skinless chicken thighs (4 to 6, depending on size)

3 tablespoons vegetable oil or unsalted butter

1 small onion, thinly sliced

½ teaspoon red pepper flakes

1 (14-ounce) can diced tomatoes

¼ cup Chicken Stock (page 218), or store-bought low-sodium chicken broth

¾ cup basmati rice, rinsed well

¾ cup water

Nonstick cooking spray, for preparing the rack

½ cup heavy (whipping) cream

¾ cup chopped fresh cilantro

PREP TIME
10 MINUTES

SEAR/SAUTÉ
5 MINUTES

PRESSURE COOK
6 MINUTES, HIGH PRESSURE

RELEASE
NATURAL FOR 8 MINUTES, THEN QUICK

BROIL
15 MINUTES

TOTAL TIME
50 MINUTES

GLUTEN-FREE, UNDER 60 MINUTES

MAKE-AHEAD TIP: The chicken can be marinated for up to 8 hours before cooking

1. In a small bowl, stir together the turmeric, garam masala, coriander, cumin, and 2 teaspoons of kosher salt (or 1 teaspoon of fine salt). Pour the yogurt into a resealable plastic bag and add half the spice mixture to it. Add half the garlic and half the ginger. Seal the bag and manipulate the ingredients to mix the spices into the yogurt. Add the chicken thighs to the bag and reseal the bag. Push the chicken around until it's coated with the marinade. Set aside. ➤

2. On your Foodi™ select Sear/Sauté and adjust to Medium to preheat the inner pot. Press Start. Allow the pot to preheat for 5 minutes. Pour in the vegetable oil and heat until shimmering. Add the remaining garlic and ginger. Cook for 1 minute, stirring occasionally, or until fragrant. Add the onion. Cook for 2 to 3 minutes or until it begins to soften. Add the red pepper flakes, tomatoes with their juice, and chicken stock. Stir to combine.

3. Place the Reversible Rack in the pot in the lower position.

4. In a medium bowl, combine the rice, water, and remaining ½ teaspoon of kosher salt (or ¼ teaspoon of fine salt). Cover the bowl with aluminum foil and place it on the rack.

5. Lock the Pressure Lid into place, making sure the valve is set to Seal. Select Pressure; adjust the pressure to High and the cook time to 6 minutes. Press Start.

6. After cooking, let the pressure release naturally for 8 minutes, then quick release any remaining pressure. Carefully unlock and remove the Pressure Lid.

7. Remove the bowl of rice and set aside. Keep covered.

8. Using tongs, remove the rack and rinse it under cold water.

9. Using an immersion blender, purée the sauce in the pot.

10. Close the Crisping Lid and select Broil; adjust the time to 2 minutes to preheat. Press Start.

11. When the rack is cool enough to handle, flip it over to the upper position and spray it with cooking spray or oil.

12. When the Foodi has preheated, set the Reversible Rack in the pot in the upper position. Remove the chicken from the marinade and arrange it on the rack.

13. Close the Crisping Lid and select Broil; adjust the cook time to 15 minutes. Press Start. Halfway through the cook time, open the lid and turn the chicken over. Continue cooking until browned and cooked through. When the chicken is finished cooking, transfer it to a cutting board and cut into bite-size pieces.

14. Add the heavy cream and cilantro to the sauce. Select Sear/Sauté and adjust to Medium. Press Start. Bring to a simmer and cook until the cream is heated through. Add the chicken and stir to coat. Serve with the rice.

Per Serving Calories: 574; Total fat: 29g; Saturated fat: 15g; Cholesterol: 210mg; Sodium: 627mg; Carbohydrates: 39g; Fiber: 3g; Protein: 40g.

Tandoori Chicken and Coconut Rice

Technically, of course, this isn't tandoori chicken, which you can get only if you have a tandoor, or clay oven that gets really hot, in your backyard. But the flavors are reminiscent of true tandoori chicken, and together with the rice, the chicken makes a really delicious weeknight meal.

1½ pounds boneless skinless chicken thighs (4 to 6, depending on size)

2½ teaspoons kosher salt (or 1¼ teaspoons fine salt), divided

1 cup plain whole-milk yogurt

1 tablespoon grated peeled fresh ginger (1- or 2-inch piece) or 1 teaspoon ground ginger

1½ teaspoons minced garlic

1 teaspoon smoked paprika

½ teaspoon cayenne pepper

½ teaspoon ground coriander

½ teaspoon ground cumin

1 teaspoon curry powder

⅛ teaspoon freshly ground black pepper

1 cup basmati rice, rinsed thoroughly and drained

¾ cup coconut milk

¼ cup water

2 or 3 green cardamom pods (optional)

½ cup frozen peas, thawed

Nonstick cooking spray, for preparing the rack

1 tablespoon chopped fresh cilantro

PREP TIME
10 MINUTES

PRESSURE COOK
3 MINUTES, HIGH PRESSURE

RELEASE
NATURAL FOR 6 MINUTES, THEN QUICK

BROIL
16 MINUTES

TOTAL TIME
45 MINUTES

GLUTEN-FREE, UNDER 60 MINUTES

MAKE-AHEAD TIP: The chicken can be marinated for up to 8 hours before cooking.

1. Sprinkle the chicken thighs on both sides with 1 teaspoon of kosher salt (or ½ teaspoon of fine salt). Place in a resealable plastic bag and set aside while you mix the marinade.

2. In a medium bowl, stir together the yogurt, 1 teaspoon of kosher salt (or ½ teaspoon of fine salt), the ginger, garlic, paprika, cayenne, coriander, cumin, curry powder, and black pepper until thoroughly combined. Pour the marinade over the chicken. Seal the bag and squish the ingredients around to coat the chicken. Set aside.

3. Pour the rice into the Foodi's™ inner pot. Add the coconut milk, water, cardamom pods (if using), and remaining ½ teaspoon of kosher salt (or ¼ teaspoon of fine salt). Stir.

4. Lock the Pressure Lid into place, making sure the valve is set to Seal. Select Pressure; adjust the pressure to High and the cook time to 3 minutes. Press Start.

5. After cooking, let the pressure release naturally for 6 minutes, then quick release any remaining pressure.

6. Carefully unlock and remove the Pressure Lid. Stir in the peas. Cover the rice with aluminum foil to keep it from drying out.

7. Spray the Reversible Rack with cooking spray or oil, making sure the rack is in the upper position. Place it in the pot, sliding the legs of the rack under the foil.

8. Remove the chicken from the marinade, letting the excess drip back into the bag. Arrange the chicken on the prepared rack in a single layer.

9. Close the Crisping Lid and select Broil. Adjust the cook time to 16 minutes. Press Start. After about 8 minutes, open the lid and check the chicken. It should be crisp and browned on the edges, and almost cooked through. If not, close the lid and broil for another 2 minutes or so. When the thighs are browned in spots, turn the chicken over and close the lid. Cook until the second side is crisp and browned on the edges. Serve the chicken and rice sprinkled with the cilantro.

Per Serving Calories: 511; Total fat: 18g; Saturated fat: 11g; Cholesterol: 147mg; Sodium: 632mg; Carbohydrates: 45g; Fiber: 3g; Protein: 41g

Chicken Shawarma with Garlic-Yogurt Sauce

SERVES 4

The Middle Eastern dish shawarma, spiced grilled meats often served in pita bread, has become a staple of food carts all over American cities. But if you can't visit a shawarma cart, you can still try this version at home. You'll be glad you did.

FOR THE CHICKEN

1½ pounds boneless skinless chicken thighs

1 teaspoon kosher salt (or ½ teaspoon fine salt)

2 tablespoons extra-virgin olive oil, divided

2 tablespoons plain Greek yogurt

2 tablespoons freshly squeezed lemon juice (from about 1 medium lemon)

3 garlic cloves, minced

1 teaspoon ground cumin

1 teaspoon smoked paprika

¼ teaspoon ground turmeric

¼ teaspoon ground allspice

¼ teaspoon ground cinnamon

¼ teaspoon freshly ground black pepper

¼ teaspoon red pepper flakes

4 pita breads, halved

Nonstick cooking spray, for preparing the rack

FOR THE SAUCE

½ cup plain Greek yogurt

½ teaspoon kosher salt (or ¼ teaspoon fine salt)

1 teaspoon extra-virgin olive oil

1 small garlic clove, minced

2 tablespoons tahini (optional)

1 tablespoon chopped fresh parsley

TO ASSEMBLE

1 or 2 large tomatoes, sliced

½ medium hothouse cucumber, sliced

PREP TIME
15 MINUTES

AIR CRISP
16 MINUTES

TOTAL TIME
35 MINUTES, PLUS MARINATING TIME

AROUND 30 MINUTES

MAKE-AHEAD TIP: You can make the marinade and salt the chicken up to 24 hours before cooking, and marinate the chicken for up to 8 hours before cooking.

To make the chicken

1. Sprinkle the chicken thighs on both sides with the salt. Place them in a resealable plastic bag and set aside while you mix the marinade.

2. In a small bowl, stir together the olive oil, yogurt, lemon juice, garlic, cumin, paprika, turmeric, allspice, cinnamon, black pepper, and red pepper flakes until thoroughly combined. Pour the marinade over the chicken. Seal the bag and manipulate the chicken to coat it with the sauce. Set aside at room temperature

for as long as you can—20 minutes is fine, an hour is better, and if longer than that, refrigerate the chicken to marinate.

3. Wrap the pita breads in aluminum foil and place them in the bottom of the pot. Spray the Reversible Rack with cooking spray or oil and place it in the pot in the upper position.

4. Close the Crisping Lid and select Air Crisp; adjust the temperature to 390°F and the time to 4 minutes to preheat. Press Start.

5. Remove the chicken from the marinade, letting the excess drip back into the bag. When the Foodi™ is preheated, open the lid and arrange the chicken on the rack in a single layer.

6. Close the Crisping Lid and select Air Crisp. Adjust the temperature to 390°F and the cook time to 16 minutes. Press Start. After about 7 minutes, open the lid and check the chicken. It should be crisp and browned on the edges and almost cooked through. If not, close the lid and cook for another 2 minutes or so. When the thighs are browned in spots, turn the chicken over and close the lid. Cook until the second side is crisp and browned on the edges, 7 to 8 minutes more. Cut into the thickest part of one of the thighs and check to make sure it's cooked all the way through. If not, cook for 2 to 3 minutes more.

7. When the chicken thighs are done, transfer them to a cutting board. Remove the pitas from the pot and set aside.

To make the sauce

While the chicken cooks, make the sauce. Spoon the yogurt into a small bowl. Add the salt, olive oil, garlic, and tahini (if using). Whisk until combined. Add the parsley and stir.

To assemble

To serve, spread 1 to 2 tablespoons of sauce into a pita half. Spoon in some chicken and add the tomato and cucumber slices.

Per Serving Calories: 405; Total fat: 17g; Saturated fat: 4g; Cholesterol: 146mg; Sodium: 1191mg; Carbohydrates: 25g; Fiber: 5g; Protein: 39g

Cajun Roasted Turkey Breast with Sweet Potatoes

SERVES 4

When you're craving Thanksgiving dinner in the middle of the summer, try this (relatively) quick recipe for spicy Cajun turkey and mashed sweet potatoes, and it will get you through to November. You won't heat up the kitchen, but you'll still get your holiday fix.

1 (4½- to 5-pound) whole bone-in turkey breast

4 teaspoons Cajun Seasoning Mix (page 223) or store-bought mix, divided

2½ teaspoons kosher salt (or 1¼ teaspoons fine salt), divided

¾ cup Chicken Stock (page 218), or store-bought low-sodium chicken broth

3 medium sweet potatoes (about 1½ pounds), scrubbed

3 tablespoons melted unsalted butter, divided

2 tablespoons heavy (whipping) cream, warmed

PREP TIME
10 MINUTES

PRESSURE COOK
13 MINUTES, HIGH PRESSURE

RELEASE
NATURAL FOR 8 MINUTES, THEN QUICK

AIR CRISP
16 MINUTES

SEAR/SAUTÉ
3 MINUTES

TOTAL TIME
1 HOUR 10 MINUTES

GLUTEN-FREE

CUSTOMIZATION TIP: If you like, skip the Cajun seasoning. Sprinkle the turkey with salt and pepper before pressure cooking and use Mustard Sauce (page 227) or Barbecue Sauce (page 226) as a glaze before roasting.

1. Pat the turkey breast dry and carefully slide your hands under the skin, separating it from the meat. In a small bowl, stir together the seasoning mix and 2 teaspoons of kosher salt (or 1 teaspoon of fine salt). Rub about half the spice mixture under the skin and in the cavity on the underside of the breast, reserving the rest.

2. Pour the chicken stock into the Foodi's™ inner pot. Place the Reversible Rack in the pot in the lower position. Place the turkey breast on its side in the center of the rack and place the sweet potatoes around it.

3. Lock the Pressure Lid into place, making sure the valve is set to Seal. Select Pressure; adjust the pressure to High and the cook time to 13 minutes. Press Start.

4. While the turkey is cooking, in a small bowl, mix the reserved spice mixture with 2 tablespoons of melted butter.

5. After cooking, let the pressure release naturally for 8 minutes, then quick release any remaining pressure. Carefully unlock and remove the Pressure Lid.

6. Using tongs, transfer the sweet potatoes to a cutting board or plate, then remove the rack with the turkey. Pour the cooking juices out of the pot into a fat separator and set aside. Return the turkey and rack to the pot.

7. Baste the exposed side of the turkey breast with half the spice-butter mixture.

8. Close the Crisping Lid and select Air Crisp; adjust the temperature to 360ºF and the cook time to 16 minutes. Press Start. After 8 minutes, open the lid and use tongs to flip the turkey breast over. Baste that side with the remaining spice-butter mixture and close the lid to continue cooking.

9. While the turkey is roasting, slip the skins off the sweet potatoes and place the flesh in a bowl. Use a potato ricer or potato masher to process the potatoes into a smooth purée. Add the remaining ½ teaspoon of kosher salt (or ¼ teaspoon of fine salt), remaining 1 tablespoon of melted butter, the heavy cream, and 2 tablespoons of the turkey cooking juices to the sweet potatoes and stir to incorporate. Taste and adjust the seasoning and cover the bowl with aluminum foil.

10. After cooking, check the internal temperature of the turkey to make sure it reads at least 150ºF. Transfer it to a cutting board, leaving the rack in the pot.

11. Pour the defatted sauce back into the pot. Select Sear/Sauté and adjust to Medium-High. Set the bowl of potatoes on the rack to keep warm while the sauce reduces. Press Start. Bring the sauce to a boil and cook for 2 to 3 minutes or until reduced by about half.

12. While the sauce reduces, slice the turkey and arrange the slices on a platter. Remove the potatoes from the pot and take the rack out. Pour the sauce over the turkey slices and serve with the sweet potatoes.

Per Serving Calories: 647; Total fat: 32g; Saturated fat: 13g; Cholesterol: 218mg; Sodium: 923mg; Carbohydrates: 22g; Fiber: 3g; Protein: 65g

Easy Chicken Cordon Bleu with Green Beans

SERVES 4

Chicken cordon bleu is one of those dishes that I rarely make at home. I love it, but it's a lot of work. While this version isn't quite as decadent as the original, it takes a fraction of the time and still gets you melty cheese and ham layered with chicken and a crisp crumb coating. And you get green beans at the same time, so you can claim you're eating healthy.

2 large (14-ounce) boneless skinless chicken breasts

¾ teaspoon kosher salt (or a scant ½ teaspoon fine salt), divided

12 ounces green beans, trimmed

3 tablespoons melted unsalted butter, divided

Nonstick cooking spray, for preparing the rack

4 teaspoons Dijon mustard

4 thin ham slices

4 thin slices Gruyère, Emmental, or other Swiss-style cheese

⅔ cup panko bread crumbs

¼ cup grated Parmesan or similar cheese

PREP TIME
15 MINUTES

PRESSURE COOK
1 MINUTE, HIGH PRESSURE

RELEASE
QUICK

AIR CRISP
4 MINUTES PLUS 10 MINUTES

TOTAL TIME
35 MINUTES

AROUND 30 MINUTES

PRESENTATION TIP: For a nicer looking and tastier crust, brown the panko in the butter before using.

1. Lay the chicken breasts on a cutting board. With your knife parallel to the board, slice through the breasts to form two thinner pieces from each breast (4 pieces total). Sprinkle the chicken with ½ teaspoon of kosher salt (or ¼ teaspoon of fine salt). Lay a piece of plastic wrap over the chicken pieces and use the heel of your hand to press the chicken into a more even thickness. This is optional but makes for a better presentation.

2. Pour 1 cup of water into the Foodi's™ inner pot. Place the Reversible Rack in the pot in the lower position. Arrange the green beans on the rack and place the chicken pieces on top.

3. Lock the Pressure Lid into place, making sure the valve is set to Seal. Select Pressure; adjust the pressure to High and the cook time to 1 minute. Press Start.

4. After cooking, use a quick pressure release. Carefully unlock and remove the Pressure Lid.

5. Remove the rack and set aside. Empty the water from the pot and return the pot to the base. Move the chicken pieces back to the cutting board and transfer the beans back to the pot. Add 1 tablespoon of melted butter to the beans and sprinkle with the remaining ¼ teaspoon of kosher salt (or ¼ teaspoon of fine salt). Stir to coat the beans with the butter.

6. Spray the Reversible Rack with cooking spray or oil and place it in the pot in the upper position.

7. Close the Crisping Lid and select Air Crisp; adjust the temperature to 360ºF and the time to 4 minutes to preheat. Press Start.

8. While the Foodi™ preheats, spread about 1 teaspoon of mustard over each chicken piece. Layer 1 ham slice and 1 cheese slice over each chicken piece.

9. In a small bowl, stir together the panko, remaining 2 tablespoons of melted butter, and the Parmesan cheese. Sprinkle the crumb mixture evenly over the chicken.

10. Open the Crisping Lid and carefully transfer the chicken pieces to the rack. Close the Crisping Lid and select Air Crisp; adjust the temperature to 360ºF and the cook time to 10 minutes. Press Start.

11. When cooking is complete, the crumbs should be crisp and a deep golden brown. Transfer the chicken pieces to a platter and serve with the green beans.

Per Serving Calories: 583; Total fat: 26g; Saturated fat: 14g; Cholesterol: 189mg; Sodium: 1367mg; Carbohydrates: 19g; Fiber: 4g; Protein: 67g

Chicken Chili Verde with Nachos

SERVES 4

I've been making pork chili verde for years; in fact, it was one of the first dishes I ever made in a pressure cooker. I don't know why it took me this long to substitute chicken for the pork, but it makes an equally good, and much faster, dish—fast enough for a weeknight. You can skip layering the nachos on top if you want, but really, do you want to?

1 tablespoon olive oil

12 ounces tomatillos, husks removed, rinsed, and halved

¾ cup Chicken Stock (page 218), or store-bought low-sodium chicken broth

1 teaspoon Mexican/Southwestern Seasoning Mix (page 224), or store-bought mix

½ teaspoon ground cumin

½ teaspoon kosher salt (or ¼ teaspoon fine salt)

1½ pounds boneless skinless chicken thighs

2 large poblano chiles, seeded and cut into chunks

2 jalapeño peppers, seeded and cut into 4 or 5 pieces each

1 small onion, sliced (about 1 cup)

2 large garlic cloves, smashed or minced

¼ cup minced fresh cilantro, divided

Nonstick cooking spray, for preparing the rack

Tortilla chips

½ cup shredded Monterey Jack cheese (or packaged shredded Mexican cheese blend)

Juice of ½ lime

PREP TIME
10 MINUTES

SEAR/SAUTÉ
5 MINUTES

PRESSURE COOK
10 MINUTES, HIGH PRESSURE

RELEASE
NATURAL FOR 5 MINUTES, THEN QUICK

AIR CRISP
5 MINUTES

TOTAL TIME
40 MINUTES

GLUTEN-FREE, UNDER 60 MINUTES

LEFTOVER TIP: Any leftover chicken can be frozen and used later for enchiladas or tacos, or as a filling for empanadas.

1. On your Foodi,™ select Sear/Sauté and adjust to High to preheat the inner pot. Press Start. Allow the pot to preheat for 5 minutes. Pour in the olive oil and heat until shimmering. Add the tomatillos, cut-side down. Cook, without moving them, for 3 to 4 minutes or until dark brown.

2. Pour the chicken stock into the pot, scraping the bottom to dissolve any browned bits. Stir in the seasoning, cumin, and salt. Add the chicken, poblanos, jalapeños, onion, garlic, and half the cilantro.

3. Lock the Pressure Lid into place, making sure the valve is set to Seal. Select Pressure; adjust the pressure to High and the cook time to 10 minutes. Press Start.

4. While the chicken cooks, spray the Reversible Rack with cooking spray or oil. Place the rack in the upper position. Cut a circle of parchment paper or aluminum foil to fit the rack and place it on the rack. Arrange a single layer of tortilla chips on the rack and sprinkle with half the cheese. Repeat with another layer of chips and cheese. Set aside.

5. After cooking, let the pressure release naturally for 5 minutes, then quick release any remaining pressure. Carefully unlock and remove the Pressure Lid.

6. Remove the chicken from the pot and set aside. Using an immersion blender, purée the sauce and vegetables, or if you prefer a chunkier chili, use a potato masher.

7. Pull the chicken into bite-size pieces and return it to the sauce. Add the remaining cilantro and the lime juice. Taste and adjust the seasoning. Carefully transfer the rack of chips to the pot.

8. Close the Crisping Lid and select Air Crisp; adjust the temperature to 375ºF and the time to 5 minutes. Press Start. When the cook time is complete, check the nachos. The cheese should be bubbling and the chips crisp at the edges. If not, cook for a couple of more minutes.

9. When cooking is complete, open the lid. Carefully remove the rack and transfer the chips to a platter. Serve the chili in bowls with the chips on the side.

Per Serving Calories: 486; Total fat: 22g; Saturated fat: 6g; Cholesterol: 157mg; Sodium: 776mg; Carbohydrates: 29g; Fiber: 4g; Protein: 41g

Coq au Vin

SERVES 4

Traditionally, French coq au vin was made with a rooster (coq). *Not only is it virtually impossible to find an actual rooster these days (even in French markets), they were so tough to cook they had to be marinated in wine for a day or so and then cooked for hours to become tender enough to eat. This modern version keeps the flavors of the traditional dish but uses economical chicken leg quarters, which cook in a fraction of the time.*

4 chicken leg quarters, skin on

1½ teaspoons kosher salt (or ¾ teaspoon fine salt), divided

2 bacon slices, cut into thirds

¼ cup sliced onion

1¼ cups dry red wine, divided (see tip)

⅓ cup Chicken Stock (page 218), or store-bought low-sodium chicken broth

1½ teaspoons tomato paste

½ teaspoon brown sugar

Freshly ground black pepper

½ cup Sautéed Mushrooms (page 220)

¾ cup frozen pearl onions, thawed and drained

PREP TIME
10 MINUTES

SEAR/SAUTÉ
20 MINUTES

PRESSURE COOK
12 MINUTES, HIGH PRESSURE

RELEASE
NATURAL FOR 8 MINUTES, THEN QUICK

BROIL
7 MINUTES

TOTAL TIME
60 MINUTES

DAIRY-FREE, GLUTEN-FREE

INGREDIENT TIP: For the wine, a Côtes du Rhône or similar blend works well, or a Malbec. Avoid anything with a heavy oak finish as it can be too pronounced in the final dish.

1. Sprinkle the chicken quarters on both sides with 1 teaspoon of kosher salt (or ½ teaspoon of fine salt) and set aside on a wire rack.

2. On your Foodi,™ select Sear/Sauté and adjust to Medium to preheat the inner pot. Press Start. Allow the pot to preheat for 5 minutes. Place the bacon in the pot in a single layer and let cook for 3 to 4 minutes or until browned on the first side. Turn and brown the other side. Using tongs, transfer the bacon to a paper towel–lined plate to drain, leaving the fat in the pot.

3. Add the chicken quarters to the pot, skin-side down. Let them cook, undisturbed, for about 5 minutes or until the skin is golden brown and some of the fat under the skin has rendered out. Turn the quarters to the other side and cook for about 2 minutes or until that side is a light golden brown. Remove the chicken to a plate.

4. Carefully pour off almost all the fat, leaving just enough to cover the bottom of the pot with a thick coat (about 1 tablespoon). Add the sliced onion to the pot. Cook for about 3 minutes, stirring, until the onion begins to brown. Add ½ cup of wine and scrape the bottom of the pan to release any browned bits. Boil the mixture until the wine reduces by about one-third in volume, about 2 minutes. Add the remaining ¾ cup of wine, the chicken stock, tomato paste, brown sugar, and a few grinds of pepper. Bring the sauce to a boil and cook for about 1 minute, stirring to make sure the tomato paste is incorporated. Add the chicken pieces, skin-side up, to the pot.

5. Lock the Pressure Lid into place, making sure the valve is set to Seal. Select Pressure; adjust the pressure to High and the cook time to 12 minutes. Press Start.

6. After cooking, let the pressure release naturally for 8 minutes, then quick release any remaining pressure. Carefully unlock and remove the Pressure Lid.

7. Remove the chicken pieces from the pot. Strain the sauce into a fat separator and let the sauce sit until the fat rises to the surface, about 5 minutes. (If you don't have a fat separator, let the sauce sit for a few minutes, then spoon or blot off any excess fat from the top of the sauce.)

8. Pour the sauce back into the pot and stir in the mushrooms and pearl onions. Place the chicken on top of the sauce, skin-side up.

9. Close the Crisping Lid and select Broil. Adjust the cook time to 7 minutes. Press Start.

10. When cooking is complete, open the lid and transfer the chicken to a serving platter. Spoon the sauce around the chicken along with the mushrooms and pearl onions and serve with the reserved bacon crumbled over the top.

Per Serving Calories: 328; Total fat: 21g; Saturated fat: 6g; Cholesterol: 89mg; Sodium: 1148mg; Carbohydrates: 7g; Fiber: 1g; Protein: 20g

Italian Wedding Soup with Turkey Sausage

SERVES 4

Contrary to what I used to think, this soup isn't traditionally served at weddings. The name "wedding soup" comes from the fact that it combines ("weds") meat and greens. Any sturdy greens can be used—escarole is typical, but I find kale more readily available.

1 pound hot Italian turkey sausage, casings removed

4 tablespoons extra-virgin olive oil, divided

3 garlic cloves, chopped

3 celery stalks, chopped

1 large onion, chopped

1 teaspoon kosher salt (or ½ teaspoon fine salt)

½ cup dry white wine

4 cups Chicken Stock (page 218), or store-bought low-sodium chicken broth

1 Parmesan or similar cheese rind (optional)

½ teaspoon fennel seeds

1 (15-oz) can cannellini (white kidney) beans, drained and rinsed

2 cups chopped kale

4 French or Italian bread slices, about ½ inch thick

½ cup grated Parmesan or similar cheese, divided

Nonstick cooking spray, for preparing the rack

PREP TIME
10 MINUTES

SEAR/SAUTÉ
8 MINUTES

PRESSURE COOK
5 MINUTES, HIGH PRESSURE

RELEASE
NATURAL FOR 5 MINUTES, THEN QUICK

BROIL
5 MINUTES

TOTAL TIME
40 MINUTES

UNDER 60 MINUTES

SUBSTITUTION TIP: If you like, use cocktail-size frozen meatballs instead of the sausage. The cooking time remains the same.

1. Break the sausage into 1-inch pieces. Wet your hands and roll the pieces into small balls.

2. On your Foodi,™ select Sear/Sauté and adjust to Medium to preheat the inner pot. Press Start. Allow the pot to preheat for 5 minutes. Pour in 2 tablespoons of olive oil and heat until shimmering. Add the Italian sausage balls. Cook for 4 minutes, turning the pieces occasionally, or until browned. The sausage does not have to be cooked all the way through.

3. Add the garlic, celery, and onion. Sprinkle with the salt and cook for 2 to 3 minutes, stirring occasionally. Pour in the wine and bring the mixture to a boil. Cook until the wine reduces by about half, scraping the bottom of the pot to get upany browned bits. Add the chicken stock, Parmesan rind (if using), fennel seeds, cannellini beans, and kale.

4. Lock the Pressure Lid into place, making sure the valve is set to Seal. Select Pressure; adjust the pressure to High and the cook time to 5 minutes. Press Start.

5. While the soup cooks, brush the bread slices with the remaining 2 tablespoons of olive oil. Sprinkle about half the cheese over the bread.

6. Once the soup finishes cooking, let the pressure release naturally for 5 minutes, then quick release any remaining pressure. Carefully unlock and remove the Pressure Lid.

7. Spray the Reversible Rack with cooking spray or oil and place it in the pot in the upper position. Lay the bread slices on the rack.

8. Close the Crisping Lid and select Broil. Adjust the cook time to 5 minutes. Press Start. When the bread is crisp and browned, transfer it from the rack to a cutting board and let cool for a couple of minutes. Cut the slices into cubes.

9. Ladle the soup into bowls and sprinkle with the remaining cheese. Divide the croutons among the bowls and serve.

Per Serving Calories: 773; Total fat: 42g; Saturated fat: 10g; Cholesterol: 199mg; Sodium: 2214mg; Carbohydrates: 58g; Fiber: 9g; Protein: 41g

Chicken Stroganoff

SERVES 4

Beef stroganoff was one of my mother's "company" dishes. It was fancy, but not too time consuming. Over the years, I've found that the basic dish is also great with other meats. The creamy sauce is a nice match for lean chicken breasts, which can dry out when overcooked. Cooking them whole prevents that from happening, and cooking the sauce, chicken, and noodles all together makes this "fancy" dish doable even on a weeknight—with or without company!

2 large (12- to 14-ounce) boneless skinless chicken breasts

1½ teaspoons kosher salt (or ¾ teaspoon fine salt), divided

2 tablespoons unsalted butter

½ cup sliced onion

1 tablespoon all-purpose flour

½ cup brandy or dry sherry or dry white wine

2 cups Chicken Stock (page 218), or store-bought low-sodium chicken broth

1½ cups water

8 ounces egg noodles

1 cup Sautéed Mushrooms (page 220)

½ teaspoon Worcestershire sauce

¼ cup sour cream

2 tablespoons fresh dill or fresh parsley for garnish (optional)

PREP TIME
10 MINUTES

SEAR/SAUTÉ
8 MINUTES

PRESSURE COOK
5 MINUTES, HIGH PRESSURE

RELEASE
QUICK

TOTAL TIME
35 MINUTES

AROUND 30 MINUTES

SUBSTITUTION TIP: If you have leftover cooked steak or pork tenderloin, substitute that for the chicken. Just add it at step 6 and simmer until it's warmed through.

1. Sprinkle the chicken breasts with ½ teaspoon of kosher salt (or ¼ teaspoon fine salt) and set aside.

2. On your Foodi,™ select Sear/Sauté and adjust to Medium to preheat the inner pot. Press Start. Allow the pot to preheat for 5 minutes. Add the butter to melt and heat until it stops foaming. Add the onion. Cook for about 4 minutes, stirring occasionally, or until the onion starts to brown. Add the flour and stir to coat the onion. Cook for 2 minutes, stirring. Deglaze the cooker by pouring in the brandy and stirring to scrape up all the browned bits from the bottom of the pot. Let the brandy simmer until it's reduced by about two-thirds.

3. Add the chicken stock, water, the remaining 1 teaspoon of kosher salt (or ½ teaspoon of fine salt), and the noodles to the pot. Lay the chicken breasts on top of the noodles.

4. Lock the Pressure Lid into place, making sure the valve is set to Seal. Select Pressure; adjust the pressure to High and the cook time to 5 minutes. Press Start.

5. After cooking, use a quick pressure release. Carefully unlock and remove the Pressure Lid.

6. Transfer the chicken breasts to a cutting board and let them cool slightly. Cut into bite-size chunks. If the chicken is not quite done in the center, return the chicken pieces to the pot. Select Sear/Sauté and adjust to Medium-Low. Press Start. Simmer the chicken until cooked through. When the chicken is done, turn the pot off and add the mushrooms and Worcestershire sauce. Stir in the sour cream as soon as the mixture stops simmering. Serve in bowls, garnished with the dill or parsley (if using).

Per Serving Calories: 550; Total fat: 15g; Saturated fat: 7g; Cholesterol: 161mg; Sodium: 598mg; Carbohydrates: 48g; Fiber: 2g; Protein: 51g

Turkey and Wild Rice Salad

SERVES 4

My oldest sister was a natural and amazingly innovative cook, especially when it came to using leftovers. I lived with her for a few years while I was in graduate school and was constantly impressed by the way she could look into the refrigerator and assemble random ingredients into a delicious meal. (I learned that technique from the best.) This salad is based on one she made from leftover Thanksgiving turkey, the contents of the crisper drawer, and a box of wild rice pilaf.

4 cups water

1 cup wild rice

2¼ teaspoons kosher salt (or 1⅛ teaspoons fine salt), divided

1 pound turkey tenderloins

3 teaspoons walnut oil or olive oil, divided

3 tablespoons apple cider vinegar

¼ teaspoon celery seeds

⅛ teaspoon freshly ground black pepper

Pinch sugar

½ cup walnut pieces, toasted

2 or 3 celery stalks, thinly sliced (about 1 cup)

1 medium Gala, Fuji, or Braeburn apple, cored and cut into ½-inch pieces

PREP TIME
10 MINUTES

PRESSURE COOK
18 MINUTES, HIGH PRESSURE

RELEASE
NATURAL FOR 10 MINUTES, THEN QUICK

BAKE/ROAST
12 MINUTES

TOTAL TIME
60 MINUTES

DAIRY-FREE, GLUTEN-FREE

MAKE-AHEAD TIP: If you have leftover turkey from the Cajun Roasted Turkey Breast with Sweet Potatoes (page 100), use that instead of cooking turkey just for this recipe, or cook the turkey on the weekend and refrigerate it for several days until you make the rest of the salad.

1. Pour the water into the Foodi's™ inner pot. Stir in the wild rice and 1 teaspoon of kosher salt (or ½ teaspoon of fine salt).

2. Lock the Pressure Lid into place, making sure the valve is set to Seal. Select Pressure; adjust the pressure to High and the cook time to 18 minutes. Press Start.

3. While the rice cooks, sprinkle the turkey tenderloins with 1 teaspoon of kosher salt (or ½ teaspoon of fine salt) and set aside.

4. After cooking the wild rice, let the pressure release naturally for 10 minutes, then quick release any remaining pressure. Carefully unlock and remove the Pressure Lid. The rice grains should be mostly split open. If not, select Sear/Sauté and adjust to Medium. Press Start. Simmer the rice for several minutes until at least half the grains have split. Drain and let cool slightly. Transfer to a large bowl to cool completely.

5. Close the Crisping Lid and select Bake/Roast; adjust the temperature to 375ºF and the time to 4 minutes to preheat. Press Start.

6. While the rice cools and the pot preheats, transfer the turkey to the Cook & Crisp™ Basket and brush with 2 teaspoons of walnut oil.

7. When the pot is preheated, place the basket in it.

8. Close the Crisping Lid and select Bake/Roast; adjust the temperature to 375ºF and the cook time to 12 minutes. Press Start.

9. While the turkey cooks, pour the remaining 1 teaspoon of walnut oil and the vinegar into a jar with a tight-fitting lid. Add the celery seed, the remaining ¼ teaspoon of kosher salt (or ⅛ teaspoon of fine salt), the pepper, and the sugar. Cover the jar and shake until the ingredients are well combined.

10. When the turkey is cooked, remove it from the basket and let cool for several minutes. Cut it into chunks and add the turkey to the rice along with the walnut pieces, celery, and apple. Pour about half the dressing over the salad and toss gently to coat, adding more dressing as desired.

Per Serving: Calories: 409; Total fat: 12g; Saturated fat: 1g; Cholesterol: 70mg; Sodium: 665mg; Carbohydrates: 41g; Fiber: 5g; Protein: 36g

5

Meat

Left: Honey-Mustard Spare Ribs, page 116

Honey-Mustard Spare Ribs

SERVES 4

Beautifully glazed, tender spare ribs are a breeze in the Foodi.™ Start them under pressure to quickly cook and tenderize them, then add a sauce and roast them for a crisp exterior and wonderfully sticky glaze. Serve with a potato salad, tossed salad, or coleslaw for a more substantial meal.

1 rack (about 3 pounds) spare ribs

1 teaspoon kosher salt (or ½ teaspoon fine salt)

1 cup Mustard Sauce (page 227)

PREP TIME
10 MINUTES

PRESSURE COOK
18 MINUTES, HIGH PRESSURE

RELEASE
QUICK

AIR CRISP
20 MINUTES

TOTAL TIME
55 MINUTES

DAIRY-FREE, GLUTEN-FREE, UNDER 60 MINUTES

SUBSTITUTION TIP: Back ribs can be used instead of spare ribs with no change to the cook time. Also, try Barbecue Sauce (page 226) or Teriyaki Sauce (page 225) instead of the mustard sauce for a change of pace.

1. Sprinkle the ribs on both sides with the salt. Cut the rack into 3 pieces. If desired, remove the membrane from the bone side of the ribs, or cut through it every couple of inches.

2. Pour 1 cup of water into the Foodi's inner pot. Place the Reversible Rack in the pot in the lower position and place the ribs on top, bone-side down.

3. Lock the Pressure Lid into place, making sure the valve is set to Seal. Select Pressure; adjust the pressure to High and the cook time to 18 minutes. Press Start.

4. After cooking, use a quick pressure release. Carefully unlock and remove the Pressure Lid. Remove the rack and ribs from the inner pot and empty the water out of the pot. Return the inner pot to the base. Place the Reversible Rack and ribs back in the pot in the lower position.

5. Close the Crisping Lid and select Air Crisp; adjust the temperature to 400ºF and the cook time to 20 minutes. Press Start.

6. After 10 minutes, open the lid and turn the ribs over. Baste the bone side of the ribs lightly with the mustard sauce and close the lid to continue cooking. After 4 minutes, open the lid and turn the ribs again. Baste the meat side of the ribs with the rest of the sauce and close the lid to continue cooking until done.

Per Serving Calories: 621; Total fat: 48g; Saturated fat: 17g; Cholesterol: 164mg; Sodium: 1419mg; Carbohydrates: 12g; Fiber: 2g; Protein: 32g

Carnitas

A favorite at Mexican restaurants and taquerias, carnitas are made by slow roasting pork shoulder and letting it brown in its own fat, resulting in deliciously tender pork chunks with crispy edges. Made the traditional way, the dish takes hours, but with the initial cooking done under pressure and the final browning under the Foodi's™ Crisping Lid, it is ready in about an hour.

2½ pounds bone-in country ribs (2 pounds if boneless)

1 teaspoon kosher salt (or ½ teaspoon fine salt)

¼ cup freshly squeezed orange juice

2 tablespoons Chicken Stock (page 218), or store-bought low-sodium chicken broth

1 tablespoon freshly squeezed lime juice

3 garlic cloves, smashed and peeled

1 small onion, cut into 8 wedges

Nonstick cooking spray, for preparing the rack

PREP TIME
5 MINUTES

PRESSURE COOK
25 MINUTES, HIGH PRESSURE

RELEASE
NATURAL FOR 12 MINUTES, THEN QUICK

AIR CRISP
6 MINUTES

TOTAL TIME
55 MINUTES

GLUTEN-FREE, UNDER 60 MINUTES

1. Sprinkle the ribs on both sides with the salt.

2. In the Foodi's inner pot, combine the orange juice, chicken stock, and lime juice. Add the garlic and onion and stir to combine. Place the ribs in the pot, arranging them in a single layer.

3. Lock the Pressure Lid into place, making sure the valve is set to Seal. Select Pressure; adjust the pressure to High and the cook time to 25 minutes. Press Start.

4. After cooking, let the pressure release naturally for 12 minutes, then quick release the remaining pressure. Carefully unlock and remove the Pressure Lid. Using tongs, transfer the ribs to a plate or baking sheet to cool slightly. Remove and discard the bones.

5. Pour the accumulated liquid in the pot into a fat separator and set aside for a few minutes. When the fat has separated, pour the sauce back into the pot, reserving the fat. (If you don't have a fat separator, spoon off as much fat as possible and remove any chunks of onion or garlic. Leave the sauce in the inner pot, reserving the fat.)

MAKE-AHEAD TIP: The initial pressure cooking can be done a day or two ahead of the final crisping. Remove the pork, let cool, then wrap in aluminum foil. Pour the sauce into a container with a lid (there's no need to separate the fat, as the fat will harden on top). Refrigerate. To finish, peel the fat off the sauce and pour the sauce into the inner pot. Continue with the recipe at step 6, either melting the fat to baste the pork or just breaking it up into bits and sprinkling it over the top.

6. Close the Crisping Lid and select Air Crisp; adjust the temperature to 400°F and the time to 3 minutes to preheat. Press Start.

7. While the Foodi™ preheats, spray the Reversible Rack with cooking spray and arrange the pork in a single layer on the rack. Baste it with the reserved fat from the sauce.

8. When the Foodi is heated, place the rack in the pot in the upper position. Close the Crisping Lid and select Air Crisp; adjust the temperature to 375°F and the cook time to 6 minutes. Press Start.

9. After cooking is complete, check the pork, which should be crisp and brown. Transfer the pork back to the sauce and use tongs to break it up into bite-size pieces. Stir the pork into the sauce. Serve the carnitas on rice, or on warmed corn or flour tortillas with chopped red onion, jalapeño, fresh cilantro, and lime wedges, or your preferred toppings.

Per Serving Calories: 442; Total fat: 27g; Saturated fat: 9g; Cholesterol: 168mg; Sodium: 725mg; Carbohydrates: 3g; Fiber: 0g; Protein: 44g

Sunday Pot Roast and Biscuits

SERVES 6

Nothing says Sunday dinner quite like pot roast. Pressure cooking yields tender, juicy beef without taking all day to get there. In this recipe, tender biscuits bake while the vegetables finish cooking and the sauce thickens into a delicious gravy.

2 tablespoons vegetable oil

1 (3- to 3½-pound) chuck roast (about 3 inches thick)

1½ teaspoons kosher salt (or ¾ teaspoon fine salt)

⅔ cup dry red wine

⅔ cup low-sodium beef broth

1 teaspoon dried thyme leaves

1 bay leaf

¼ teaspoon freshly ground black pepper

1 small onion, peeled and quartered

1 pound small red potatoes, scrubbed and quartered

2 carrots, peeled and cut into 1-inch pieces

¾ cup frozen pearl onions

6 refrigerated biscuits, or frozen biscuits, thawed

PREP TIME
10 MINUTES

SEAR/SAUTÉ
8 MINUTES

PRESSURE COOK
35 MINUTES PLUS 2 MINUTES, HIGH PRESSURE

RELEASE
QUICK

BAKE/ROAST
15 MINUTES

TOTAL TIME
1 HOUR 15 MINUTES

DAIRY-FREE

SUBSTITUTION TIP: If you can't find pearl onions, use one medium onion, coarsely chopped.

1. On your Foodi™ select Sear/Sauté and adjust to Medium-High to preheat the inner pot. Press Start. Allow the pot to preheat for 5 minutes. Add the vegetable oil and heat until shimmering. Sprinkle the beef on both sides with the salt. Blot the roast dry and add it to the pot. Let it cook, undisturbed, for 3 minutes or until deeply browned. Turn the roast over and brown the other side for 3 minutes. Transfer the beef to a wire rack.

2. Pour off the oil from the pot. Return the pot to the base and add the wine. Stir, scraping the bottom of the pot to dissolve the browned bits. Bring to a boil and cook for 1 to 2 minutes or until the wine has reduced by about half. Add the beef broth, thyme, bay leaf, pepper, and onion. Stir to combine.

3. Add the beef with any accumulated juices.

4. Lock the Pressure Lid in place and select Pressure; adjust the pressure to High and the cook time to 35 minutes. Press Start.

5. After cooking, use a quick pressure release. Carefully unlock and remove the Pressure Lid.

6. Add the potatoes, carrots, and pearl onions to the pot.

7. Lock the Pressure Lid into place and select Pressure; adjust the pressure to High and the cook time to 2 minutes. Press Start.

8. After cooking, use a quick pressure release. Carefully unlock and remove the Pressure Lid. Transfer the beef to a cutting board and tent with aluminum foil.

9. Place the Reversible Rack in the upper position and cover with foil or a parchment paper circle. Place the biscuits on the rack and place the rack in the pot.

10. Close the Crisping Lid and select Bake/Roast; adjust the temperature to 300ºF and the cook time to 15 minutes. Press Start. After 8 minutes, open the lid and carefully turn the biscuits over. After baking, remove the rack and biscuits and let the biscuits cool for a few minutes before serving.

11. While the biscuits cook, untent the beef and cut it against the grain into slices about ⅓ inch thick. Carefully remove the bay leaf. Transfer the beef to a serving platter. Spoon the vegetables and the sauce over the beef and serve with the biscuits on the side.

FROM SCRATCH

For the easiest homemade biscuits ever, mix 8 ounces self-rising flour (about 1⅔ cups) with 8 fluid ounces (1 cup) heavy (whipping) cream. Turn the dough out onto a floured cutting board and knead briefly. Pat the dough into an oval about ½ inch thick. Cut with a (2-inch) biscuit cutter, rerolling the scraps as necessary.

Per Serving Calories: 817; Total fat: 51g; Saturated fat: 19g; Cholesterol: 150mg; Sodium: 933mg; Carbohydrates: 37g; Fiber: 3g; Protein: 49g

Beefy Onion Soup with Cheese Croutons

SERVES 4

Oxtails are a cut of beef with extraordinary flavor and an unctuous texture, and they turn this soup into an amazing version of French onion soup. I like to reserve some of the sautéed onions until right before serving so they keep their texture, but if you prefer softer onions, add them all before pressure cooking.

2 cups (¾-inch) bread cubes

1 pound bone-in oxtails

½ teaspoon kosher salt (or ¼ teaspoon fine salt), plus more as needed

3 tablespoons unsalted butter, divided

2 or 3 medium white or yellow onions, thinly sliced (about 3 cups)

⅓ cup dry or medium-dry sherry

4 cups low-sodium beef broth

½ teaspoon dried thyme leaves or 2 thyme sprigs

1 bay leaf

1 recipe Caramelized Onions (page 222)

2 teaspoons Worcestershire sauce

1 teaspoon sherry vinegar (optional)

2 cups shredded Gruyère, Emmental, or other Swiss-style cheese

PREP TIME
10 MINUTES

SEAR/SAUTÉ
15 MINUTES

PRESSURE COOK
40 MINUTES, HIGH PRESSURE

RELEASE
NATURAL FOR 10 MINUTES, THEN QUICK

AIR CRISP
8 MINUTES

TOTAL TIME
1 HOUR 25 MINUTES

SUBSTITUTION TIP: If you can't find oxtails, bone-in short ribs make a fine substitute

1. Spread the bread cubes on a baking sheet to dry out. Season the oxtails on all sides with the salt and set aside.

2. On your Foodi,™ select Sear/Sauté and adjust to Medium-High to preheat the inner pot. Press Start. Allow the pot to preheat for 5 minutes. Add the butter to melt and heat until foaming. Add the sliced onions and stir to coat with the butter. Spread the onions into a single layer as much as possible and let them cook, without stirring, for 2 to 4 minutes until they start to brown.

3. Stir the onions and repeat the cooking process until most of the pieces are browned. Remove from the pot and set aside.

4. Place the oxtails into the pot. Let cook for several minutes, or until browned on one side. Add the sherry. Bring to a simmer, scraping up any browned bits from the bottom of the

pot. Cook until the sherry has reduced by about half. Add the beef broth, thyme, and bay leaf. Stir in the caramelized onions (but not the reserved onions from step 3).

5. Lock the Pressure Lid into place, making sure the valve is set to Seal. Select Pressure; adjust the pressure to High and the cook time to 40 minutes. Press Start.

6. After cooking, let the pressure release naturally for 10 minutes, then quick release any remaining pressure. Carefully unlock and remove the Pressure Lid.

7. Using tongs, remove the oxtails. The meat should be falling off the bones. Set aside until cool enough to handle. Remove and discard the bay leaf and thyme sprigs (if used).

8. Let the soup sit for a few minutes to allow the fat to come to the surf ace. Skim or spoon off as much as possible.

9. When the oxtails are cool enough to handle, shred the meat, discarding the bones and tendons and any remaining fat. Return the meat to the soup along with the reserved onions and the Worcestershire sauce. Taste and add salt if needed. If the soup seems sweet, add the optional sherry vinegar. (If the soup has cooled off, bring it back to a simmer by selecting Sear/Sauté, Medium setting, and pressing Start.)

10. Sprinkle about one-third of the cheese over the top of the soup. Arrange the bread cubes over the cheese. Top with the remaining cheese.

11. Close the Crisping Lid and select Air Crisp; adjust the temperature to 400°F and the cook time to 8 minutes. Press Start. Check the soup after about 6 minutes. The cheese should be melted and the bread crisp around the edges. If not, cook for a few minutes longer. Ladle into bowls and serve immediately.

Per Serving Calories: 608; Total fat: 31g; Saturated fat: 18g; Cholesterol: 91mg; Sodium: 1266mg; Carbohydrates: 41g; Fiber: 3g; Protein: 36g.

Kielbasa with Braised Cabbage and Noodles

SERVES 4

With German grandparents on both sides, my family ate many German-inspired meals, and sausages with cabbage were a favorite dinner. I still love smoked sausages such as kielbasa, and often pair them with noodles and cabbage, cooked with a bit of bacon for good measure.

3 ounces bacon, diced (about 3 slices)

1 small onion, sliced (about 1 cup)

⅓ cup dry white wine

1 cup Chicken Stock (page 218), or store-bought low-sodium chicken broth

1 teaspoon kosher salt (or ½ teaspoon fine salt) (Use ½ teaspoon kosher salt or ¼ teaspoon fine salt if using store-bought broth)

¼ teaspoon freshly ground black pepper

5 ounces wide egg noodles

4 cups shredded cabbage or coleslaw mix

1½ pounds kielbasa or other smoked sausage, cut into 4 pieces

Nonstick cooking spray, for preparing the rack

PREP TIME
10 MINUTES

SEAR/SAUTÉ
8 MINUTES

PRESSURE COOK
3 MINUTES, HIGH PRESSURE

RELEASE
QUICK

BAKE/ROAST
8 MINUTES

TOTAL TIME
35 MINUTES

DAIRY-FREE, GLUTEN-FREE OPTION, AROUND 30 MINUTES

SUBSTITUTION TIP: To make the dish gluten-free, use small red potatoes, quartered, in place of the noodles. Decrease the chicken stock to ⅓ cup.

1. On your Foodi,™ select Sear/Sauté and adjust to Medium to preheat the inner pot. Press Start. Allow the pot to preheat for 5 minutes. Add the bacon. Cook for about 6 minutes until most of the fat has rendered and the bacon is crisp. Using tongs or a slotted spoon, transfer the bacon to a paper towel–lined plate to drain, leaving the fat in the pot.

2. Add the onion to the pot. Stir to coat with the bacon fat. Cook for about 2 minutes, stirring, until the onion starts to soften. Add the wine. Bring to a simmer, scraping the bottom of the pot to get up any browned bits. Let the wine reduce slightly.

3. Add the chicken stock, salt, and noodles. Stir, submerging the noodles as much as possible in the liquid. Place the cabbage on top of the noodles and the sausages on top of the cabbage.

4. Lock the Pressure Lid into place, making sure the valve is set to Seal. Select Pressure; adjust the pressure to High and the cook time to 3 minutes.

5. After cooking, use a quick pressure release. Carefully unlock and remove the Pressure Lid.

6. Stir the cabbage and noodles and taste for seasoning.

7. Spray the Reversible Rack with cooking spray or oil and place it in the pot in the upper position. Using tongs, transfer the sausages to the rack.

8. Close the Crisping Lid and select Bake/Roast; adjust the temperature to 390ºF and the cook time to 8 minutes. Press Start. After 4 minutes, open the lid and check the sausages. They should be browned on top. If not, close the lid and cook for 1 to 2 minutes more. When browned, turn them, close the lid, and cook to brown the other side.

9. Spoon the cabbage and noodles into a bowl and top with the bacon. Serve with the sausages.

Per Serving Calories: 667; Total fat: 42g; Saturated fat: 14g; Cholesterol: 164mg; Sodium: 2467mg; Carbohydrates: 40g; Fiber: 3g; Protein: 32g

Pork Ragu with Penne

SERVES 6

Long-simmered pork ragu is probably tied with Bolognese sauce for the best-known and tastiest Italian meat sauce. Italian sausage and pork shoulder braise in a flavorful tomato sauce to make the perfect topping for pasta or polenta. Here, I cook the ragu with pasta, then sprinkle with cheese and broil for a crisp, browned top.

1 pound boneless pork shoulder country ribs

1 teaspoon kosher salt (or ½ teaspoon fine salt), divided

2 tablespoons olive oil

4 ounces Italian sausage (usually 1 link), sweet or hot, casings removed

1 medium onion, chopped (about 1¼ cups)

1 medium carrot, peeled and chopped (about ½ cup)

1 celery stalk, diced (about ½ cup)

2 garlic cloves, minced or pressed

½ cup dry red wine

1 (28-ounce) can crushed tomatoes

2 tablespoons tomato paste

⅛ teaspoon red pepper flakes

2 teaspoons dried Italian herbs (thyme, oregano, basil, or a combination)

1 cup water, divided

12 ounces penne pasta

½ cup grated Parmesan or similar cheese, plus more for serving

PREP TIME
10 MINUTES

SEAR/SAUTÉ
10 MINUTES

PRESSURE COOK
20 MINUTES PLUS 4 MINUTES, HIGH PRESSURE

RELEASE
NATURAL FOR 10 MINUTES, THEN QUICK

BROIL
7 MINUTES

TOTAL TIME
1 HOUR 10 MINUTES

MAKE-AHEAD TIP: The ragu can be made through step 4 and refrigerated for up to 3 days or frozen for up to 1 month. Bring to a simmer and continue with the recipe.

1. Sprinkle the pork with ½ teaspoon of kosher salt (or ¼ teaspoon of fine salt).

2. On your Foodi,™ select Sear/Sauté and adjust to Medium to preheat the inner pot. Press Start. Allow the pot to preheat for 5 minutes. Pour in the olive oil and heat until shimmering. When the pot is hot, add the pork. Sear on one side for about 4 minutes or until browned. Add the sausage, stirring to break it up a little. Add the onion, carrot, celery, and garlic. Cook for about 2 minutes, stirring, until the vegetables just start to soften. Stir in the wine, scraping up any browned bits from the bottom of the pot. Cook for 2 to 3 minutes until the wine has reduced by at least half. Add the tomatoes, tomato paste, red pepper flakes, remaining ½ teaspoon of kosher salt (or ¼ teaspoon of fine salt), and the dried herbs. Stir to combine.

3. Lock the Pressure Lid into place, making sure the valve is set to Seal. Select Pressure; adjust the pressure to High and the cook time to 20 minutes. Press Start.

4. After cooking, let the pressure release naturally for 10 minutes, then quick release any remaining pressure. Carefully unlock and remove the Pressure Lid. Stir the sauce and use two forks to shred the pork and break the sausage apart.

5. Add the water and the penne.

6. Lock the Pressure Lid into place again, making sure the valve is set to Seal. Select Pressure; adjust the pressure to High and the cook time to 4 minutes. Press Start.

7. After cooking, use a quick pressure release. Carefully unlock and remove the Pressure Lid.

8. Sprinkle the cheese over the pasta and sauce.

9. Close the Crisping Lid and select Broil. Adjust the time to 7 minutes. Press Start. After cooking, open the lid; the cheese should be browned and crisp. Let cool slightly. Serve with a salad on the side, if desired.

Per Serving Calories: 679; Total fat: 25g; Saturated fat: 8g; Cholesterol: 85mg; Sodium: 1914mg; Carbohydrates: 80g; Fiber: 10g; Protein: 38g

Chorizo-Stuffed Peppers

SERVES 4

Forget the boring stuffed peppers you grew up with. These are spicy and cheesy, with a Mexican accent from the chorizo. They cook quickly under pressure, and a few minutes under the Crisping Lid is all it takes to finish this beautiful, delicious entrée.

4 large bell peppers (red, yellow, or green)

2 teaspoons olive oil

¾ pound chorizo

1 small onion, diced (about 1 cup)

⅔ cup diced fresh or canned tomatoes

1½ cups cooked rice

1 cup grated Monterey Jack cheese or shredded Mexican blend cheese, divided

PREP TIME
10 MINUTES

SEAR/SAUTÉ
5 MINUTES

PRESSURE COOK
12 MINUTES, HIGH PRESSURE

RELEASE
QUICK

BROIL
5 MINUTES

TOTAL TIME
40 MINUTES

UNDER 60 MINUTES

1. Cut about ¼ to ⅓ inch off the top of each pepper, setting the tops aside. With a paring knife, cut through the ribs on the insides of the peppers and pull out the core. Using the knife and your fingers, remove as much of the ribs as possible, leaving a hollow shell. Take the pepper tops and cut the flesh away from the stem. Trim off any white pithy parts from the inside, and dice the flesh. You should have ½ to ⅔ cup.

2. On your Foodi™ select Sear/Sauté and adjust to Medium to preheat the inner pot. Press Start. Allow the pot to preheat for 5 minutes. Pour in the oil and heat until shimmering. Add the chorizo and use a spatula to break the meat up. Cook until just starting to brown, about 2 minutes. Add the onion and bell pepper and cook, stirring, until the vegetables are softening and the chorizo is browned, about 3 minutes.

3. Turn the Foodi off and scoop the chorizo and vegetables into a medium bowl. Add the tomatoes, rice, and ½ cup of the cheese and stir to combine.

4. Scoop the stuffing mixture into the hollowed out bell peppers, packing the filling in and heaping it slightly over the tops of the peppers.

INGREDIENT TIP: For the chorizo, if you don't have access to a Hispanic market, Johnsonville is a good brand found in most grocery stores. Make sure you get fresh Mexican chorizo and not the cured Spanish or Portuguese versions.

SUBSTITUTION TIP: If you can't find Mexican chorizo, substitute 1 pound of ground beef or pork seasoned with 3 tablespoons of Mexican/Southwestern Seasoning Mix (page 224).

5. Wash or wipe out the inner pot and return it to the base. Pour 1 cup of water into the pot and place the rack in the pot in the lower position. Place the peppers on the rack and cover the tops loosely with a piece of aluminum foil.

6. Lock the Pressure Lid into place, making sure the valve is set to Seal. Select Pressure; adjust the pressure to High and the time to 12 minutes. Press Start.

7. After cooking, quick release the pressure. Carefully unlock and remove the Pressure Lid.

8. Remove the foil from the top of the peppers and divide the remaining ½ cup of cheese over the tops.

9. Close the Crisping Lid and select Broil. Adjust the time to 5 minutes. Press Start. After 4 minutes, open the lid and check the peppers. The cheese should be melted and beginning to brown a bit. If not, close the lid and continue cooking.

10. Let the peppers cool for several minutes before serving.

Per Serving Calories: 656; Total fat: 45g; Saturated fat: 18g; Cholesterol: 105mg; Sodium: 1233mg; Carbohydrates: 32g; Fiber: 3g; Protein: 31g

Southwestern Shepherd's Pie

SERVES 6

Okay, technically this isn't shepherd's pie. No lamb and no mashed potatoes. But I like to think the spirit is the same. A savory braised beef dish gets a topping that's a cross between corn pudding and corn bread for a delicious, hearty, one-pot dinner, Southwestern-style.

FOR THE BEEF

2 pounds chuck roast, cut into strips 3 inches wide and 2 inches thick

1 teaspoon kosher salt (or ½ teaspoon fine salt)

2 tablespoons vegetable oil

1 large onion, coarsely chopped

2 garlic cloves, minced

3 tablespoons Mexican/ Southwestern Seasoning Mix (page 224), or store-bought mix

1 (14-ounce) can diced tomatoes with juice

2 tablespoons low-sodium beef broth

1 medium poblano or Anaheim chile, diced

FOR THE TOPPING

¾ cup all-purpose flour

¾ cup cornmeal

3 teaspoons baking powder

½ teaspoon kosher salt (or ¼ teaspoon fine salt)

⅓ cup whole milk

1 large egg

2 tablespoons melted unsalted butter

1 (14-ounce) can creamed corn

PREP TIME
10 MINUTES

SEAR/SAUTÉ
6 MINUTES

PRESSURE COOK
35 MINUTES, HIGH PRESSURE

RELEASE
QUICK

BAKE/ROAST
20 MINUTES

TOTAL TIME
1 HOUR 15 MINUTES

CUSTOMIZATION TIP: Make the beef filling from this recipe and use it in empanadas.

To make the beef

1. Season the beef on all sides with the salt.

2. On your Foodi,™ select Sear/Sauté and adjust to Medium to preheat the inner pot. Press Start. Allow the pot to preheat for 5 minutes. Pour in the vegetable oil and heat until shimmering. Add the beef. Cook, without turning, for 4 minutes or until browned. Turn the beef strips over and move them to the sides. Add the onion and garlic. Cook for 1 to 2 minutes, stirring, until slightly softened. Scrape up any browned bits from the bottom of the pot. Add the seasoning, tomatoes with their juice, and beef broth. Stir to combine.

3. Lock the Pressure Lid into place, making sure the valve is set to Seal. Select Pressure; adjust the pressure to High and the cook time to 35 minutes. Press Start.

To make the topping

1. While the beef cooks, make the topping. In a medium bowl, combine the flour, cornmeal, baking powder, and salt.

2. In a small bowl, whisk the milk, egg, and melted butter. Stir in the creamed corn. Fold the wet ingredients into the dry ingredients until well combined.

To finish the dish

1. Once the beef finishes cooking, use a quick pressure release. Carefully unlock and remove the Pressure Lid.

2. Transfer the strips of beef from the pot to a cutting board. Pour the liquid into a fat separator and let sit for several minutes until the fat has risen to the surface (or spoon or blot off the fat from the surface of the sauce). Return the sauce to the pot.

3. Shred the beef into bite-size chunks, discarding any fat or gristle. Return it to the pot. Add the diced chile. Stir to combine.

4. Spoon the corn topping over the beef.

5. Close the Crisping Lid and select Bake/Roast; adjust the temperature to 200°F and the cook time to 10 minutes. Press Start.

6. When cooking is complete, open the lid. The topping should be set but not browned on top. Close the Crisping Lid and select Bake/Roast again; adjust the temperature to 360°F and the cook time to 10 minutes. Press Start.

Per Serving Calories: 627; Total fat: 38g; Saturated fat: 15g; Cholesterol: 146mg; Sodium: 789mg; Carbohydrates: 37g; Fiber: 4g; Protein: 35g

Sausage and Pepper Calzones

SERVES 4

Calzones, a sort of folded-over pizza, are easy to make once you get the hang of working with pizza dough. I use refrigerated dough from the grocery store and press it out rather than rolling it. Using parchment paper makes it much easier—the dough sticks to it just enough to keep it from shrinking, but it peels right off after baking.

2 tablespoons olive oil, divided, plus more as needed

1 small red bell pepper, seeded and coarsely chopped

2 or 3 Italian sausages (about 12 ounces)

1 pound pizza dough or thawed frozen bread dough

¼ cup Marinara Sauce (page 228) or your favorite store-bought sauce

1 cup shredded mozzarella cheese or mozzarella blend

PREP TIME
10 MINUTES

SEAR/SAUTÉ
7 MINUTES

PRESSURE COOK
4 MINUTES, HIGH PRESSURE

RELEASE
QUICK

BAKE/ROAST
12 MINUTES PER BATCH

TOTAL TIME
35 MINUTES

UNDER 60 MINUTES

CUSTOMIZATION TIP:
Feel free to substitute your favorite pizza toppings in these calzones; just don't fill them too full or they can split. For a vegetarian version, mushrooms and spinach make a good combination.

1. On your Foodi™ select Sear/Sauté and adjust to Medium-High to preheat the inner pot. Press Start. Allow the pot to preheat for 5 minutes. Pour in 1 tablespoon of olive oil and heat until shimmering. Add the bell pepper. Cook for 1 minute, stirring occasionally, or until just starting to soften. Using a slotted spoon, remove the pepper and set aside. Add the sausages. Let brown for 2 to 3 minutes on one side. Turn and brown the other side.

2. Add ¾ cup of water to the inner pot.

3. Lock the Pressure Lid into place, making sure the valve is set to Seal. Select Pressure; adjust the pressure to High and the cook time to 4 minutes. Press Start.

4. After cooking, use a quick pressure release. Carefully unlock and remove the Pressure Lid.

5. Using tongs, transfer the sausages from the pot to a cutting board. Let them cool for several minutes. Pour the water out of the pot, wipe the pot dry, and return it to the base. When the sausages have cooled, slice them into ¼-inch rounds.

6. Cut four pieces of parchment paper about 8 inches on a side. Divide the pizza dough into four equal pieces. One at a time, on a piece of parchment, press one piece of dough into a circle about 6 to 7 inches in diameter. You may find it easier if you coat your fingers with a bit of olive oil. It might help to press one piece of dough out and let it rest while you start on another piece. Once the dough relaxes a bit, it's usually easier to get it into the right size. Repeat with the remaining dough pieces.

7. Close the Crisping Lid and select Bake/Roast; adjust the temperature to 400ºF and the time to 5 minutes to preheat. Press Start.

8. While the Foodi™ preheats, make the calzones. One at a time, spread 1 tablespoon of marinara sauce over half of a dough circle, leaving a ½-inch clear border. Lay the sausage rounds in a single layer and sprinkle one-fourth of the red peppers over the top. Top with ¼ cup of cheese. Use the parchment to pull the other side of the dough over the filling and pinch the edges together to seal. Repeat with one more dough round.

9. Cut the parchment around each calzones so it is about ½ inch larger than the calzone all around. Brush the calzones with some of the remaining 1 tablespoon of olive oil. Using a large spatula, transfer the two calzones to the Reversible Rack set in the lower position. Open the lid and place the rack in the pot. ➤

Sausage and Pepper Calzones continued

10. Close the Crisping Lid and select Bake/Roast; adjust the temperature to 400ºF and the cook time to 12 minutes. Press Start. After 6 minutes, check the calzones, which should be a dark golden brown. Remove the rack and carefully flip the calzones over. Peel off the parchment paper and brush the tops with a little olive oil. Return the rack to the pot. Close the lid and resume cooking for the last 6 minutes.

11. While the first two calzones bake, assemble the remaining two.

12. When the first calzones are done, transfer them to a wire rack or cutting board to cool while you bake the second batch. (If they cool too much, just return them to the warm Foodi™ while the second batch cools.) They come out much too hot to eat, so the cooling process is essential.

Per Serving Calories: 715; Total fat: 42g; Saturated fat: 14g; Cholesterol: 86mg; Sodium: 793mg; Carbohydrates: 55g; Fiber: 3g; Protein: 25g

Simple Potato Gratin with Ham and Peas

SERVES 4

This is one of my go-to potato dishes when I don't want to go to all the trouble of a traditional potato gratin, but I do want something a little special. The addition of ham and peas turns this gratin into an easy but tasty weeknight dinner.

1½ pounds red potatoes, quartered

½ teaspoon kosher salt, or more to taste

⅛ teaspoon freshly ground black pepper (several grinds)

½ cup heavy (whipping) cream, or more to taste

1 cup shredded sharp Cheddar cheese (about 2 ounces)

10 ounces ham, diced

¾ cup frozen peas, thawed

½ cup grated Parmesan or similar cheese

3 tablespoons chopped fresh chives or scallions

PREP TIME
10 MINUTES

PRESSURE COOK
4 MINUTES, HIGH PRESSURE

RELEASE
QUICK

BAKE/ROAST
10 MINUTES

TOTAL TIME
30 MINUTES

GLUTEN-FREE, AROUND 30 MINUTES

CUSTOMIZATION TIP:
Use other meats, cheeses, or vegetables in this dish. Bacon, Swiss-style cheese, and mushrooms are a good combination, or spice it up with Italian sausage, mozzarella, and roasted red peppers.

1. Place the potatoes on the Reversible Rack or in a steamer basket. Pour 1 cup of water into the Foodi's™ inner pot. Place the rack in the pot in the lower position.

2. Lock the Pressure Lid into place, making sure the valve is set to Seal. Select Pressure; adjust the pressure to High and the cook time to 4 minutes. Press Start.

3. After cooking, use a quick pressure release. Carefully unlock and remove the Pressure Lid.

4. Remove the rack. Empty the water out of the pot and return the pot to the base. Return the potatoes to the pot and sprinkle with the salt and pepper. Use a large fork or potato masher to break up the potatoes into pieces about ½ inch on a side. Stir in the heavy cream, Cheddar cheese, and ham. Add more cream if necessary to coat the ingredients, but not enough to pool on the bottom of the pot. Gently stir in the peas.

5. Sprinkle the mixture with the Parmesan cheese. ➤

Simple Potato Gratin with Ham and Peas continued

6. Close the Crisping Lid and select Bake/Roast; adjust the temperature to 400ºF and the cook time to 10 minutes. Press Start.

7. When the top of the gratin is browned and the interior is bubbling slightly, sprinkle with the chives and serve.

Per Serving: Calories: 582; Total fat: 35g; Saturated fat: 19g; Cholesterol: 125mg; Sodium: 1363mg; Carbohydrates: 36g; Fiber: 3g; Protein: 32g

Pork Lo Mein with Vegetables

Traditionally, lo mein is made by quickly stir-frying meat and vegetables and then mixing in cooked noodles and sauce. In my version, the noodles and vegetables simmer together while the pork slices cook above, under the broiler. It's a little unconventional, but easy, and it works.

¼ cup soy sauce

1 tablespoon oyster sauce or hoisin sauce

1 tablespoon sesame oil

1 (12- to 14-ounce) pork tenderloin, cut into ¼-inch-thick slices

8 ounces Chinese wheat noodles or ramen noodles

2 cups Chicken Stock (page 218), store-bought low-sodium chicken broth, or water

1 garlic clove, minced

4 or 5 scallions, chopped, greens and white parts separated

1 cup snow peas, trimmed

Nonstick cooking spray, for preparing the rack

1 large carrot, peeled and cut into strips (about ½ cup)

1 small red bell pepper, cut into strips (about ⅔ cup)

½ cup Sautéed Mushrooms (page 220)

PREP TIME
15 MINUTES

PRESSURE COOK
1 MINUTE, LOW PRESSURE

RELEASE
QUICK

AIR CRISP
4 MINUTES PLUS 8 MINUTES

TOTAL TIME
30 MINUTES

DAIRY-FREE, AROUND 30 MINUTES

CUSTOMIZATION TIP: Slices of chicken breast or peeled raw shrimp can be substituted for the pork slices. Cook the chicken for the same amount of time; cook the shrimp for about 6 minutes.

SUBSTITUTION TIP: If you can't find Chinese wheat noodles, substitute ramen noodles. Just leave out the seasoning packet.

1. In a small bowl, whisk together the soy sauce, oyster sauce, and sesame oil (or pour the ingredients into a jar with a tight-fitting lid, cover, and shake to combine).

2. Place the pork slices in a resealable plastic bag and add 2 tablespoons of the sauce. Seal the bag and move the pork around until it's evenly coated. Set aside.

3. Pour the chicken stock into the Foodi's™ inner pot. Add the garlic, white parts of the scallions, and 2 teaspoons of the sauce. Break the noodles up and put them in the pot in a single layer as much as possible. Spread the snow peas over the noodles.

4. Lock the Pressure Lid into place, making sure the valve is set to Seal. Select Pressure; adjust the pressure to Low and the cook time to 1 minute. Press Start. ➤

5. While the noodles cook, spray the Reversible Rack with cooking spray or oil, making sure the rack is in the upper position. Arrange the pork slices on it.

6. When cooking is complete, use a quick pressure release. Carefully unlock and remove the Pressure Lid.

7. Stir the noodles and snow peas, breaking up any clumps of noodles. Layer the carrot and bell pepper over the noodle mixture.

8. Close the Crisping Lid and select Air Crisp; adjust the temperature to 400°F and the cook time to 4 minutes. Press Start.

9. When cooking is complete, open the lid and stir in the mushrooms. Place the rack with the pork in the pot in the upper position. Close the Crisping Lid again and select Air Crisp; set the time for 8 minutes. Press Start. Halfway through the cook time, open the lid and flip the pork. Close the lid and continue cooking.

10. When cooking is complete, remove the rack and pork. Stir the remaining sauce into the noodles and add the pork. Gently stir to combine. Serve garnished with the scallion greens.

Per Serving Calories: 519; Total fat: 25g; Saturated fat: 4g; Cholesterol: 58mg; Sodium: 1546mg; Carbohydrates: 46g; Fiber: 5g; Protein: 28g

Meatloaf and Mashed Potatoes

SERVES 4

Cooking meatloaf under pressure not only speeds the process but also keeps it very juicy. This recipe takes a little time to put together, but it's so good, it's definitely worth it. Plus, you get mashed potatoes at the same time, in the same pot.

1 tablespoon vegetable or olive oil

1 cup chopped onion

2 garlic cloves, minced

12 ounces meatloaf mix (or 8 ounces ground chuck and 4 ounces ground pork)

2 teaspoons kosher salt (or 1 teaspoon fine salt), divided

½ teaspoon freshly ground black pepper

3 tablespoons chopped fresh parsley

¼ teaspoon dried thyme

12 individual saltine crackers, put in a resealable plastic bag and crushed to crumbs

1¾ cups whole milk, divided

2 large eggs

1 teaspoon Creole mustard or other grainy mustard

1 teaspoon Worcestershire sauce

½ cup heavy (whipping) cream

2 pounds russet potatoes, peeled and cut into large chunks (3 inches or so)

3 tablespoons unsalted butter

¼ cup Barbecue Sauce (page 226)

PREP TIME
20 MINUTES

SEAR/SAUTÉ
2 MINUTES

PRESSURE COOK
25 MINUTES, HIGH PRESSURE

RELEASE
QUICK

BROIL
7 MINUTES

TOTAL TIME
55 MINUTES

UNDER 60 MINUTES

MAKE-AHEAD TIP: You can make the meatloaf ahead of time and refrigerate it, covered in plastic wrap, overnight. Once cooked, leftovers can be frozen.

1. On your Foodi™ select Sear/Sauté and adjust to Medium to preheat the inner pot. Press Start. Allow the pot to preheat for 5 minutes. Pour in the vegetable oil and heat until shimmering. Add the onion and garlic. Cook for about 2 minutes, stirring, until the onion softens. Remove the onion and garlic and set aside.

2. In a large bowl, break the meatloaf mix into small pieces. Over the meat, sprinkle 1 teaspoon of kosher salt (or ½ teaspoon of fine salt), the pepper, parsley, and thyme. Add the sautéed onion and garlic. Sprinkle the crushed saltines over the meat and seasonings. ➤

3. In a small bowl or measuring cup, whisk ¼ cup of milk, the eggs, mustard, and Worcestershire sauce. Pour the mixture over the layer of cracker crumbs. Using your hands or a large spoon, gently mix together all the ingredients in the bowl. Everything should be thoroughly combined, but avoid over-working the mixture or it may get tough as it cooks. Shape the meat mixture into an 8-inch round.

4. Cover the Reversible Rack in the lower position with nonstick aluminum foil (or regular foil sprayed with cooking spray). Carefully transfer the meatloaf to the rack.

5. Pour the remaining 1½ cups of milk and the heavy cream into the inner pot. Add the potatoes, butter, and remaining 1 teaspoon of kosher salt (or ½ teaspoon of fine salt). Place the rack with the meatloaf on top of the potatoes.

6. Lock the Pressure Lid into place, making sure the valve is set to Seal. Select Pressure; adjust the pressure to High and the cook time to 25 minutes. Press Start.

7. After cooking, use a quick pressure release. Carefully unlock and remove the Pressure Lid.

8. Brush the barbecue sauce over the top of the meatloaf.

9. Close the Crisping Lid and select Broil. Adjust the cook time to 7 minutes. Press Start.

10. When the top is browned and glazed, remove the rack and transfer the meatloaf to a platter or cutting board. Use a potato masher to mash the potatoes in the pot. Slice the meatloaf and serve with the potatoes.

Per Serving Calories: 718; Total fat: 43g; Saturated fat: 21g; Cholesterol: 235mg; Sodium: 808mg; Carbohydrates: 56g; Fiber: 4g; Protein: 29g

Jerk Pork

SERVES 4

Jerk pork is traditionally made from a whole pork shoulder, roasted and basted with a spicy, slightly sweet rub. Not only does it take a long time, it's also enough meat to feed an entire neighborhood. Using country ribs, which are strips of pork shoulder, and pressure cooking to give the meat a head start solves both problems and still produces a relatively authentic dish. A traditional Jamaican dish, "rice and peas," is actually a mixture of rice and red beans. It goes well with the pork.

2½ pounds boneless country ribs

1 teaspoon kosher salt (or ½ teaspoon fine salt)

¼ cup Chicken Stock (page 218), or store-bought low-sodium chicken broth

1 habanero chile, seeded and minced

2 garlic cloves, minced

2 tablespoons grated peeled fresh ginger

2 tablespoons packed brown sugar

2 tablespoons sherry vinegar

2 teaspoons ground allspice

1 teaspoon dried thyme leaves

½ teaspoon ground cinnamon

1 (15-ounce) can kidney beans, drained and rinsed

2 cups cooked rice

PREP TIME
10 MINUTES

PRESSURE COOK
25 MINUTES, HIGH PRESSURE

RELEASE
QUICK

BROIL
10 MINUTES

TOTAL TIME
55 MINUTES

DAIRY-FREE, GLUTEN-FREE, UNDER 60 MINUTES

SUBSTITUTION TIP: If you can't find habanero chiles, use 2 serranos, seeded and minced, plus 1 tablespoon of minced red bell pepper.

1. Sprinkle the ribs on all sides with the salt and set aside.

2. Pour the chicken stock into the Foodi's™ inner pot. Add the habanero, garlic, ginger, brown sugar, vinegar, allspice, thyme, and cinnamon. Stir to combine. Transfer the ribs to the pot.

3. Lock the Pressure Lid into place, making sure the valve is set to Seal. Select Pressure; adjust the pressure to High and the cook time to 25 minutes. Press Start.

4. After cooking, use a quick pressure release. Carefully unlock and remove the Pressure Lid.

5. Carefully transfer the ribs to the Reversible Rack set in the upper position. Stir the beans and rice into the sauce. Place the rack in the pot. ➤

Jerk Pork continued

6. Close the Crisping Lid and select Broil. Adjust the cook time to 10 minutes. Press Start. After 5 minutes, open the lid and turn the ribs over. When the ribs are browned on both sides, remove them and the rack from the pot.

7. If desired, thicken the sauce by selecting Sear/Sauté and adjusting to Medium. Press Start. Bring to a simmer and cook until the sauce reaches the desired consistency. Taste and adjust the seasoning. Transfer the country ribs to a platter and serve with the beans and rice.

Per Serving Calories: 381; Total fat: 22g; Saturated fat: 8g; Cholesterol: 137mg; Sodium: 409mg; Carbohydrates: 8g; Fiber: 1g; Protein: 36g

Japanese Pork Cutlets (Tonkatsu) with Ramen

SERVES 4

Tonkatsu, or Japanese breaded pork cutlets, are usually made from pork loin chops, cut thin and pounded out to tenderize them, then reshaped before breading. Using pork tenderloin means you can skip that step, since it's so tender to begin with. You can find tonkatsu sauce in the Asian section of most grocery stores, or see the sidebar (page 144) for a recipe to make your own.

1 small (12-ounce) pork tenderloin

½ teaspoon kosher salt (or ¼ teaspoon fine salt)

3 tablespoons vegetable oil

2 cups panko bread crumbs

4 cups Chicken Stock (page 218), or store-bought low-sodium chicken broth

⅓ cup all-purpose flour

1 large egg, beaten

1 tablespoon soy sauce

1 tablespoon sesame oil

½ teaspoon granulated garlic

2 packages ramen noodles, seasoning packets discarded

½ cup frozen peas, thawed

2 scallions, chopped

1 medium carrot, peeled and grated

½ cup tonkatsu sauce

PREP TIME
10 MINUTES

SEAR/SAUTÉ
5 MINUTES

PRESSURE COOK
0 MINUTES, LOW PRESSURE

RELEASE
QUICK

BROIL
10 MINUTES

TOTAL TIME
35 MINUTES

DAIRY-FREE, AROUND 30 MINUTES

INGREDIENT TIP: While toasting the panko is not necessary, it results in much nicer looking cutlets, with a crisper texture.

SUBSTITUTION TIP: Thin slices of chicken breast can be used instead of pork if you prefer.

1. Slice the tenderloin into pieces about ⅓ inch thick. Use the heel of your hand to flatten each piece slightly, to about ¼ inch thick. Season the slices on both sides with the salt. Set aside.

2. On your Foodi,™ select Sear/Sauté and adjust to Medium to preheat the inner pot. Press Start. Allow the pot to preheat for 5 minutes. Pour in the vegetable oil and heat until shimmering. Once hot, add the panko and stir to coat with the oil. Cook for about 3 minutes, stirring, until the crumbs are a light golden brown. Transfer them to a shallow dish to cool. Set aside.

3. Return the pot to the base, select Sear/Sauté, and adjust to Medium. Pour in the chicken stock to warm. ➤

4. Place the flour in a shallow bowl and the beaten egg in another shallow bowl. While the stock heats, dredge each pork piece in flour to coat completely. Pat off the excess. Then place it in the egg and turn to coat both sides. Transfer to the panko, pressing the pork into the panko to make sure it adheres. Place the tenderloin slices on the Reversible Rack set in the upper position and set the rack aside.

5. Add the soy sauce, sesame oil, and granulated garlic to the warm stock. Break up each block of noodles into 3 or 4 pieces and put them in the pot in a single layer as much as possible.

6. Lock the Pressure Lid into place, making sure the valve is set to Seal. Select Pressure; adjust the pressure to Low and the cook time to 0 minutes (the time it takes for the unit to come to pressure is enough cooking time). Press Start.

7. After cooking, use a quick pressure release. Carefully unlock and remove the Pressure Lid.

8. Stir in the peas, scallions, and carrot.

9. Place the rack with the pork in the pot in the upper position.

10. Close the Crisping Lid and select Broil. Adjust the cook time to 10 minutes. Press Start. After 5 minutes, open the lid. The cutlets should be crisp and browned. Turn them over and close the lid. Continue cooking until the second side is crisp. Serve with the tonkatsu sauce and a bowl of vegetables and noodles on the side.

FROM SCRATCH

To make your own tonkatsu sauce, in a small bowl, whisk together 2 tablespoons ketchup, 2 tablespoons Worcestershire sauce, 2 teaspoons soy sauce, 2 teaspoons oyster sauce, 1 teaspoon sugar, and 1 teaspoon Dijon-style mustard until combined.

Per Serving Calories: 787; Total fat: 31g; Saturated fat: 5g; Cholesterol: 115mg; Sodium: 1643mg; Carbohydrates: 88g; Fiber: 5g; Protein: 35g

Beef Satay with Peanut Sauce

SERVES 4

A favorite at Thai restaurants, satays are Indonesian in origin. Marinated meat is threaded on to skewers and grilled, then served with various dipping sauces, peanut sauce being one of the most common. Quick-pickled cucumbers are a refreshing accompaniment. In this version, I skip the skewers and marinate the skirt steak in one piece, making it easier to broil without overcooking.

FOR THE BEEF

1 pound skirt steak

½ teaspoon kosher salt (or ¼ teaspoon fine salt)

1 tablespoon freshly squeezed lime juice (from about ½ lime)

1½ teaspoons Thai red curry paste

1 tablespoon soy sauce

1 tablespoon coconut oil or vegetable oil

FOR THE CUCUMBER RELISH

½ English (hothouse) cucumber

½ cup rice vinegar

¼ cup water

2 tablespoons sugar

1 teaspoon kosher salt (or ½ teaspoon fine salt)

1 serrano chile, cut into thin rounds (optional)

FOR THE SAUCE

1 tablespoon coconut oil or vegetable oil

1 tablespoon finely minced onion

1 teaspoon finely minced garlic

1 cup coconut milk

2 teaspoons Thai red curry paste

1 teaspoon brown sugar

⅓ cup water

½ cup peanut butter

1 tablespoon freshly squeezed lime juice

PREP TIME
10 MINUTES

SEAR/SAUTÉ
2 MINUTES

PRESSURE COOK
0 MINUTES, HIGH PRESSURE

RELEASE
QUICK

BROIL
14 MINUTES

TOTAL TIME
30 MINUTES, NOT INCLUDING MARINATING TIME

DAIRY-FREE, AROUND 30 MINUTES

INGREDIENT TIP: Substitute boneless skinless chicken thighs for the steak. The cook time remains the same.

MAKE-AHEAD TIP: The cucumber relish can be made up to 1 day in advance and kept refrigerated. The steak can be marinated for up to 8 hours before cooking.

To make the beef

1. Sprinkle the skirt steak on both sides with the salt. Place in a resealable plastic bag and set aside while you make the marinade.

2. In a small bowl, whisk together the lime juice, curry paste, soy sauce, and coconut oil. Pour over the steak, seal the bag, and squish the bag around to coat the steak. Set aside for 20 minutes. ➤

Beef Satay with Peanut Sauce continued

To make the cucumber relish

1. While the steak marinates, prepare the cucumber relish. Cut the cucumber into ¼-inch slices, then cut each slice into quarters.

2. In a medium bowl, whisk together the vinegar, water, sugar, and salt until the sugar and salt dissolve. Add the cucumber pieces and serrano (if using). Refrigerate until needed.

To make the sauce

1. On your Foodi,™ select Sear/Sauté and adjust to Medium-High to preheat the inner pot. Press Start. Allow the pot to preheat for 5 minutes. Pour in the coconut oil and heat until shimmering. Add the onion and garlic. Cook for 1 to 2 minutes, stirring, or until fragrant and slightly softened.

2. Stir in the coconut milk, curry paste, and brown sugar.

3. Lock the Pressure Lid into place, making sure the valve is set to Seal. Select Pressure; adjust the pressure to High and the cook time to 0 minutes (the time it takes for the unit to come to pressure is enough cooking time). Press Start.

4. After cooking, use a quick pressure release. Carefully unlock and remove the Pressure Lid. Stir in the water.

5. Remove the steak from the marinade and place it on the Reversible Rack set to the upper position. Place the rack with the steak in the pot.

6. Close the Crisping Lid and select Broil. Adjust the cook time to 14 minutes. Press Start. After about 7 minutes, open the lid and flip the steak over. Close the lid and continue cooking. (If you have a thin cut of skirt steak—less than 1 inch—it may take only 12 minutes total.)

7. Transfer the steak to a cutting board or a wire rack set on a baking sheet and let it rest for a few minutes.

8. While the steak rests, stir the peanut butter and lime juice into the sauce. Taste and adjust the seasoning.

9. Cut the steak against the grain into thin slices and serve with the peanut sauce and cucumber relish on the side.

Per Serving Calories: 551; Total fat: 43g; Saturated fat: 18g; Cholesterol: 38mg; Sodium: 895mg; Carbohydrates: 18g; Fiber: 3g; Protein: 27g

Italian Beef Sandwiches

SERVES 4

A Chicago specialty, Italian beef sandwiches are cousin to the French dip—beef cooked in seasoned broth, then piled onto rolls with sweet or hot peppers and the Italian pickled vegetables called giardiniera. In Chicago, it's customary to dip the whole sandwich into the broth after assembly, which is delicious but really messy. I prefer to drizzle mine with a bit of broth to start, then dip as I go.

1½ pounds sirloin or flatiron steak

½ teaspoon kosher salt (or ¼ teaspoon fine salt)

½ teaspoon freshly ground black pepper

3 cups good-quality beef broth or stock

2 tablespoons dry red wine

1 teaspoon Italian herb mix (or ½ teaspoon dried basil and ½ teaspoon dried oregano)

1 dried bay leaf

2 garlic cloves, smashed

1 large green bell pepper, seeded and sliced

4 sandwich or hoagie rolls, sliced

1½ cups giardiniera (Italian pickled vegetables), drained and chopped coarsely

½ cup sliced pepperoncini (optional)

PREP
10 MINUTES

PRESSURE COOK
1 MINUTE, HIGH PRESSURE

RELEASE
QUICK

BROIL
12 MINUTES

TOTAL TIME
30 MINUTES

DAIRY-FREE, AROUND 30 MINUTES

INGREDIENT TIP: Since the jus reduces while the steak cooks, make sure you use beef broth that's either unsalted or low-sodium. Don't add salt until after the steak is done cooking or you might end up with oversalted jus. (I use unsalted College Inn brand Bold Beef Stock if I don't have my own on hand.)

1. Sprinkle the salt and pepper over both sides of the steak and place it on the Reversible Rack set in the upper position. Set aside.

2. Pour the beef broth into the inner pot. Add the red wine, herb mix, bay leaf, and garlic. Lock the Pressure Lid into place, making sure the valve is set to Seal. Select Pressure; adjust the pressure to High and the time to 1 minute. Press Start.

3. After cooking, quick release the pressure. Carefully unlock and remove the Pressure Lid. Add the bell pepper to the beef broth mixture in the pot.

4. Place the rack and steak in the pot. Close the Crisping Lid and select Broil. Adjust the time to 12 minutes. Press Start. After about 6 minutes, open the lid and flip the steak over. Close the lid and continue cooking.

5. When the steak is finished, remove the rack and transfer the steak to a cutting board. Let rest for 5 minutes, and then slice against the grain as thin as possible (the steak interior should be very rare; it will cook again briefly in the broth).

6. Slice the sandwich rolls in half, removing some of the soft bread from the interior if you like.

7. Remove the bay leaf and garlic cloves from the broth. Add the steak slices to the broth, making sure that the slices are submerged. Warm the meat by leaving it in the broth for about 1 minute, then remove and arrange the steak slices and green pepper slices on the bottom halves of the sandwich rolls. Drizzle with a few spoonfuls of broth. Top the sandwiches with the pickled vegetables and pepperoncini (if using). Slice the sandwiches in half before serving, and serve the extra broth for dipping.

Per Serving Calories: 521; Total fat: 21g; Saturated fat: 8g; Cholesterol: 70mg; Sodium: 1132mg; Carbohydrates: 34g; Fiber: 2g; Protein: 45g

Deviled Short Ribs with Noodles

SERVES 4

There's not a dish much better than braised short ribs, unless it's braised short ribs finished with a crisp and spicy coating. Noodles cooked in the beefy cooking liquid are the perfect side dish for the ribs. The noodles in this dish get a bit crisp on top as the short ribs roast. I like that texture, but if you don't, cover the noodles with aluminum foil before roasting the ribs.

4 pounds bone-in short ribs (or 3 pounds boneless short ribs)

2½ teaspoons kosher salt (or 1¼ teaspoons fine salt), divided

Low-sodium beef broth or water, as needed

6 ounces egg noodles

6 tablespoons Dijon-style mustard

2 tablespoons prepared horseradish

1 garlic clove, pressed or minced

½ teaspoon freshly ground black pepper

3 tablespoons melted unsalted butter

1½ cups panko bread crumbs

PREP TIME
10 MINUTES

PRESSURE COOK
25 MINUTES PLUS
4 MINUTES, HIGH PRESSURE

RELEASE
NATURAL FOR 5 MINUTES,
THEN QUICK

BAKE/ROAST
15 MINUTES

TOTAL TIME
1 HOUR 5 MINUTES

DAIRY-FREE

SUBSTITUTION TIP: If you can find beef back ribs (which are cut from rib roasts), they're also great cooked this way.

1. Sprinkle the short ribs on all sides with 1½ teaspoons of kosher salt (or ¾ teaspoon of fine salt).

2. Pour 1 cup of water into the inner pot. Place the Reversible Rack in the pot in the lower position and arrange the short ribs on top.

3. Lock the Pressure Lid into place, making sure the valve is set to Seal. Select Pressure; adjust the pressure to High and the time to 25 minutes. Press Start.

4. After cooking, let the pressure release naturally for 5 minutes, then quick release any remaining pressure. Carefully unlock and remove the Pressure Lid. Carefully remove the rack and short ribs.

5. Pour the cooking liquid into a measuring cup. You want 2 cups—if there is more, discard any extra, and if there is less, add beef broth or water to make 2 cups. Return the liquid to the pot.

6. Pour in the egg noodles and add the remaining 1 teaspoon of kosher salt (or ½ teaspoon of fine salt). Stir, submerging the noodles as much as possible.

7. Lock the Pressure Lid into place, making sure the valve is set to Seal. Select Pressure; adjust the pressure to High and the cook time to 4 minutes. Press Start.

8. While the noodles cook, in a small bowl, stir together the mustard, horseradish, garlic, and pepper. Brush this sauce over all sides of the short ribs, reserving any extra sauce. In a medium bowl, stir the melted butter into the panko. Coat the sauced ribs with the crumbs. Place the short ribs back on the rack.

9. After cooking, use a quick pressure release. Carefully unlock and remove the Pressure Lid. Stir the noodles, which may not be quite done but will continue cooking.

10. Return the rack and beef to the pot in the upper position.

11. Close the Crisping Lid and select Bake/Roast; adjust the temperature to 400°F and the cook time to 15 minutes. Press Start. After 8 minutes, open the lid and turn the ribs over. Close the lid and continue cooking. Serve the beef and noodles, with the extra sauce on the side, if desired.

Per Serving Calories: 978; Total fat: 48g; Saturated fat: 21g; Cholesterol: 234mg; Sodium: 1518mg; Carbohydrates: 62g; Fiber: 4g; Protein: 71g

Carbonnade Flamande

SERVES 4

Carbonnade flamande is a Belgian dish of beef braised in dark beer with onions. It's a natural for pressure cooking and results in meltingly tender beef with an amazing sauce. I love it over mashed potatoes, but it's also wonderful with noodles.

2 pounds chuck roast, cut into 2 or 3 pieces

½ teaspoon kosher salt (or ¼ teaspoon fine salt)

1 tablespoon olive or vegetable oil

1 large onion, sliced (about 1½ cups)

8 fluid ounces porter or stout

¼ teaspoon dried thyme leaves

¼ cup low-sodium beef broth

½ teaspoon Dijon-style mustard

½ teaspoon brown sugar, or more to taste

2 tablespoons chopped fresh parsley

PREP TIME
10 MINUTES

SEAR/SAUTÉ
5 MINUTES

PRESSURE COOK
35 MINUTES, HIGH PRESSURE

RELEASE
NATURAL FOR 10 MINUTES, THEN QUICK

TOTAL TIME
1 HOUR 10 MINUTES

DAIRY-FREE

CUSTOMIZATION TIP: Some versions of this dish are more like a stew, with vegetables added. If you want to try that version, cut the seared chuck roast into 1-inch pieces. Add quartered red potatoes and carrot chunks, and cook on high pressure for 20 minutes with a quick pressure release.

1. Season the beef on all sides with the salt.

2. On your Foodi™ select Sear/Sauté and adjust to Medium to preheat the inner pot. Press Start. Allow the pot to preheat for 5 minutes. Pour in the olive oil and heat until shimmering. Add the beef. Cook, without turning, for 4 minutes or until browned. Turn the beef over and move the pieces to the sides. Add the onion. Cook, stirring, for 1 to 2 minutes or until slightly softened. Add the porter, scraping up any browned bits from the bottom of the pot. Bring to a simmer and cook until the beer has reduced by about half. Add the thyme and beef broth.

3. Lock the Pressure Lid into place, making sure the valve is set to Seal. Select Pressure; adjust the pressure to High and the cook time to 35 minutes. Press Start.

4. After cooking, let the pressure release naturally for 10 minutes, then quick release any remaining pressure. Carefully unlock and remove the Pressure Lid.

5. Transfer the beef to a cutting board.

6. If there is much fat on the sauce, spoon or blot it off. Stir in the mustard and brown sugar. Select Sear/Sauté and adjust to Medium. Press Start. Bring the sauce to a simmer and cook until reduced to the consistency of a thin gravy. Taste and adjust the seasoning.

7. Slice the beef and return it to the sauce to reheat. Serve over mashed potatoes or noodles, if desired, garnished with the parsley.

Per Serving Calories: 625; Total fat: 44g; Saturated fat: 17g; Cholesterol: 150mg; Sodium: 319mg; Carbohydrates: 6g; Fiber: 1g; Protein: 45g

Pork Tenderloin with Peppers and Roasted Potatoes

SERVES 4

I got the idea for this combination from a recipe by Bruce Aidells, which uses sweet and pickled peppers for a sauce served over sautéed pork medallions. Cooking a whole tenderloin under pressure is easier and very fast, and adding potatoes makes it a complete dinner.

1 large (about 1¼-pound) pork tenderloin, cut into 2 pieces

2 teaspoons kosher salt (or 1 teaspoon fine salt)

¼ teaspoon freshly ground black pepper

2 tablespoons vegetable oil

½ cup dry white wine

1 pound small red potatoes, quartered

¼ cup Chicken Stock (page 218), or store-bought low-sodium chicken broth

1 rosemary sprig

2 medium garlic cloves, finely minced (about 2 teaspoons)

1 small roasted red bell pepper, cut into strips

5 or 6 pickled sweet cherry peppers, stemmed and seeded, quartered

2 teaspoons pickling liquid from the peppers

2 tablespoons unsalted butter

PREP TIME
10 MINUTES

SEAR/SAUTÉ
8 MINUTES PLUS 5 MINUTES

PRESSURE COOK
0 MINUTES, HIGH PRESSURE

RELEASE
NATURAL FOR 5 MINUTES, THEN QUICK

TOTAL TIME
35 MINUTES

GLUTEN-FREE, AROUND 30 MINUTES

SUBSTITUTION TIP: If you don't have fresh rosemary, use ½ teaspoon dried thyme leaves, or 1 bay leaf, or ½ teaspoon dried sage. Dried rosemary tends to be flavorless, so I would avoid it.

1. Season the pork pieces on all sides with the salt and pepper.

2. On your Foodi,™ select Sear/Sauté and adjust to Medium-High to preheat the inner pot. Press Start. Allow the pot to preheat for 5 minutes. Pour in the vegetable oil and heat until shimmering. Once hot, add the pork pieces. Let sear, without moving, for 3 minutes or until browned. Turn and brown at least one more side. Transfer the pork to a plate. Pour the wine into the pot and scrape up any browned bits from the bottom. Let the wine cook until reduced by about one-third.

3. Add the potatoes, chicken stock, rosemary sprig, and garlic to the wine. Return the pork to the pot.

4. Lock the Pressure Lid into place, making sure the valve is set to Seal. Select Pressure; adjust the pressure to High and the cook time to 0 minutes (the time it takes for the unit to come to pressure is enough cooking time). Press Start.

5. After cooking, let the pressure release naturally for 5 minutes, then quick release any remaining pressure. Carefully unlock and remove the Pressure Lid.

6. Remove the pork and check the internal temperature with a meat thermometer. It should read about 140ºF. If not, return it to the pot, cover the pot with the lid, and let sit for another minute or so. Let the pork rest while you finish the sauce.

7. Remove and discard the rosemary sprig. Select Sear/Sauté and adjust to Medium. Press Start. Bring the sauce to a simmer and let the potatoes cook for 2 to 4 minutes or until tender. Add the roasted pepper and pickled peppers, along with the pickling liquid. Taste and adjust the seasoning. Right before serving, turn off the heat and stir in the butter.

8. While the sauce and potatoes cook, slice the tenderloin and arrange it on a platter. Spoon the peppers and potatoes around the pork and pour the sauce over.

Per Serving Calories: 393; Total fat: 18g; Saturated fat: 6g; Cholesterol: 107mg; Sodium: 664mg; Carbohydrates: 23g; Fiber: 2g; Protein: 32g

Sloppy Joes

I'm not ashamed to admit that I love these sandwiches, even though they're supposed to be kids' fare. I like mine a bit spicy, so I add a splash of Tabasco, but you can omit that if you prefer. I do recommend making your own sauce for this; my recipe is much less sweet than most commercial versions.

1¼ pounds ground beef

½ cup chopped onion

1 teaspoon kosher salt (or ½ teaspoon fine salt), plus more as needed

½ medium red or green bell pepper, chopped (about ⅓ cup)

1 garlic clove, minced or pressed

1 cup Barbecue Sauce (page 226) or your favorite store-bought barbecue sauce

¼ teaspoon Tabasco

1 tablespoon apple cider vinegar (optional)

1 tablespoon packed brown sugar (optional)

4 hamburger buns, split

PREP TIME
10 MINUTES

SEAR/SAUTÉ
5 MINUTES

PRESSURE COOK
12 MINUTES, HIGH PRESSURE

RELEASE
QUICK

TOTAL TIME
35 MINUTES

DAIRY-FREE, AROUND 30 MINUTES

CUSTOMIZATION TIP: If you prefer toasted buns, place the Reversible Rack in the pot in the upper position (you will probably have to work in batches). Place the buns on the rack, cut-side up, and close the Crisping Lid. Select Broil and press Start. Check the buns after 2 to 3 minutes. Repeat with the remaining buns. If you choose this option, the sloppy joe mixture will thicken as you heat the buns.

1. On your Foodi,™ select Sear/Sauté and adjust to Medium-High to preheat the inner pot. Press Start. Allow the pot to preheat for 5 minutes. Put a large handful of ground beef in the pot and let it cook, undisturbed, for about 4 minutes or until very brown on the bottom. Add the onion and salt. Stir to scrape the beef from the bottom of the pot. Add the remaining beef and stir to break up the meat. Add the bell pepper, garlic, and barbecue sauce. Stir to combine and ensure that no beef is stuck to the bottom of the pot.

2. Lock the Pressure Lid into place, making sure the valve is set to Seal. Select Pressure; adjust the pressure to High and the cook time to 12 minutes. Press Start.

3. After cooking, use a quick pressure release. Carefully unlock and remove the Pressure Lid.

4. Stir in the Tabasco. Taste the sauce. You may need the optional vinegar, especially if you've used commercial sauce, which tends to be sweet. Add salt and brown sugar as necessary.

5. If there is much fat on the surface of the meat, spoon or blot it off. If the sauce is very thin, select Sear/Sauté and adjust to Medium. Press Start. Bring the sloppy joe mixture to a simmer and cook until you get the consistency you like. Serve it on the buns.

Per Serving Calories: 497; Total fat: 20g; Saturated fat: 8g; Cholesterol: 88mg; Sodium: 1294mg; Carbohydrates: 46g; Fiber: 2g; Protein: 32g

6
Seafood

Left: Bow Tie Pasta with Shrimp and Arugula, page 160

Bow Tie Pasta with Shrimp and Arugula

Years ago, I saw Jamie Oliver making the rounds through the morning shows to promote a new book. He made a quick pasta dish with spaghetti, shrimp, sun-dried tomatoes, and arugula, which he (being British) called "rocket." This is my version of the dish, spiced up a bit. Whenever we make it, we always call arugula "rocket" in our poor attempt at British accents in honor of Jamie.

1¼ pounds medium raw shrimp (41 to 50 count), peeled and deveined

1½ teaspoons kosher salt (or ¾ teaspoon fine salt), divided

1 tablespoon extra-virgin olive oil

2 large garlic cloves, peeled and minced or pressed, divided

¼ cup white wine

10 ounces farfalle (aka bow tie, or butterfly, pasta)

2½ cups water

⅓ cup sun-dried tomato purée

½ teaspoon red pepper flakes, or more to taste

1 tablespoon freshly squeezed lemon juice

1 teaspoon grated lemon zest

6 cups arugula

PREP TIME
10 MINUTES

AIR CRISP
6 MINUTES

SEAR/SAUTÉ
2 MINUTES

PRESSURE COOK
5 MINUTES, HIGH PRESSURE

RELEASE
QUICK

TOTAL TIME
30 MINUTES

DAIRY-FREE, AROUND 30 MINUTES

SUBSTITUTION TIP: If you can't find or don't like arugula, spinach makes a great alternative

1. Place the shrimp in the Cook & Crisp™ Basket. Add ½ teaspoon of kosher salt (or ¼ teaspoon of fine salt), the olive oil, and 1 minced garlic clove. Toss to coat.

2. Place the basket in the Foodi's™ inner pot and then close the Crisping Lid and select Air Crisp; adjust the temperature to 400°F and the cook time to 6 minutes. Press Start. After 3 minutes, open the lid and toss the shrimp. Close the lid and continue cooking. When done, the shrimp should be opaque and pink. It's okay if they are not quite done, as they'll finish cooking later. Remove the basket and set aside.

3. On your Foodi™ select Sear/Sauté and adjust to High to preheat the inner pot. Press Start. Allow the pot to preheat for 5 minutes. Pour in the wine and bring it to a boil. Simmer for 1 to 2 minutes to cook off some of the alcohol. Add the pasta, water, remaining 1 teaspoon of kosher salt (or ½ teaspoon of fine salt), remaining 1 minced garlic clove, tomato purée, and red pepper flakes. Stir to combine.

4. Lock the Pressure Lid into place, making sure the valve is set to Seal. Select Pressure; adjust the pressure to High and the cook time to 5 minutes. Press Start.

5. After cooking, use a quick pressure release. Carefully unlock and remove the Pressure Lid.

6. Stir in the lemon juice and zest. Add the arugula by big handfuls and toss it in the sauce to wilt. Stir in the shrimp. Let sit for a few minutes to reheat the shrimp. Serve immediately.

Per Serving Calories: 483; Total fat: 8g; Saturated fat: 1g; Cholesterol: 215mg; Sodium: 683mg; Carbohydrates: 58g; Fiber: 3g; Protein: 39g

Lax Pudding

This oddly named dish is Swedish in origin. Rather than a pudding as we think of that term, this comfort food consists of layered potatoes and smoked salmon held together with a rich custard. Paired with a salad, it makes a great brunch dish. Use either hot-smoked salmon cut into chunks, or slices of cold-smoked salmon (lox). It's delicious either way.

1 pound Yukon gold potatoes (3 or 4 medium potatoes), peeled and cut into ¼-inch slices

¾ teaspoon kosher salt (or a scant ½ teaspoon fine salt), divided

3 large eggs

⅔ cup whole milk

½ cup heavy (whipping) cream

¼ teaspoon freshly ground black pepper, plus more for finishing

3 tablespoons melted unsalted butter, divided

6 ounces smoked salmon, cut into chunks

3 tablespoons chopped fresh dill, divided

PREP TIME
10 MINUTES

PRESSURE COOK
3 MINUTES PLUS 15 MINUTES, HIGH PRESSURE

RELEASE
QUICK, THEN NATURAL FOR 10 MINUTES FOLLOWED BY ANOTHER QUICK RELEASE

BROIL
5 MINUTES

TOTAL TIME
50 MINUTES

GLUTEN-FREE, UNDER 60 MINUTES

MAKE-AHEAD TIP: If you have leftover boiled potatoes, slice them and use them, and skip the first 2 steps

1. Pour 1 cup of water into the Foodi's™ inner pot. Place the potato slices on the Reversible Rack, or in a steaming basket, and place the rack in the pot in the lower position.

2. Lock the Pressure Lid into place, making sure the valve is set to Seal. Select Pressure; adjust the pressure to High and the cook time to 3 minutes. Press Start.

3. When cooking is complete, use a quick pressure release. Carefully unlock and remove the Pressure Lid. Remove the rack, sprinkle the potatoes with ¼ teaspoon of kosher salt (or ⅛ teaspoon of fine salt), and let them cool. Pour the water out of the pot.

4. While the potatoes cook and cool, in a large bowl, whisk the eggs, milk, heavy cream, remaining ½ teaspoon of kosher salt (or ⅜ teaspoon of fine salt), and the pepper.

5. Grease a 1-quart, high-sided, round dish with 2 teaspoons or so of melted butter. Lay one-third of the potatoes on the base of the dish, spread with half the salmon, and sprinkle with 1 tablespoon of dill. Top with another third of the potatoes, the remaining salmon spread over the top, and 1 tablespoon of dill followed by the remaining third of the potatoes. Pour the custard over; it should come up just to the top layer of potatoes but not cover them. (You may not need all the custard).

6. Pour 1 cup of water into the inner pot. Place the Reversible Rack in the pot in the lower position and place the baking dish on top.

7. Lock the Pressure Lid into place, making sure the valve is set to Seal. Select Pressure; adjust the pressure to High and the cook time to 15 minutes. Press Start.

8. After cooking, let the pressure release naturally for 10 minutes, then quick release any remaining pressure. Carefully unlock and remove the Pressure Lid.

9. Remove the baking dish and rack from the inner pot and empty the water out of the pot. Return the inner pot to the base and place the rack back in the pot in the lower position. Close the Crisping Lid and select Broil. Adjust the time to 2 minutes to preheat. Press Start.

10. While the Foodi™ preheats, drizzle the remaining melted butter over the top of the potatoes. Open the Crisping Lid and place the dish on the rack. Close the lid, select Broil, and set the cook time to 5 minutes. Press Start.

11. When the broiling is complete, open the lid and carefully remove the pudding. Let cool for a few minutes. Sprinkle with the remaining 1 tablespoon of dill and season with additional pepper as desired.

Per Serving Calories: 344; Total fat: 21g; Saturated fat: 11g; Cholesterol: 221mg; Sodium: 706mg; Carbohydrates: 24g; Fiber: 1g; Protein: 17g

Warm Potato and Green Bean Salad with Tuna

SERVES 4

Reminiscent of a salade Niçoise, this dish combines roasted green beans and potatoes with canned tuna and vegetables for a casual, easy summertime dinner. If you like, serve this with garlic cheese toasts (see page 56), which can toast while you prepare the salad.

1½ pounds red potatoes, quartered

3 tablespoons olive oil, divided

1 teaspoon kosher salt (or ½ teaspoon fine salt), divided, plus more as needed

8 ounces haricot verts (thin green beans), trimmed

2 tablespoons red wine vinegar, divided

¼ teaspoon freshly ground black pepper

½ cup coarsely chopped roasted red peppers

½ cup pitted Kalamata olives

2 tablespoons chopped fresh parsley

2 (5- or 6-ounce) cans tuna, drained

½ cup crumbled feta cheese (optional)

PREP TIME
10 MINUTES

PRESSURE COOK
4 MINUTES, HIGH PRESSURE

RELEASE
QUICK

AIR CRISP
12 MINUTES

TOTAL TIME
35 MINUTES

DAIRY-FREE OPTION, GLUTEN-FREE, AROUND 30 MINUTES

1. Place the potatoes in the Cook & Crisp™ Basket. Pour 1 cup of water into the inner pot and place the basket in the pot.

2. Lock the Pressure Lid into place, making sure the valve is set to Seal. Select Pressure; adjust the pressure to High and the cook time to 4 minutes. Press Start.

3. After cooking, use a quick pressure release. Carefully unlock and remove the Pressure Lid. Remove the basket. Empty the water from the inner pot and return it to the base.

4. Close the Crisping Lid and select Air Crisp; adjust the temperature to 375°F and the time to 2 minutes to preheat. Press Start.

5. Meanwhile, drizzle 2 teaspoons of olive oil over the potatoes and sprinkle with ½ teaspoon of kosher salt (or ¼ teaspoon of fine salt). Gently toss the potatoes.

INGREDIENT TIP: I think this salad is best with Italian tuna packed in oil; I prefer Genova yellowfin tuna. Use whatever brand and style you prefer, but if you use a water-packed tuna, you will probably want to increase the olive oil in the dressing by 1 tablespoon or so.

MAKE-AHEAD TIP: While this salad is best served warm or at room temperature, you can make it ahead and refrigerate for several hours. Let it come to room temperature before serving, if possible.

6. Lay the beans over the potatoes and drizzle with 1 teaspoon of olive oil and sprinkle with ¼ teaspoon of kosher salt (or ⅛ teaspoon of fine salt).

7. Place the basket in the preheated Foodi.™ Close the Crisping Lid and select Air Crisp; adjust the temperature to 375°F and the cook time to 12 minutes. Press Start.

8. After 8 minutes, open the lid and check the vegetables. The beans should be starting to get crisp and browned. Toss the beans and potatoes gently and close the lid. Continue to cook for the remaining 4 minutes.

9. Remove the basket and transfer the beans and potatoes to a large bowl. Sprinkle with 1 tablespoon of vinegar and toss to coat. Let the vegetables cool until just warm.

10. Pour the remaining 2 tablespoons of olive oil and the remaining 1 tablespoon of vinegar into a small jar with a tight-fitting lid. Add the remaining ¼ teaspoon of kosher salt (or ⅛ teaspoon of fine salt) and the pepper. Cover the jar and shake to combine.

11. When the potatoes and beans have cooled slightly, add the roasted red peppers, olives, parsley, tuna, and feta (if using; omit for a dairy-free dish). Pour the dressing over the salad and toss to coat. Adjust the seasoning. If you've omitted the cheese, you may need more salt. Serve immediately.

Per Serving Calories: 292; Total fat: 13g; Saturated fat: 2g; Cholesterol: 13mg; Sodium: 664mg; Carbohydrates: 32g; Fiber: 6g; Protein: 15g

Teriyaki Salmon and Vegetables

SERVES 4

A quick stint under pressure is the first step in this easy and tasty Japanese-inspired dish. Then with a few minutes under the broiler, dinner is served. Feel free to substitute any quick-cooking green vegetables you like for the peas; bok choy is a nice substitute.

4 (5-ounce) skin-on salmon fillets

½ teaspoon kosher salt (or ¼ teaspoon fine salt)

2 cups snow peas or snap peas

½ medium red bell pepper, cut into chunks

⅓ cup Teriyaki Sauce (page 225), plus 1 tablespoon

¼ cup water

2 scallions, chopped

½ cup Sautéed Mushrooms (page 220)

PREP TIME
10 MINUTES

PRESSURE COOK
1 MINUTE, HIGH PRESSURE

RELEASE
QUICK

BROIL
7 MINUTES

TOTAL TIME
25 MINUTES

DAIRY-FREE, AROUND 30 MINUTES

CUSTOMIZATION TIP: If you would like to serve a starch with this, add 6 ounces of Chinese wheat noodles to the snow peas and bell pepper in the bottom of the pot. Add 1½ cups of water and ¼ teaspoon of kosher salt (or ⅛ teaspoon of fine salt).

1. Sprinkle the salmon fillets with the salt and place them on the Reversible Rack set in the upper position.

2. Place the snow peas and bell pepper in the Foodi's™ inner pot. Drizzle with 1 tablespoon of teriyaki sauce and pour in the water. Place the rack with the salmon in the pot in the upper position.

3. Lock the Pressure Lid into place, making sure the valve is set to Seal. Select Pressure; adjust the pressure to High and the cook time to 1 minute. Press Start.

4. After cooking, use a quick pressure release. Carefully unlock and remove the Pressure Lid.

5. Brush about half the remaining ⅓ cup of teriyaki sauce over the salmon.

6. Close the Crisping Lid and select Broil. Adjust the cook time to 7 minutes. Press Start. Check the salmon after 5 minutes. It should just flake apart when done. Cook for the remaining 2 minutes if necessary.

7. When cooking is complete, remove the rack with the salmon and set aside.

8. Add the scallions and mushrooms to the vegetables in the pot and stir to heat through. If the sauce is too thin, select Sear/Sauté and adjust to High. Press Start. Simmer until the sauce is the consistency you like. Divide the vegetables among four plates and top with the salmon, drizzling the remaining teriyaki sauce over.

Per Serving Calories: 255; Total fat: 9g; Saturated fat: 1g; Cholesterol: 77mg; Sodium: 1123mg; Carbohydrates: 10g; Fiber: 2g; Protein: 32g

Shrimp and Vegetable Egg Rolls

If you've never made egg rolls, I think you'll find it surprisingly easy and fun. While the list of ingredients is long, there's not much prep if you start with coleslaw mix. The filling cooks very quickly; some people even serve the filling with crisped wonton skins and call the dish "inside-out egg rolls," but I think that misses the best part of these appetizers (apart from eating them): rolling them. Serve these alongside hot and sour soup if you want a more substantial meal.

2 tablespoons soy sauce

1 tablespoon dry sherry

2 teaspoons rice vinegar

3 cups shredded cabbage or coleslaw mix

3 scallions, chopped

1 large carrot, peeled and shredded

2 garlic cloves, minced

1 teaspoon grated peeled fresh ginger

1 teaspoon sugar

2 teaspoons sesame oil

¼ teaspoon freshly ground black pepper

8 ounces shrimp, peeled and coarsely chopped

½ cup Sautéed Mushrooms (page 220), coarsely chopped

1 teaspoon cornstarch

1 tablespoon water

8 to 10 egg roll wrappers

Nonstick cooking spray, for cooking the egg rolls

PREP TIME
10 MINUTES

PRESSURE COOK
2 MINUTES, HIGH PRESSURE

RELEASE
QUICK

SEAR/SAUTÉ
5 MINUTES

AIR CRISP
15 MINUTES

TOTAL TIME
40 MINUTES

DAIRY-FREE, UNDER 60 MINUTES

CUSTOMIZATION TIP: Pork is a common addition to egg rolls. If you like, sauté 4 ounces of ground pork before adding the other egg roll ingredients to the inner pot. This will give you enough filling for 10 to 12 egg rolls.

MAKE-AHEAD TIP: The filling can be prepared and refrigerated up to 3 days ahead. The egg rolls, once rolled, will keep refrigerated for a couple of hours covered in plastic wrap, but any longer than that and they start to get mushy

1. In the Foodi's™ inner pot, combine the soy sauce, sherry, and rice vinegar. Add the cabbage, scallions, carrot, garlic, ginger, sugar, and sesame oil to the pot.

2. Lock the Pressure Lid into place, making sure the valve is set to Seal. Select Pressure; adjust the pressure to High and the cook time to 2 minutes. Press Start.

3. After cooking, use a quick pressure release. Carefully unlock and remove the Pressure Lid.

4. Add the pepper, shrimp, and mushrooms to the pot. Select Sear/Sauté and adjust to Medium-High. Press Start. Bring the mixture to a simmer to cook the shrimp and warm the mushrooms. Continue simmering for about 5 minutes until most of the liquid has evaporated. Transfer the filling to a bowl and set aside to cool. Wipe out the inner pot and return it to the base.

5. To form the egg rolls, in a small bowl, stir together the cornstarch and water. Lay a wrapper on your work surface positioned with a corner pointed toward you. Lightly moisten the edges of the wrapper with the cornstarch mixture. Using a slotted spoon, scoop a scant ¼ cup of filling just below the center of the wrapper. As you scoop the filling out, leave as much liquid behind as possible. You want the rolls to be dry inside, not soggy.

6. Fold the bottom corner of the wrapper over the filling and tuck it under the filling. Roll once and then fold both sides in. Continue to roll up tightly. Repeat with the remaining wrappers and filling on the other side.

7. Close the Crisping Lid and select Air Crisp; adjust the temperature to 390ºF and the time to 5 minutes to preheat. Press Start.

8. Place 6 to 8 egg rolls in the Cook & Crisp™ Basket and spray with the cooking spray. Turn them over and spray the other sides. When the pot has preheated, place the basket in the inner pot. ➤

Shrimp and Vegetable Egg Rolls continued

9. Close the Crisping Lid and select Air Crisp; adjust the temperature to 390°F and the cook time to 15 minutes. Press Start. After 6 minutes, open the lid and check the egg rolls. They should be golden brown and crisp on top. If not, close the lid and cook for 1 to 2 minutes more. Turn the rolls when the tops are crisp and cook for 5 to 6 minutes more or until crisp on the other side.

10. Repeat with any uncooked egg rolls. Let the rolls cool on a wire rack for 8 to 10 minutes, as the interiors will be very hot. Serve with plum sauce, sweet and sour sauce, or Chinese mustard as desired.

FROM SCRATCH

To make your own dipping sauce, whisk together 1 teaspoon orange juice concentrate, 1½ teaspoons grated peeled fresh ginger, 1 teaspoon soy sauce, 2 tablespoons rice vinegar, 1 tablespoon Thai sweet chili sauce (or 1 teaspoon chile-garlic paste), 1 teaspoon hoisin sauce, and 1 tablespoon toasted sesame oil.

Per Serving Calories: 181; Total fat: 4g; Saturated fat: 1g; Cholesterol: 87mg; Sodium: 726mg; Carbohydrates: 21g; Fiber: 3g; Protein: 17g

Clam Chowder with Parmesan Crackers

If I admit that the main reason I make clam chowder is so I can eat these Parmesan oyster crackers that go along with it, will you think less of me?

2 cups oyster crackers

2 tablespoons melted unsalted butter

¼ cup finely grated Parmesan or similar cheese

½ teaspoon granulated garlic

1 teaspoon kosher salt (or ½ teaspoon fine salt), divided

2 thick bacon slices, cut into thirds

1 medium onion, chopped (about ¾ cup)

2 celery stalks, chopped (about ⅔ cup)

1 tablespoon all-purpose flour

¼ cup white wine

1 cup clam juice

3 (6-ounce) cans chopped clams, drained, liquid reserved

1 pound Yukon gold potatoes, peeled and cut into 1-inch chunks

1 teaspoon dried thyme leaves

1 bay leaf

1½ cups half-and-half

2 tablespoons chopped fresh parsley or chives

PREP TIME
10 MINUTES

AIR CRISP
6 MINUTES

SEAR/SAUTÉ
7 MINUTES

PRESSURE COOK
4 MINUTES, HIGH PRESSURE

RELEASE
NATURAL FOR 5 MINUTES, THEN QUICK

TOTAL TIME
40 MINUTES

UNDER 60 MINUTES

MAKE-AHEAD TIP: The crackers can be made ahead and kept in an airtight container for up to a week. That is, if you can resist snacking on them.

1. Close the Crisping Lid and select Air Crisp; adjust the temperature to 375°F and the time to 2 minutes to preheat. Press Start.

2. While the Foodi™ preheats, pour the oyster crackers into a medium bowl. Drizzle with the melted butter and sprinkle with the Parmesan, granulated garlic, and ½ teaspoon of kosher salt (or ¼ teaspoon of fine salt). Toss to coat the crackers. Transfer them to the Cook & Crisp™ Basket.

3. Once the pot is heated, open the Foodi's lid and insert the basket. Close the lid and select Air Crisp; adjust the temperature to 375°F and the cook time to 6 minutes. Press Start. After 3 minutes, open the lid and stir the crackers. Close the lid and continue cooking until lightly browned and crisp. Remove the basket and set aside to cool. ➤

Clam Chowder with Parmesan Crackers continued

4. On your Foodi™ select Sear/Sauté and adjust to Medium. Press Start. Allow the pot to preheat for 5 minutes. Place the bacon in the pot and cook for about 5 minutes, turning once or twice, until the bacon is crisp and the fat is rendered. Using tongs or a slotted spoon, transfer the bacon to a paper towel–lined plate to drain and set aside. Leave the fat in the pot.

5. Add the onion and celery to the pot. Cook for about 1 minute, stirring, until the vegetables begin to soften. Add the flour and stir to coat the vegetables. Pour in the wine and bring to a simmer. Cook for about 1 minute or until reduced by about one-third. Add the clam juice, the reserved clam liquid (but not the clams), potatoes, remaining ½ teaspoon of kosher salt (or ¼ teaspoon of fine salt), thyme, and bay leaf.

6. Lock the Pressure Lid into place, making sure the valve is set to Seal. Select Pressure; adjust the pressure to High and the cook time to 4 minutes. Press Start.

7. After cooking, let the pressure release naturally for 5 minutes, then quick release any remaining pressure. Carefully unlock and remove the Pressure Lid.

8. Stir in the clams and half-and-half. Select Sear/Sauté and adjust to Medium. Press Start. Bring the soup to a simmer to heat the clams through. Carefully remove the bay leaf. Ladle the soup into bowls and crumble the bacon over the top. Garnish with the parsley and a handful of crackers, serving the remaining crackers on the side.

Per Serving Calories: 483; Total fat: 28g; Saturated fat: 14g; Cholesterol: 67mg; Sodium: 989mg; Carbohydrates: 47g; Fiber: 5g; Protein: 13g

Crab and Roasted Asparagus Risotto

SERVES 4

Having lived much of my adult life on the West Coast and having spent countless summer vacations on the Oregon coast, I grew up with Dungeness crab. It wasn't until I moved to Atlanta that I realized blue crabs were a real thing. I'm still kind of spoiled, but I've learned to like the crab from this side of the country, too. Risotto is a great way to stretch a little of this expensive ingredient.

1 pound asparagus, trimmed and cut into 1-inch pieces

1 tablespoon olive oil

1 teaspoon kosher salt (or ½ teaspoon fine salt), divided

2 tablespoons unsalted butter

1 small onion, chopped (about ½ cup)

1 cup arborio rice

⅓ cup white wine

2¾ to 3 cups Roasted Vegetable Stock (page 219) or low-sodium vegetable broth

8 ounces lump crabmeat

⅓ cup grated Parmesan or similar cheese

PREP TIME
10 MINUTES

AIR CRISP
10 MINUTES

SEAR/SAUTÉ
8 MINUTES

PRESSURE COOK
8 MINUTES, HIGH PRESSURE

RELEASE
QUICK

TOTAL TIME
45 MINUTES

GLUTEN-FREE, UNDER 60 MINUTES

CUSTOMIZATION TIP: Like the Risotto with Chard, Caramelized Onions, and Mushrooms (page 66), this recipe is easy to alter depending on your taste and what you have on hand. Shrimp or leftover salmon can stand in for the crab. I particularly like smoked salmon when I have it on hand.

MAKE-AHEAD TIP: The asparagus can be cooked ahead and refrigerated for a day or so.

1. Close the Crisping Lid and select Air Crisp; adjust the temperature to 375°F and the time to 2 minutes to preheat. Press Start.

2. While the unit preheats, place the asparagus in the Cook & Crisp™ Basket. Drizzle with the olive oil. Sprinkle with ½ teaspoon of kosher salt (or ¼ teaspoon of fine salt) and toss.

3. Place the basket in the Foodi's™ inner pot. Close the Crisping Lid and select Air Crisp; adjust the temperature to 375°F and the cook time to 10 minutes. Press Start. After 5 minutes, open the lid and stir the asparagus, then continue cooking.

4. When cooking is complete, remove the basket and set aside. ➤

5. On your Foodi, select Sear/Sauté and adjust to Medium. Press Start. Add the butter to melt, and cook until it stops foaming. Add the onion. Cook for about 5 minutes, stirring, until softened. Add the rice, stir to coat, and cook for about 1 minute. Add the wine. Cook for 2 to 3 minutes, stirring, until it's almost evaporated.

6. Add 2½ cups of vegetable stock and the remaining ½ teaspoon of kosher salt (or ¼ teaspoon of fine salt) and stir to combine.

7. Lock the Pressure Lid into place, making sure the valve is set to Seal. Select Pressure; adjust the pressure to High and the cook time to 8 minutes. Press Start.

8. After cooking, use a quick pressure release. Carefully unlock and remove the Pressure Lid.

9. Test the risotto; the rice should be soft with a slightly firm center and the sauce should be creamy, but it will probably not be quite done. If not, add another ¼ to ½ cup of stock. Select Sear/Sauté and adjust to Medium-Low. Press Start. Bring to a simmer and cook for 2 to 3 minutes until done. If the rice is done but too dry, add enough stock to loosen it up.

10. Gently stir in the asparagus and crabmeat and let it heat for a minute or so. Stir in the Parmesan. Taste and adjust the seasoning. Serve immediately.

Per Serving Calories: 361; Total fat: 11g; Saturated fat: 4g; Cholesterol: 44mg; Sodium: 1435mg; Carbohydrates: 45g; Fiber: 4g; Protein: 20g

Thai Fish Curry

With a can of coconut milk and a good commercial Thai curry paste, this dish comes together quickly but tastes like you spent all afternoon making it. I use the Mae Ploy brand of curry paste; if you can't find it, you may need to adjust the seasoning with additional lime juice or sugar. The final dish, like many Thai dishes, should have a good balance of salty, sweet, and sour.

1 (14-ounce) can coconut milk (not "lite")

Vegetable or coconut oil, as needed

1 tablespoon Thai red curry paste, or more to taste

½ cup seafood stock or water

1 medium zucchini, cut into ¼-inch rounds

1 small onion, sliced

1 small red bell pepper, seeded and cut into bite-size pieces

1 pound frozen cod or grouper fillets

1 teaspoon freshly squeezed lime juice (optional)

1 teaspoon sugar (optional)

1 small (5-ounce) bag baby spinach

1 cup cherry tomatoes, halved

2 tablespoons chopped fresh basil

¼ cup coarsely chopped roasted salted cashews

PREP TIME
10 MINUTES

SEAR/SAUTÉ
2 MINUTES

PRESSURE COOK
3 MINUTES, LOW PRESSURE

RELEASE
QUICK

TOTAL TIME
20 MINUTES

DAIRY-FREE, GLUTEN-FREE, AROUND 30 MINUTES

CUSTOMIZATION TIP: Use shrimp instead of fish for this dish, adding them at the end to cook after the pressure is released. Or you can cook them before as in the recipe for Bow Tie Pasta with Shrimp and Arugula (page 160) or Shrimp and Sausage Gumbo (page 182). If you prefer chicken, use bite-size chunks of boneless breasts and decrease the time under pressure to 2 minutes.

1. On your Foodi™ select Sear/Sauté and adjust to Medium to preheat the inner pot. Press Start. Allow the pot to preheat for 5 minutes.

2. Open the can of coconut milk without shaking it. Depending on the brand, you should see a thick layer of almost solid coconut "cream" on top. If yes, scoop out 2 to 3 tablespoons and add it to the inner pot. If no, add enough vegetable or coconut oil to the pot to form a thick coat on the bottom. Heat until shimmering. Add the curry paste and smash it down into the oil to fry it slightly, cooking for about 2 minutes. Add the remaining coconut milk and stir to dissolve.

3. Add the seafood stock, zucchini, onion, bell pepper, and fish fillets. ➤

4. Lock the Pressure Lid into place, making sure the valve is set to Seal. Select Pressure; adjust the pressure to Low and the cook time to 3 minutes. Press Start.

5. After cooking, use a quick pressure release. Carefully unlock and remove the Pressure Lid.

6. Using a fork, break the fish fillets into bite-size chunks. Taste the sauce. If needed, add the optional lime juice or sugar to balance the flavor.

7. Stir in the spinach and tomatoes to heat through. Serve over rice, if desired, garnished with the basil and cashews.

Per Serving Calories: 400; Total fat: 29g; Saturated fat: 22g; Cholesterol: 42mg; Sodium: 129mg; Carbohydrates: 13g; Fiber: 3g; Protein: 26g

Blackened Salmon with Creamy Grits

Grits cook quickly under pressure, but it's difficult to keep them from scorching if you put them directly in the pot. In a separate bowl they take a bit longer but are still much faster than on the stovetop—and you don't have to stir them. They go really well with the spicy salmon. A cucumber salad with a tangy vinaigrette makes a good foil to the rich fish and grits.

¾ cup grits (not instant or quick cooking)

1½ cups milk

1½ cups Chicken Stock (page 218), or store-bought low-sodium chicken broth

3 tablespoons unsalted butter, divided

2 teaspoons kosher salt (or 1 teaspoon fine salt), divided

3 tablespoons Cajun Seasoning Mix (page 223) or store-bought mix

1 tablespoon packed brown sugar

4 (5-ounce) salmon fillets, skin removed

Nonstick cooking spray

PREP TIME
10 MINUTES

PRESSURE COOK
15 MINUTES, HIGH PRESSURE

RELEASE
NATURAL FOR 10 MINUTES, THEN QUICK

BAKE/ROAST
12 MINUTES

TOTAL TIME
55 MINUTES

GLUTEN-FREE, UNDER 60 MINUTES

SUBSTITUTION TIP: If you can find trout fillets, they're excellent in this dish in place of the salmon. They tend to be thinner so won't need quite as long under the Crisping Lid.

1. Pour the grits into a heat-proof bowl that holds at least 6 cups. Add the milk, chicken stock, 1 tablespoon of butter, and ½ teaspoon of kosher salt (or ¼ teaspoon of fine salt). Stir. Cover the bowl with aluminum foil.

2. Pour 1 cup of water into the inner pot. Place the Reversible Rack in the pot in the lower position and place the bowl on top.

3. Lock the Pressure Lid into place, making sure the valve is set to Seal. Select Pressure; adjust the pressure to High and the cook time to 15 minutes. Press Start.

4. While the grits cook, in a shallow bowl that fits one or two fillets at a time, stir together the seasoning, brown sugar, and remaining 1½ teaspoons of kosher salt (or ¾ teaspoon of fine salt). ➤

Blackened Salmon with Creamy Grits continued

5. Spray the fillets on one side with cooking spray and transfer one or two at a time, sprayed-side down, to the spice mixture. Spray the exposed sides of the fillets and turn over to coat that side in the seasoning. Repeat with the remaining fillets.

6. Once the grits cook, let the pressure release naturally for 10 minutes, then quick release any remaining pressure. Carefully unlock and remove the Pressure Lid.

7. Remove the rack and bowl from the pot. Add the remaining 2 tablespoons of butter to the grits and stir to incorporate. Re-cover with the foil and return the bowl to the pot (without the rack).

8. Reverse the rack to the upper position. Place the salmon fillets on the rack and place the rack in the pot.

9. Close the Crisping Lid and select Bake/Roast; adjust the temperature to 400°F and the cook time to 12 minutes. Press Start. After 6 minutes, open the lid and carefully turn the fillets over. Close the lid and continue cooking. When the salmon is cooked and flakes easily with a fork, remove the rack. Remove the bowl of grits and uncover. Stir them again and serve immediately with the salmon.

Per Serving Calories: 486; Total fat: 22g; Saturated fat: 9g; Cholesterol: 111mg; Sodium: 969mg; Carbohydrates: 36g; Fiber: 1g; Protein: 36g

Salmon Cakes

SERVES 4

For a long time, I thought of salmon cakes as the poor cousins of the crab cake—a dish that was okay, but only if you couldn't have the real thing. But made well, salmon cakes are objectively delicious, tender, and moist with a bit of crunch from the vegetables and a crisp exterior. These are mostly salmon, held together with potato flakes, and uncoated so the salmon flavor really shines. They're great alone, or as "salmon burgers" on a bun, or under poached eggs for brunch.

1 pound fresh salmon

1 teaspoon kosher salt (or ½ teaspoon fine salt), divided

1 tablespoon unsalted butter

2 teaspoons olive oil

1 small onion, diced (about ½ cup)

1 large celery stalk, diced (about ½ cup)

½ small red bell pepper, diced (about ½ cup)

½ teaspoon Worcestershire sauce

¼ teaspoon hot pepper sauce

1 teaspoon Cajun Seasoning Mix (page 223) or store-bought mix

¼ cup mayonnaise

1 teaspoon Dijon mustard

1 large egg, beaten

½ cup instant mashed potato flakes

PREP TIME
10 MINUTES

PRESSURE COOK
3 MINUTES, HIGH PRESSURE

RELEASE
QUICK

SEAR/SAUTÉ
12 MINUTES

BAKE/ROAST
7 MINUTES

BROIL
4 MINUTES

TOTAL TIME
45 MINUTES, NOT INCLUDING CHILLING TIME

GLUTEN-FREE, UNDER 60 MINUTES

SUBSTITUTION TIP: If you don't have time to cook the salmon, use canned instead.

1. Sprinkle the salmon on both sides with ½ teaspoon of kosher salt (or ¼ teaspoon of fine salt) and place it on the Reversible Rack in the lower position. Pour 1 cup of water into the inner pot. Place the rack in the pot.

2. Lock the Pressure Lid into place, making sure the valve is set to Seal. Select Pressure; adjust the pressure to High and the cook time to 3 minutes. Press Start.

3. After cooking, use a quick pressure release. Carefully unlock and remove the Pressure Lid.

4. Remove the salmon and the rack and let the salmon rest until cool enough to handle. Pour the water out of the pot and return the pot to the base.

5. Flake the salmon into a large bowl and place it in the refrigerator. (If the salmon has skin, remove and discard it.) ➤

6. On your Foodi™ select Sear/Sauté and adjust to Medium to preheat the inner pot. Press Start. Allow the pot to preheat for 5 minutes. Add the butter and oil. Once those ingredients stop foaming, add the onion, celery, and bell pepper. Sprinkle with the remaining ½ teaspoon of kosher salt (or ¼ teaspoon of fine salt). Stir to coat the vegetables in the fat and cook for 10 minutes, stirring occasionally.

7. Add the Worcestershire sauce, hot pepper sauce, and seasoning. Adjust the heat to Medium-High and cook for 2 minutes more.

8. Remove the salmon from the refrigerator and transfer the sautéed vegetables to the bowl.

9. In a small bowl, whisk together the mayonnaise and mustard. Whisk in the egg.

10. Add the mayonnaise mixture to the salmon and vegetables. Add the potato flakes. Gently but thoroughly mix the ingredients. Chill for 30 minutes.

11. Shape the mixture into four cakes. If you have egg rings, they come in very handy for shaping the cakes. If not, make the cakes about 1 inch thick and 3½ inches across.

12. Cover the Reversible Rack set in the upper position with nonstick aluminum foil (or regular foil sprayed with cooking spray). Carefully transfer the salmon cakes to the rack.

13. Close the Crisping Lid and select Bake/Roast; adjust the temperature to 325ºF and the time to 2 minutes to preheat. Press Start.

14. When the Foodi™ is preheated, place the rack and salmon into the pot. Close the Crisping Lid and select Bake/Roast; leave the temperature at 325ºF and adjust the cook time to 7 minutes. Press Start.

15. When cooking is complete, select Broil and set the time for 4 minutes. Press Start. Cook until the tops of the cakes are brown and crisp. Serve with a salad for a light dinner, or serve on buns with tartar sauce or the piquillo sauce for empanadas.

FROM SCRATCH

Make a spicy lemon butter sauce while the salmon cakes cook. Melt 2 tablespoons unsalted butter in a saucepan over low heat. Stir in 1 teaspoon Cajun Seasoning Mix (page 223) or store-bought mix, and 1 tablespoon freshly squeezed lemon juice. Bring to a simmer and stir in 1 tablespoon heavy cream.

Per Serving Calories: 332; Total fat: 20g; Saturated fat: 5g; Cholesterol: 127mg; Sodium: 590mg; Carbohydrates: 13g; Fiber: 1g; Protein: 25g.

Shrimp and Sausage Gumbo

SERVES 4

I'd never made gumbo until I moved to Atlanta. In fact, I think I'd only had it once or twice. I'd thought it was a dish that took all day, and some recipes do indeed take lots of time. But by borrowing Paul Prudhomme's bold method for making a roux quickly, and then pressure cooking, I can turn out a pretty great gumbo in less than an hour—and so can you. Plus, there's a bonus: You can cook the rice at the same time as the gumbo.

1 pound medium shrimp

1½ teaspoons kosher salt (or ¾ teaspoon fine salt), divided

¼ cup vegetable oil, plus 2 teaspoons

⅓ cup all-purpose flour

1½ teaspoons Cajun Seasoning Mix (page 223) or store-bought mix

1 medium onion, chopped (about 1 cup)

1 or 2 celery stalks, chopped (about ⅔ cup)

1 small red bell pepper, chopped (about ⅔ cup)

2 garlic cloves, minced

1 small jalapeño pepper, seeded and minced (optional)

2½ cups Chicken Stock (page 218), or store-bought low-sodium chicken broth

6 ounces andouille sausage, cut in ¼-inch rounds, then into half-moons

¾ cup long-grain white rice, rinsed

¾ cup water

2 scallions, finely sliced (about ⅓ cup)

PREP TIME
15 MINUTES

AIR CRISP
6 MINUTES

SEAR/SAUTÉ
5 MINUTES

PRESSURE COOK
6 MINUTES, HIGH PRESSURE

RELEASE
NATURAL FOR 8 MINUTES, THEN QUICK

TOTAL TIME
50 MINUTES

DAIRY-FREE, UNDER 60 MINUTES

SUBSTITUTION TIP: If you don't like or don't eat sausage, omit it and increase the shrimp to 1½ pounds. Or add 8 ounces of crabmeat at step 9 if you want to get fancy.

1. Place the shrimp in the Cook & Crisp™ Basket. Add ½ teaspoon of kosher salt (or ¼ teaspoon of fine salt), and 2 teaspoons of vegetable oil. Toss to coat. Place the basket in the Foodi's™ inner pot.

2. Close the Crisping Lid and select Air Crisp; adjust the temperature to 400°F and the cook time to 6 minutes. Press Start. After 3 minutes, open the lid and toss the shrimp. Close the lid and continue cooking. When done, the shrimp should be opaque and pink. It's okay if they are not quite done, as they'll finish cooking later. Remove the basket and set aside.

3. On your Foodi™ select Sear/Sauté and adjust to High. Press Start. Pour in the remaining ¼ cup of vegetable oil and heat until the oil begins to smoke. Whisk in the flour. Switch to a wooden spoon and cook the roux for 3 to 5 minutes, stirring constantly, until the roux is the color of peanut butter. Turn off the Foodi.

4. Quickly add the seasoning, onion, celery, bell pepper, garlic, and jalapeño (if using). Stir for about 5 minutes until the mixture cools a little. Add the chicken stock and sausage.

5. Pour the rice into a 1½-quart heat-proof bowl. Add the water and the remaining 1 teaspoon of kosher salt (or ½ teaspoon of fine salt). Cover the bowl with aluminum foil.

6. Place the Reversible Rack in the pot in the lower position and place the bowl on top.

7. Lock the Pressure Lid into place, making sure the valve is set to Seal. Select Pressure; adjust the pressure to High and the cook time to 6 minutes. Press Start.

8. After cooking, let the pressure release naturally for 8 minutes, then quick release any remaining pressure. Carefully unlock and remove the Pressure Lid.

9. Remove the rack and bowl and set aside. Stir the shrimp into the gumbo to heat it up, about 3 minutes.

10. Fluff the rice with a fork and place a scoop of it in the middle of each of four bowls. Ladle the gumbo around the rice and garnish with the scallions.

Per Serving Calories: 635; Total fat: 32g; Saturated fat: 7g; Cholesterol: 201mg; Sodium: 1377mg; Carbohydrates: 48g; Fiber: 2g; Protein: 36g

Tilapia Veracruz

Traditionally made with a whole red snapper, this dish shows the definite Spanish influence common to Veracruz (Mexico) cooking: olives, capers, and parsley. Since snapper can be difficult to find, I generally make the dish with whatever mild white fish is available. Cooking the fish frozen is perfect for pressure cooking—the fish doesn't overcook in the time it takes for the sauce to cook.

4 (6-ounce) frozen tilapia fillets

¼ teaspoon kosher salt (or ⅛ teaspoon fine salt)

3 tablespoons olive oil

½ small onion, sliced (about ½ cup)

2 large garlic cloves, minced

1 small jalapeño pepper, seeded and minced (about 1 tablespoon)

1 (14.5-ounce) can diced tomatoes, drained

1 bay leaf

½ teaspoon dried oregano leaves

⅓ cup sliced green olives

¼ cup chopped fresh parsley, divided

3 tablespoons capers, divided

PREP TIME
10 MINUTES

SEAR/SAUTÉ
5 MINUTES

PRESSURE COOK
3 MINUTES, LOW PRESSURE

RELEASE
QUICK

TOTAL TIME
25 MINUTES

DAIRY-FREE, GLUTEN-FREE, AROUND 30 MINUTES

MAKE-AHEAD TIP: You can make the sauce ahead of time. In fact, I often make a double batch and freeze half. It will keep in the refrigerator for several days or in the freezer for 1 month. Just thaw (if necessary), add to the pot along with the tilapia, and start at step 4.

1. Sprinkle the fish fillets with the salt and place them in the refrigerator while you make the sauce.

2. On your Foodi™ select Sear/Sauté and adjust to Medium to preheat the inner pot. Press Start. Allow the pot to preheat for 5 minutes. Pour in the olive oil and heat until shimmering. Add the onion, garlic, and jalapeño. Cook for 5 minutes, stirring occasionally, or until just starting to brown.

3. Add the tomatoes, bay leaf, oregano, olives, half the parsley, and half the capers to the pot. Stir to combine. Place the fish fillets on top.

4. Lock the Pressure Lid into place, making sure the valve is set to Seal. Select Pressure; adjust the pressure to Low and the cook time to 3 minutes. Press Start.

5. After cooking, use a quick pressure release. Carefully unlock and remove the Pressure Lid. Remove and discard the bay leaf. Transfer the fish fillets to a platter and spoon the sauce over. Sprinkle with the remaining parsley and capers.

Per Serving Calories: 305; Total fat: 16g; Saturated fat: 3g; Cholesterol: 84mg; Sodium: 610mg; Carbohydrates: 6g; Fiber: 2g; Protein: 35g

Cheesy Tuna Noodle Casserole

SERVES 4

Using a pressure cooker for tuna noodle casserole not only makes it faster but also keeps the dish nice and creamy instead of all dried out the way it can get in the oven. I know people say you should not mix cheese with fish, but I've always liked tuna melts with Cheddar cheese, so why not add it to tuna casserole?

1 tablespoon vegetable oil

1 medium onion, chopped (about 1 cup)

1 large celery stalk, chopped (about ½ cup)

6 ounces wide egg noodles

1 (12-ounce) can evaporated milk, divided

1 cup water

1 teaspoon kosher salt (or ½ teaspoon fine salt)

2 cups shredded Cheddar cheese (about 4 ounces)

2 teaspoons cornstarch

2 (5- to 6-ounce) cans tuna, drained

1 cup frozen peas, thawed

2½ cups panko bread crumbs

3 tablespoons unsalted butter, melted

PREP TIME
10 MINUTES

SEAR/SAUTÉ
1 MINUTE PLUS 2 MINUTES

PRESSURE COOK
5 MINUTES, LOW PRESSURE

RELEASE
QUICK

BROIL
5 MINUTES

TOTAL TIME
35 MINUTES

AROUND 30 MINUTES

SUBSTITUTION TIP: Some people like crushed potato chips on top of tuna noodle casserole, so if you are one of those people, substitute them for the buttered panko and broil for just 1 to 2 minutes.

1. On your Foodi™ select Sear/Sauté and adjust to Medium to preheat the inner pot. Press Start. Allow the pot to preheat for 5 minutes. Pour in the vegetable oil and heat until shimmering. Once the pot is hot, add the onion and celery. Cook for about 1 minute, stirring, until softened.

2. Add the noodles, ¾ cup of evaporated milk, the water, and salt to the pot. Stir to combine and submerge the noodles in the liquid.

3. Lock the Pressure Lid in place, making sure the valve is set to Seal. Select Pressure; adjust the pressure to Low and the cook time to 5 minutes. Press Start.

4. After cooking, use a quick pressure release. Carefully unlock and remove the Pressure Lid.

5. On your Foodi™ select Sear/Sauté and adjust to Less for low heat. Press Start. Pour the remaining ¾ cup of evaporated milk into the noodles.

6. In a medium bowl, toss together the cheese and cornstarch to coat. Add the cheese mixture by large handfuls, stirring, until the cheese melts and the sauce thickens. Add the tuna and peas and gently stir. Let the tuna and peas heat for 1 to 2 minutes.

7. In another medium bowl, stir together the panko and melted butter. Spread the crumbs evenly over the casserole.

8. Close the Crisping Lid and select Broil. Adjust the cook time to 5 minutes. Press Start. When done, the topping should be brown and crisp. If not, broil for 1 to 2 minutes more. Serve immediately.

Per Serving Calories: 997; Total fat: 43g; Saturated fat: 23g; Cholesterol: 163mg; Sodium: 1522mg; Carbohydrates: 96g; Fiber: 7g; Protein: 55g

Potato-Crusted Cod with Succotash

SERVES 4

If you're like me, you might be thinking, "Potato flakes? Really?" I used to shun them, after the one disappointing time I used them for mashed potatoes. But it turns out they're very good for other things, like coating fish fillets. For this recipe, consider buying frozen vacuum-sealed fish fillets—they're portioned evenly, with a uniform thickness, which ensures they all cook at the same rate.

1 tablespoon vegetable or olive oil

½ small onion, chopped (about ½ cup)

1 garlic clove, minced

1 medium jalapeño, seeded and chopped

1½ cups frozen corn

1½ cups frozen baby lima beans

¼ teaspoon cayenne pepper

1 bay leaf

½ teaspoon Worcestershire sauce

¼ cup Chicken Stock (page 218), Roasted Vegetable Stock (page 219), or low-sodium chicken or vegetable broth

1 teaspoon kosher salt (or ½ teaspoon fine salt), divided

4 (4-ounce) cod fillets (or other firm white fish), at least 1 inch thick

¼ cup mayonnaise

1 tablespoon Dijon-style mustard

1½ cups instant mashed potato flakes

1 large tomato, seeded and chopped (about ½ cup)

¼ cup chopped fresh parsley

Nonstick cooking spray

PREP TIME
10 MINUTES

SEAR/SAUTÉ
4 MINUTES

PRESSURE COOK
5 MINUTES, HIGH PRESSURE

RELEASE
QUICK

BAKE/ROAST
8 MINUTES

TOTAL TIME
35 MINUTES

DAIRY-FREE, GLUTEN-FREE, AROUND 30 MINUTES

CUSTOMIZATION TIP: If you like bacon, dice and sauté 2 slices before cooking the onion and garlic. Remove the bacon and use the bacon fat to sauté the vegetables. Stir in the cooked bacon right before serving.

1. On your Foodi™ select Sear/Sauté and adjust to Medium to preheat the inner pot. Press Start. Allow the pot to preheat for 5 minutes. Pour in the vegetable oil and heat until shimmering. Add the onion, garlic, and jalapeño. Cook for 4 minutes, stirring occasionally, or until the vegetables are softened.

2. Add the corn, lima beans, cayenne, bay leaf, Worcestershire sauce, chicken stock, and ½ teaspoon of kosher salt (or ¼ teaspoon of fine salt).

3. Lock the Pressure Lid into place, making sure the valve is set to Seal. Select Pressure; adjust the pressure to High and the cook time to 5 minutes. Press Start. While the succotash cooks, season the fish fillets with the remaining ½ teaspoon of kosher salt (or ¼ teaspoon of fine salt). In a small bowl, stir together the mayonnaise and mustard. Pour the potato flakes into a shallow bowl.

4. Using a basting brush, paint the mayonnaise mixture on all sides of the fillets and then roll them in the potato flakes to coat.

5. Once the succotash is cooked, use a quick pressure release. Carefully unlock and remove the Pressure Lid. Stir in the tomato and parsley. Carefully remove the bay leaf.

6. Cover the Reversible Rack set in the upper position with nonstick aluminum foil (or regular foil sprayed with cooking spray). Carefully transfer the fish fillets to the rack and place the rack in the pot.

7. Spray the tops of the fillets with cooking spray.

8. Close the Crisping Lid and select Bake/Roast; adjust the temperature to 375°F and the cook time to 8 minutes. Press Start. After 4 minutes, open the lid. Carefully turn the fillets over and spray the other side with cooking spray. Close the lid and continue cooking. The fish should flake apart easily when done. Serve the fillets with the succotash.

Per Serving Calories: 410; Total fat: 10g; Saturated fat: 1g; Cholesterol: 45mg; Sodium: 535mg; Carbohydrates: 54g; Fiber: 8g; Protein: 29g

Quinoa Pilaf with Smoked Trout and Corn

SERVES 4

I love the combination of smoked trout and corn—the sweetness of the corn is a nice foil for the rich, smoky, salty fish. They pair well with the nuttiness of quinoa in this easy but elegant dish, and pecans add the perfect finishing touch. If you can't find smoked trout, any hot-smoked white fish or salmon can be used instead.

½ cup pecan pieces

1 tablespoon vegetable oil

4 scallions, chopped, green and white parts separated

1 cup quinoa, rinsed briefly and drained

1 cup frozen corn, thawed

3 cups water

1 teaspoon kosher salt (or ½ teaspoon fine salt)

1 smoked trout or salmon fillet (about 8 ounces), flaked

1 medium tomato, seeded and diced

2 teaspoons prepared horseradish

PREP
10 MINUTES

SEAR/SAUTÉ
4 MINUTES

PRESSURE COOK
3 MINUTES, HIGH PRESSURE

RELEASE
NATURAL FOR 4 MINUTES, THEN QUICK

AIR CRISP
5 MINUTES

TOTAL TIME
35 MINUTES

GLUTEN FREE, DAIRY FREE, AROUND 30 MINUTES

CUSTOMIZATION TIP: Once you get the basic technique of quinoa pilaf down, you can add whatever meat and vegetables you like. Chopped ham and peas are a great combination!

1. Pour the pecans into a heat-proof bowl that fits in the Cook & Crisp™ Basket. Place the basket in the inner pot and the bowl in the basket. Close the Crisping Lid and select Air Crisp; adjust the temperature to 375ºF and the time to 5 minutes. Press Start. When the pecans are toasted, carefully remove the bowl and basket from the pot and set aside.

2. On your Foodi™ select Sear/Sauté and adjust to Medium to preheat the inner pot. Add the oil and heat until shimmering. Add the white part of the scallions, and cook for about a minute, or until starting to soften. Stir in the quinoa and cook, stirring occasionally for 2 to 3 minutes, or until it's starting to smell nutty. Add the corn, water, and salt.

3. Lock the Pressure Lid in place, making sure the valve is set to Seal. Select Pressure; adjust the pressure to High and the cook time to 3 minutes. Press Start.

4. After cooking, let the pressure release naturally for 5 minutes, then quick release the remaining pressure. Carefully unlock and remove the Pressure Lid.

5. Gently fluff the quinoa using a large fork. Stir in the flaked trout, green parts of the scallions, and the tomato. Stir in the horseradish. Let sit for a few minutes to warm through.

6. Serve in bowls topped with the toasted pecans.

Per serving: Calories: 286; Total fat: 10g; Saturated fat: 2g; Cholesterol: 11g; Sodium: 617mg; Carbohydrates 38g; Fiber 5g; Protein 12g

Trout Florentine

At a wonderful South American restaurant in San Francisco, I used to order whole trout stuffed with spinach and wrapped in bacon, then roasted until crisp. It was delicious, but too time-consuming to make at home. This is a much simpler dish with similar flavors, still delicious, but easy enough to make on a weeknight. If you can't find trout, you can use another mild fish such as tilapia, sole, or flounder.

3 slices bacon, chopped

½ small onion, chopped (about ⅓ cup)

2 (5- to 6-ounce) bags baby spinach

½ teaspoon kosher salt (or ¼ teaspoon fine salt), divided

½ cup heavy cream

4 (4- to 6-ounce) trout, tilapia, sole, or flounder fillets

3 tablespoons unsalted butter, melted and divided

¼ teaspoon fresh ground black pepper

1 cup panko breadcrumbs

2 tablespoons chopped fresh parsley

PREP: 10 MINUTES

SEAR/SAUTÉ: 15 MINUTES

BAKE/ROAST: 9 MINUTES

TOTAL TIME: 35 MINUTES

AROUND 30 MINUTES

SUBSTITUTION TIP: Any mild fish fillets can be used instead of trout—just make sure that they aren't more than about ¾ of an inch thick. Thicker fillets can be used, but will need to be cooked longer.

1. On your Foodi,™ select Sear/Sauté and adjust to Medium to preheat the inner pot. Press Start. Add the bacon and cook until most of the fat has rendered and the bacon is crisp, about 6 minutes. Add the onions to the pot and cook, stirring occasionally, for about 2 minutes or until the onion pieces start to soften. Sprinkle with half of the salt.

2. Add about a quarter of the spinach and cooking, stir frequently until wilted, about 1 minute. Repeat with the remaining spinach, adding it in 3 more batches. When all the spinach is wilted, cook for another 2 to 3 minutes, or until most of the liquid is evaporated. Stir in the cream.

3. Lay the trout fillets over the spinach in a single layer. Brush 1 tablespoon of the melted butter over the fillets and sprinkle with the remaining salt and the pepper.

4. Close the Crisping Lid and select Bake/Roast. Adjust the temperature to 300ºF and the cook time to 3 minutes. Press Start.

5. While the fish cooks, stir together the remaining butter, the panko breadcrumbs, and the parsley.

6. When the cooking is complete, open the Crisping Lid. The fillets should be opaque and mostly, but not entirely, cooked. Cover the fillets with the panko mixture.

7. Close the Crisping Lid and select Bake/Roast. Adjust the temperature to 400°F and the cook time to 6 minutes. Press Start. After about 4 minutes, open the lid and check the fish. The panko should be golden brown and crisp. If not, close the lid and continue to cook for an additional 2 minutes.

Per serving: Calories: 617; Total fat: 37g; Saturated fat: 17g; Cholesterol: 123g; Sodium: 1544mg; Carbohydrates 32g; Fiber 16g; Protein 51g

7

Desserts

Left: Chocolate Marble Cheesecake, page 200

Mixed Berry Crisp

SERVES 6

Crisps are among the easiest fruit desserts to make. No crust or dough to roll out, just a topping to sprinkle over. And pressure cooking the filling makes this crisp not only easy but quick as well.

FOR THE BASE

2 (10-ounce) bags frozen mixed berries

⅓ cup granulated sugar

1 tablespoon all-purpose flour

1 teaspoon grated lemon zest

FOR THE TOPPING

⅔ cup gluten-free quick-cooking oatmeal

½ cup packed brown sugar

½ cup all-purpose flour

¼ cup blanched slivered almonds

1 teaspoon ground cinnamon

Pinch kosher salt (or small pinch fine salt)

6 tablespoons unsalted butter, at room temperature

PREP TIME
10 MINUTES

PRESSURE COOK
3 MINUTES, HIGH PRESSURE

RELEASE
QUICK

BAKE/ROAST
12 MINUTES

TOTAL TIME
25 MINUTES

GLUTEN-FREE OPTION, VEGETARIAN, UNDER 60 MINUTES

MAKE-AHEAD TIP: Prepare the topping ahead of time and freeze it.

SUBSTITUTION TIP: For a gluten-free dessert, substitute gluten-free flour in the base and topping, or just omit the flour in the topping and use an extra ½ cup of oatmeal.

To make the base

1. Empty the bags of berries into the Foodi's™ inner pot. Add the granulated sugar, flour, and lemon zest. Stir to combine.

2. Lock the Pressure Lid into place, making sure the valve is set to Seal. Select Pressure; adjust the pressure to High and the cook time to 3 minutes. Press Start.

3. After cooking, use a quick pressure release. Carefully unlock and remove the Pressure Lid.

To make the topping

1. In a food processor, combine the oatmeal, brown sugar, flour, almonds, cinnamon, and salt. Pulse just until blended. Add the butter and pulse again until the mixture is crumbly but holds together when you pinch a bit between your fingers. Spread the topping over the berry mixture in the pot.

2. Close the Crisping Lid and select Bake/Roast; adjust the temperature to 375°F and the cook time to 12 minutes. Press Start. Check the crisp after about 8 minutes; the topping should be browned and crisp. Let cool before serving, but serve warm.

Per Serving Calories: 365; Total fat: 15g; Saturated fat: 8g; Cholesterol: 31mg; Sodium: 86mg; Carbohydrates: 58g; Fiber: 5g; Protein: 4g

Peach Cobbler

SERVES 4

Cobblers, fruit desserts topped with a sweetened biscuit-like dough, are good with almost any fruits, but one of my favorites is peaches, either alone or with blueberries or raspberries. You can, of course, make this with fresh peaches when they are in season, but frozen peaches are delicious and much easier.

FOR THE BASE
2 (10- to 12-ounce) bags frozen peaches
3 tablespoons cornstarch
1 cup sugar

FOR THE TOPPING
1 cup self-rising flour
5 tablespoons granulated sugar, divided
¼ teaspoon ground cinnamon
⅔ cup cream, plus more as needed
1 tablespoon melted unsalted butter
1 tablespoon heavy (whipping) cream

PREP TIME
10 MINUTES

PRESSURE COOK
3 MINUTES, HIGH PRESSURE

RELEASE
QUICK

BAKE/ROAST
12 MINUTES

TOTAL TIME
35 MINUTES

VEGETARIAN, AROUND 30 MINUTES

CUSTOMIZATION TIP: Vanilla ice cream or whipped cream makes an indulgent but delicious topping.

SUBSTITUTION TIP: If you like, substitute one bag of frozen blueberries or raspberries for one of the bags of peaches.

To make the base

1. Empty the bags of peaches into the Foodi's™ inner pot. Add the cornstarch and sugar. Stir to combine.

2. Lock the Pressure Lid into place, making sure the valve is set to Seal. Select Pressure; adjust the pressure to High and the cook time to 3 minutes. Press Start.

3. After cooking, use a quick pressure release. Carefully unlock and remove the Pressure Lid.

To make the topping

1. In a small bowl, whisk the flour, 3 tablespoons of sugar, and the cinnamon. In another small bowl, whisk the cream and melted butter. Add the cream mixture to the dry ingredients. Stir just until combined. If the mixture is too dry to come together, add a little more cream, 1 teaspoon at a time, until the dough holds together in a ball but is very sticky.

2. Using two spoons or a disher, scoop out 2 to 3 tablespoons of dough and place the scoop over the peaches. Scoop out the rest in similar-size portions and arrange evenly over the top of the fruit. As much as possible, smooth out the tops of the dough balls and spread them out slightly. Brush the topping with the heavy cream and sprinkle with the remaining 2 tablespoons of sugar.

3. Close the Crisping Lid and select Bake/Roast; adjust the temperature to 325ºF and the cook time to 12 minutes. Press Start. Check after about 8 minutes; if the dough doesn't seem to be cooking evenly, rotate the pot about 90 degrees. When done, the topping should be lightly browned and cooked through (use a skewer to check; it should come out with no raw dough clinging to it). Let cool before serving, but serve warm.

Per Serving Calories: 523; Total fat: 9g; Saturated fat: 6g; Cholesterol: 28mg; Sodium: 39mg; Carbohydrates: 109g; Fiber: 4g; Protein: 6g

Chocolate Marble Cheesecake

SERVES 8

For those times when you can't decide between chocolate and vanilla, this is the cheesecake to make. Luscious dark chocolate gets swirled into a rich, creamy vanilla cheesecake base. Chocolate cookie crumbs make the perfect crust for this company-worthy dessert.

4 ounces chocolate wafer cookies, crushed into crumbs (about 1 cup crumbs)

2 tablespoons unsalted butter, melted

16 ounces cream cheese, at room temperature

½ cup sugar

2 tablespoons sour cream

2 tablespoons heavy (whipping) cream

2 teaspoons vanilla extract

2 large eggs

3 ounces bittersweet chocolate chips, melted

PREP TIME
15 MINUTES

AIR CRISP
6 MINUTES

PRESSURE COOK
25 MINUTES, HIGH PRESSURE

RELEASE
NATURAL FOR 10 MINUTES, THEN QUICK

TOTAL TIME
60 MINUTES, PLUS CHILLING TIME

GLUTEN-FREE OPTION, VEGETARIAN

SUBSTITUTION TIP: For a gluten-free treat, choose gluten-free cookies to make the crumbs for the crust.

1. In a small bowl, stir together the cookie crumbs and melted butter. Press the crumbs into the bottom of a 7-inch springform pan and about ½ inch up the sides.

2. Set the Reversible Rack in the inner pot in the lower position and place the springform pan on top.

3. Close the Crisping Lid and select Air Crisp; adjust the temperature to 350°F and the cook time to 6 minutes. Press Start. Bake until fragrant and set. Remove and let cool.

4. In a medium bowl, use a handheld electric mixer to beat the cream cheese until very smooth. Add the sugar and beat until blended. Add the sour cream, heavy cream, and vanilla. Beat to combine. One at a time, add the eggs and beat just to blend.

5. Scoop ½ cup of the cheesecake filling into a small bowl. Stir in the melted chocolate.

6. Pour the vanilla cheesecake filling into the springform pan. Drop spoonfuls of the chocolate mixture evenly on top of the filling. Run the tip of a small knife or a skewer through the filling to form a swirled ("marbleized") pattern on the top of the cheesecake. Cover the cheesecake with aluminum foil.

7. Pour 1 cup of water into the inner pot. Place the Reversible Rack in the pot in the lower position and place the pan on top.

8. Lock the Pressure Lid into place, making sure the valve is set to Seal. Select Pressure; adjust the pressure to High and the cook time to 25 minutes. Press Start.

9. After cooking, let the pressure release naturally for 10 minutes, then quick release any remaining pressure.

10. Carefully unlock and remove the Pressure Lid. Carefully remove the cheesecake from the pot and remove the foil. The cheesecake should be set, with the center slightly softer than the edges.

11. Let the cheesecake rest at room temperature for 15 to 20 minutes. Refrigerate the cooled cake for 3 to 4 hours until thoroughly chilled.

Per Serving Calories: 428; Total fat: 32g; Saturated fat: 17g; Cholesterol: 129mg; Sodium: 285mg; Carbohydrates: 30g; Fiber: 2g; Protein: 7g

Crème Brûlée

I first had crème brûlée during a junior high school "field trip" with my French class. We went to the only French restaurant in town, and it was on the menu. I felt so sophisticated. And you know what? I still feel sophisticated when I eat it.

8 large egg yolks
1 teaspoon vanilla extract
½ cup sugar

2 cups heavy (whipping) cream
6 tablespoons packed light brown sugar, sifted

PREP TIME
10 MINUTES

PRESSURE COOK
6 MINUTES, HIGH PRESSURE

RELEASE
NATURAL FOR 10 MINUTES, THEN QUICK

BROIL
5 MINUTES

TOTAL TIME
35 MINUTES, PLUS CHILLING TIME

GLUTEN-FREE, VEGETARIAN, AROUND 30 MINUTES

MAKE-AHEAD TIP: The custards can be cooked and refrigerated, covered with plastic wrap, for 2 days.

1. In a medium bowl, combine the egg yolks, vanilla, and sugar. Using a handheld electric mixer, beat until the sugar is dissolved. Add the heavy cream and beat briefly to combine. Pour the custard into 4 small ramekins or custard cups. (You may find it easier to do this if you transfer the custard to a measuring cup with a lip.) Cover the ramekins with small squares of aluminum foil.

2. Pour 1 cup of water into the inner pot. Place the Reversible Rack in the pot in the lower position and place the ramekins on top, stacking them if necessary.

3. Lock the Pressure Lid into place, making sure the valve is set to Seal. Select Pressure; adjust the pressure to High and the cook time to 6 minutes. Press Start.

4. After cooking, let the pressure release naturally for 10 minutes, then quick release any remaining pressure. Carefully unlock and remove the Pressure Lid.

5. Using tongs, carefully remove the custards from the pot. Remove the foil from the custards. Let cool at room temperature for 20 minutes or so, then refrigerate until chilled, about 2 hours.

6. Sprinkle the brown sugar evenly over the custards.

7. Place the Reversible Rack in the pot in the upper position. Transfer the ramekins to the rack, working in batches if necessary.

8. Close the Crisping Lid and select Broil. Adjust the time to 5 minutes. Press Start. Cook until the sugar is browned and bubbling on top of the custards. Let cool slightly before eating.

Per Serving Calories: 695; Total fat: 53g; Saturated fat: 31g; Cholesterol: 583mg; Sodium: 67mg; Carbohydrates: 50g; Fiber: 0g; Protein: 8g

Lemon Bars

SERVES 4

This recipe takes some time, it's true, but in my opinion, it's well worth it. Most lemon bars are too sweet for my taste, with a lemon topping that's too much like pudding. These are tart, creamy, crunchy, and absolutely delicious.

FOR THE SHORTBREAD

8 tablespoons (1 stick) unsalted butter, at room temperature

2 tablespoons confectioners' sugar

2 tablespoons granulated sugar

½ teaspoon vanilla extract

Pinch kosher salt (or tiny pinch fine salt)

1¼ cups all-purpose flour

FOR THE LEMON CURD

¾ cup granulated sugar

4 tablespoons (½ stick) unsalted butter, at room temperature

4 large egg yolks

6 tablespoons freshly squeezed lemon juice (from 2 or 3 large lemons)

Zest of 2 lemons

Pinch kosher salt (or tiny pinch fine salt)

TO FINISH

¼ cup confectioners' sugar

PREP TIME
15 MINUTES

BAKE/ROAST
40 MINUTES PLUS 8 MINUTES

PRESSURE COOK
10 MINUTES, HIGH PRESSURE

RELEASE
NATURAL FOR 10 MINUTES, THEN QUICK

TOTAL TIME
1 HOUR 30 MINUTES, PLUS COOLING TIME

VEGETARIAN

MAKE-AHEAD TIP: Make the curd ahead of time and refrigerate it for several days. Bring it to room temperature to make it easier to spread over the shortbread.

To make the shortbread

1. Line an 8-inch round cake pan with nonstick aluminum foil (or regular foil coated with cooking spray).

2. In the bowl of a stand mixer with the paddle attachment, or a medium bowl using a hand mixer, mix together the butter, confectioners' and granulated sugars, vanilla, and salt until thoroughly blended, light colored, and creamy. Add half the flour. Mix on low speed to combine. Add the remaining flour and mix until combined. The dough will be very crumbly and will look dry.

3. Dump the dough mixture into the prepared pan and press firmly into the pan to form an even layer. If necessary, use an offset spatula or the back of a bench scraper to even it out. Prick the surface of the dough lightly all over with a fork.

4. Place the Reversible Rack in the pot in the lower position and place the cake pan on top. Close the Crisping Lid and select Bake/Roast; adjust the temperature to 275°F and the cook time to 20 minutes. Press Start.

5. When the time is up, select Bake/Roast again; increase the temperature to 325°F and adjust the time to 20 minutes. Press Start.

6. When cooking is complete, open the lid. The shortbread should be a pale golden brown. Remove and set aside.

To make the lemon curd

1. In a heat-proof bowl that will fit into the Foodi™ pot, use a handheld electric mixer to beat the sugar and butter until the sugar has mostly dissolved and the mixture is light colored and fluffy. Add the egg yolks and beat until combined. Add the lemon juice, zest, and salt and beat to combine. The mixture will probably appear grainy, but don't worry. Cover the bowl with foil.

2. Pour 1 cup of water into the inner pot. Place the Reversible Rack in the pot in the lower position and place the bowl on top.

3. Lock the Pressure Lid into place. Select Pressure; adjust the pressure to High and the cook time to 10 minutes. Press Start.

4. When cooking is complete, let the pressure release naturally for 10 minutes, then quick release any remaining pressure.

5. Carefully unlock and remove the Pressure Lid. Carefully remove the bowl from the pot and remove the foil. Pour the water out of the pot and return the pot to the base with the rack in place in the lower position. ➤

6. The curd will appear clumpy and curdled. Whisk it until smooth. Place a fine strainer over a medium bowl and pour the curd through it, pressing down with a flexible spatula to pass the curd through, leaving the zest and any curdled egg bits behind. Scrape any curd on the bottom of the strainer into the bowl.

To finish

1. Pour the curd over the shortbread base. Place the pan on the rack and close the Crisping Lid. Select Bake/Roast; adjust the temperature to 325°F and the cook time to 8 minutes. Press Start.

2. When the time is complete, open the lid and remove the pan and rack. Let cool for 30 minutes. Place the confectioners' sugar in a small sieve and sprinkle over the top. Lift the dessert out of the pan before slicing into wedges or bars.

Per Serving Calories: 740; Total fat: 42g; Saturated fat: 25g; Cholesterol: 308mg; Sodium: 24mg; Carbohydrates: 87g; Fiber: 1g; Protein: 7g

Tarte Tatin

SERVES 4

I know what you're going to say: Tarte tatin is made in a skillet, on the stovetop, with apples on the bottom and crust on the top. Then it's baked so the crust gets brown and crisp. Then you flip it over so the crust is on the bottom. And you're absolutely correct. But that doesn't mean you can't make this variation—it's faster, easier, and just as good.

5 Granny Smith apples, peeled and cut into slices about ¼ inch thick

2 teaspoons ground cinnamon

¼ cup packed brown sugar

2 tablespoons brandy or apple brandy

1 refrigerated piecrust

2 tablespoons heavy (whipping) cream

¼ cup granulated sugar

PREP TIME
10 MINUTES

PRESSURE COOK
4 MINUTES, HIGH PRESSURE

RELEASE
NATURAL FOR 5 MINUTES, THEN QUICK

BAKE/ROAST
12 MINUTES

TOTAL TIME
35 MINUTES

VEGETARIAN, AROUND 30 MINUTES

SUBSTITUTION TIP: Frozen puff pastry can be substituted for the piecrust. Thaw according to the package directions and roll out to fit the top of the filling (you may have to piece the two sheets together, depending on size).

1. Place the apples in the Foodi's™ inner pot. Sprinkle with the cinnamon and brown sugar. Pour in the brandy. Stir to coat the apples.

2. Lock the Pressure Lid into place, making sure the valve is set to Seal. Select Pressure; adjust the pressure to High and the cook time to 4 minutes. Press Start.

3. After cooking, let the pressure release naturally for 5 minutes, then quick release any remaining pressure. Carefully unlock and remove the Pressure Lid.

4. Unroll the piecrust over the filling. Brush with the heavy cream and sprinkle with the granulated sugar.

5. Close the Crisping Lid and select Bake/Roast; adjust the temperature to 325°F and the cook time to 12 minutes. Press Start. Check the tarte tatin after 8 minutes. The crust should be crisp and browned. If not, cook a little longer.

6. To serve, cut a wedge of the tart and invert onto a dessert plate so the crust is on the bottom. Repeat with the remaining pieces. Serve warm.

Per Serving Calories: 481; Total fat: 18g; Saturated fat: 7g; Cholesterol: 10mg; Sodium: 241mg; Carbohydrates: 82g; Fiber: 4g; Protein: 2g

Blueberry Cream Tart

SERVES 4

I make this tart for a French Bistro cooking class my partner and I teach, and the students love it—making it, and especially eating it. This version simplifies it somewhat by substituting a cream cheese layer for the cooked crème pâtissière *we make in class. The dessert still takes some time. Make it on a weekend when you want to impress some guests. I guarantee you won't be disappointed.*

1 refrigerated piecrust

FOR THE BLUEBERRIES
2½ cups fresh blueberries, divided
1 tablespoon cornstarch
2 tablespoons water
¼ cup granulated sugar
1 teaspoon freshly squeezed lemon juice

¼ teaspoon grated lemon zest
Pinch kosher salt (or tiny pinch fine salt)

FOR THE CREAM FILLING
8 ounces cream cheese, at room temperature
1 teaspoon vanilla extract
½ cup confectioners' sugar
¼ cup heavy (whipping) cream

PREP TIME
20 MINUTES

BAKE/ROAST
15 MINUTES PLUS 4 MINUTES

PRESSURE COOK
2 MINUTES, HIGH PRESSURE

RELEASE
QUICK

TOTAL TIME
55 MINUTES, PLUS CHILLING TIME

VEGETARIAN, UNDER 60 MINUTES

SUBSTITUTION TIP: If you want to save some time, use a purchased graham cracker crust instead of baking the piecrust.

1. Unroll the piecrust and fit it into an 8-inch pie pan or tart pan. Try not to stretch the dough or it will shrink when cooking. Prick the bottom of the crust all over with a fork.

2. Place the Reversible Rack in the pot in the lower position and set the pie pan on top.

3. Close the Crisping Lid and select Bake/Roast; adjust the temperature to 250°F and the cook time to 15 minutes. Press Start.

4. When cooking is complete, open the lid and check the crust. It should be set and just starting to turn light brown around the edges.

5. Close the Crisping Lid again. Adjust the temperature to 375°F and the cook time to 4 minutes. Press Start. After 3 minutes, check the crust. It should be a deep golden brown. If not, cook for the remaining 1 minute. Remove the rack and set the crust aside to cool.

To make the blueberries

1. Sort through the blueberries to remove any bits of stem. Measure 1 cup of berries, including any that are particularly soft, and put them in the Foodi's™ inner pot. In a cup or small bowl, whisk the cornstarch and water until blended. Add this slurry to the berries, along with the granulated sugar, lemon juice, lemon zest, and salt. Stir to distribute the cornstarch mixture.

2. Lock the Pressure Lid into place, making sure the valve is set to Seal. Select Pressure; adjust the pressure to High and the cook time to 2 minutes. Press Start.

3. After cooking, use a quick pressure release. Carefully unlock and remove the Pressure Lid. The berries should be split and very soft. Add the remaining 1½ cups of blueberries, stirring to coat with the cooked mixture. Let cool.

To make the cream filling

1. In a large bowl using a handheld electric mixer, or in the bowl of a stand mixer fitted with the paddle attachment, combine the cream cheese and vanilla. Beat for several minutes until smooth. Add the confectioners' sugar and beat again until the sugar is completely incorporated and the mixture is smooth and light. ➤

Blueberry Cream Tart continued

2. In a separate bowl with clean beaters, beat the heavy cream until soft peaks form. Fold the whipped cream into the cream cheese mixture: Start by adding about half the whipped cream to the cream cheese mixture. Gently stir the two together. Add the remaining whipped cream and fold it in by scooping through the mixture with a spatula and turning it over, turning and repeating until the mixture is homogenous.

To assemble

Spoon the cream filling into the cooled pie shell. Top with the berries. To get the cleanest slices, chill the tart for 20 to 30 minutes before cutting and serving.

Per Serving Calories: 664; Total fat: 40g; Saturated fat: 20g; Cholesterol: 82mg; Sodium: 421mg; Carbohydrates: 74g; Fiber: 3g; Protein: 6g

Caramel-Pecan Brownies

SERVES 4

These brownies are the ultra-fudgy kind, which, in my opinion, is the only kind of brownie worth making. Topping them with caramel and pecans sends them halfway into turtle territory, and what's wrong with that?

8 tablespoons (1 stick) unsalted butter

8 ounces dark chocolate

1 cup sugar

2 teaspoons vanilla extract

Pinch kosher salt (or small pinch fine salt)

2 large eggs, at room temperature

¾ cup all-purpose flour

Nonstick cooking spray, for preparing the pan

½ cup caramel sauce

½ cup pecans

PREP TIME
10 MINUTES

BAKE/ROAST
10 MINUTES PLUS
48 MINUTES

TOTAL TIME
1 HOUR 10 MINUTES, PLUS
COOLING TIME

VEGETARIAN

CUSTOMIZATION TIP: I make a version of these brownies that's inspired by Mexican chocolate desserts. Mix 1 teaspoon ground cinnamon and ¼ teaspoon cayenne pepper into the flour before adding it to the chocolate mixture. Omit the caramel-nut topping but bake for the same amount of time.

MAKE-AHEAD TIP: The brownies can be stored in an airtight container for 3 to 4 days at room temperature, or frozen for up to 1 month.

1. In a small bowl, put the butter and chocolate. Pour 1 cup of water into the inner pot. Place the Reversible Rack in the pot in the lower position and place the bowl on top. Close the Crisping Lid and select Bake/Roast; adjust the temperature to 375°F and the cook time to 10 minutes to melt the chocolate and butter. Press Start. (You can do this in the microwave if you prefer.) Check after 5 minutes and stir. As soon as the chocolate is melted, remove the bowl from the pot.

2. Scrape the chocolate mixture into a medium bowl (this helps cool the chocolate slightly). Stir in the sugar, vanilla, and salt. One at a time, add the eggs and stir until blended after each addition.

3. Add the flour to the chocolate mixture and mix until smooth, about 1 minute.

4. Spray an 8-inch round cake pan with cooking spray. If you like, line the pan with parchment paper or aluminum foil to make the brownies easier to remove. Pour the batter into the prepared pan. Place the pan in the pot on the rack. ➤

5. Close the Crisping Lid and select Bake/Roast; adjust the temperature to 250°F and the cook time to 25 minutes. Press Start. When the time is up, open the lid and check the brownies. The top should be just set. If butter is pooling on the top, blot it off with a paper towel.

6. Close the Crisping Lid again and adjust the temperature to 300°F and the cook time to 15 minutes. Press Start.

7. When the time is up, open the lid and check the brownies. A toothpick inserted into the center should come out with crumbs sticking to it but no raw batter.

8. Drizzle the caramel sauce over the brownies and sprinkle with the pecans. Close the Crisping Lid again and adjust the temperature to 325°F and the cook time to 8 minutes. Press Start. When the caramel is bubbling and the nuts are brown, remove the brownies and let cool for at least 30 minutes.

9.   If you lined the pan, pick up the edges of the foil or parchment and carefully lift the brownies out of the pan. Peel off the foil and let cool for another 5 minutes or longer. Cut into squares.

Per Serving Calories: 1054; Total fat: 59g; Saturated fat: 30g; Cholesterol: 167mg; Sodium: 193mg; Carbohydrates: 123g; Fiber: 8g; Protein: 12g

Mocha Pots de Crème

SERVES 4

Pots de crème is a fancy name for custards originally cooked in little covered pots. But you don't need fancy pots to cook them, just small custard dishes or ramekins. This version is a nice blend of coffee and chocolate, not too sweet and not too rich. You could even eat them for breakfast, right?

1 large egg

3 large egg yolks

¾ cup sugar

½ teaspoon vanilla extract

1 cup whole milk

1 cup heavy (whipping) cream

2 tablespoons instant espresso powder

1 tablespoon cocoa powder

PREP TIME
10 MINUTES

PRESSURE COOK
6 MINUTES, HIGH PRESSURE

RELEASE
NATURAL FOR 10 MINUTES, THEN QUICK

TOTAL TIME
30 MINUTES, PLUS CHILLING TIME

GLUTEN-FREE, VEGETARIAN, AROUND 30 MINUTES

MAKE-AHEAD TIP: Like most custards, these keep well in the refrigerator for 2 to 3 days, as long as they're covered in plastic wrap so they don't dry out.

1. In a medium bowl, use a handheld mixer to beat the egg, egg yolks, sugar, and vanilla until the sugar dissolves. Add the milk, heavy cream, espresso powder, and cocoa powder. Beat briefly to combine. Pour the mixture into four small ramekins or custard cups. (You may find it easier to do this if you transfer the custard to a measuring cup with a lip.) Place a square of aluminum foil over each and crimp to seal.

2. Pour 1 cup of water into the Foodi's™ inner pot. Place the Reversible Rack in the pot in the lower position and place the ramekins on top, stacking them if necessary.

3. Lock the Pressure Lid into place, making sure the valve is set to Seal. Select Pressure; adjust the pressure to High and the cook time to 6 minutes. Press Start.

4. After cooking, let the pressure release naturally for 10 minutes, then quick release any remaining pressure. Carefully unlock and remove the Pressure Lid.

5. Carefully remove the custards from the pot. Remove the foil from the tops. Let cool at room temperature for 20 minutes or so, then cover with plastic wrap and refrigerate until chilled, about 2 hours.

Per Serving Calories: 450; Total fat: 29g; Saturated fat: 17g; Cholesterol: 298mg; Sodium: 71mg; Carbohydrates: 44g; Fiber: 0g; Protein: 7g

Spiced Poached Pears

SERVES 4

Poached pears make an elegant, easy dessert, one that's perfect for guests who are vegan or gluten sensitive. For an extra-luxurious version, stir a little heavy cream into the sauce before serving.

1 cup medium-sweet Moscato wine (or Riesling or Gewürztraminer)

1 cup water

⅓ cup sugar

1 strip lemon peel

Juice of 1 lemon

1 cinnamon stick

4 or 5 whole cloves

4 or 5 peppercorns

4 large ripe but firm pears, peeled, cored, and halved

1. In the Foodi's™ inner pot, combine the wine, water, sugar, lemon peel, lemon juice, cinnamon stick, cloves, and peppercorns. Select Sear/Sauté and adjust the heat to Medium-High. Press Start. Bring the mixture to a simmer, stirring until the sugar dissolves. Add the pears and stir to coat.

2. Lock the Pressure Lid into place, making sure the vent is set to Seal; adjust the pressure to High and the cook time to 5 minutes. Press Start.

PREP TIME
5 MINUTES

SEAR/SAUTÉ
4 MINUTES PLUS 4 MINUTES

PRESSURE
5 MINUTES, HIGH PRESSURE

RELEASE
QUICK

TOTAL TIME
25 MINUTES

DAIRY-FREE, GLUTEN-FREE, VEGAN, VEGETARIAN, AROUND 30 MINUTES

SUBSTITUTION TIP: If pears are not in season, apples work great in their place. They need to cook a minute or so longer, but that's the only change you'll need to make.

3. After cooking, use a quick pressure release. Carefully unlock and remove the Pressure Lid. Using tongs or a large slotted spoon, transfer the pears to a serving bowl.

4. Select Sear/Sauté and adjust the heat to High. Press Start. Bring the cooking liquid to a boil. Cook for about 4 minutes until it's reduced to a thin syrup. Remove and discard the lemon peel and whole spices. Pour the warm syrup over the pears and serve.

Per Serving Calories: 244; Total fat: 0g; Saturated fat: 0g; Cholesterol: 0mg; Sodium: 2mg; Carbohydrates: 54g; Fiber: 7g; Protein: 1g

8

Kitchen Staples

Left: Roasted Vegetable Stock, page 219

Chicken Stock

If you haven't used a pressure cooker to make chicken stock, you'll be amazed at what 90 minutes and a little work will get you. This makes a very gelatinous stock with deep flavor. For recipes when I don't want a strong chicken flavor, I dilute it by half.

2 pounds meaty chicken bones (backs, wing tips, leg quarters)

¼ teaspoon kosher salt (or ⅛ teaspoon fine salt)

3½ cups water

1. Place the chicken parts in the Foodi's™ inner pot and sprinkle with the salt. Add the water; don't worry if it doesn't cover the chicken.

2. Lock the Pressure Lid into place, making sure the valve is set to Seal. Select Pressure; adjust the pressure to High and the cook time to 90 minutes. Press Start.

3. After cooking, let the pressure release naturally for 15 minutes, then quick release any remaining pressure. Carefully unlock and remove the Pressure Lid.

4. Line a colander with cheesecloth or a clean cotton towel (you'll never get the towel completely clean, so don't use a nice one) and place it over a large bowl. Pour the chicken parts and stock into the colander to strain out the chicken and bones. Let the stock cool. Refrigerate it for several hours, or overnight so the fat hardens on top of the stock.

5. Peel the layer of fat off the stock. Measure the amount of stock. If you have much more than 1 quart, pour the stock back into the Foodi pot. Select Sear/Sauté and adjust to High. Press Start. Bring the stock to a boil and cook until reduced to 1 quart.

Per Serving (1 cup) Calories: 51; Total fat: 3g; Saturated fat: 1g; Cholesterol: 7mg; Sodium: 56mg; Carbohydrates: 0g; Fiber: 0g; Protein: 6g

PREP TIME
10 MINUTES

PRESSURE COOK
90 MINUTES, HIGH PRESSURE

RELEASE
NATURAL FOR 15 MINUTES, THEN QUICK

TOTAL TIME
2 HOURS

DAIRY-FREE, GLUTEN-FREE

CUSTOMIZATION TIP: If you like, roast the bones before beginning the stock. Place them in the Cook & Crisp™ Basket and the basket in the inner pot. Close the Crisping Lid. Select Bake/Roast and adjust the temperature to 400°F. Press Start. Roast for about 20 minutes until golden and dark brown in many places.

MAKE-AHEAD TIP: The stock can be refrigerated for several days or frozen for several months. When freezing, I like to divide it into 1-cup portions so I can take out just what I need for a particular recipe.

Roasted Vegetable Stock

MAKES 1 QUART

Like Chicken Stock (page 218), vegetable stock is a breeze to make in a pressure cooker. Roasting the onion and carrots adds layers of flavor to the stock, and mushrooms give it a savory base that can stand up to any meat stock.

1 onion, quartered

2 large carrots, peeled, cut into 1-inch pieces

1 tablespoon vegetable oil

12 ounces mushrooms, sliced

¼ teaspoon kosher salt (or ⅛ teaspoon fine salt)

3½ cups water

1. Making sure that the Cook & Crisp™ Basket is out of the inner pot, close the Crisping Lid on your Foodi™ and select Bake/Roast; adjust the temperature to 400ºF and the time to 3 minutes to preheat. Press Start.

2. While the pot preheats, place the onion and carrot chunks in the Cook & Crisp Basket and drizzle with the vegetable oil. Toss to coat.

3. Place the basket in the inner pot. Close the Crisping Lid and select Bake/Roast; adjust the temperature to 400ºF and the cook time to 15 minutes. Press Start. Halfway through the cook time, open the lid and stir the vegetables.

4. Remove the basket from the pot and add the onions and carrots. Add the mushrooms and sprinkle with the salt. Add the water.

5. Lock the Pressure Lid into place, making sure the valve is set to Seal. Select Pressure; adjust the pressure to High and the cook time to 60 minutes. Press Start.

6. After cooking, let the pressure release naturally for 15 minutes, then quick release any remaining pressure. Carefully unlock and remove the Pressure Lid.

7. Line a colander with cheesecloth or a clean cotton towel and place it over a large bowl. Pour the vegetables and stock into the colander and let the stock strain through to the bowl. Discard the vegetables.

PREP TIME
5 MINUTES

BAKE/ROAST
15 MINUTES

PRESSURE COOK
60 MINUTES, HIGH PRESSURE

RELEASE
NATURAL FOR 15 MINUTES, THEN QUICK

TOTAL TIME
1 HOUR 40 MINUTES

DAIRY-FREE, GLUTEN-FREE, VEGAN, VEGETARIAN

MAKE-AHEAD TIP: The stock can be refrigerated for several days or frozen for several months. When freezing, I like to divide it into 1-cup portions so I can take out just what I need for a particular recipe.

Per Serving (1 cup) Calories: 45; Total fat: 4g; Saturated fat: 0g; Cholesterol: 0mg; Sodium: 32mg; Carbohydrates: 3g; Fiber: 0g; Protein: 0g

Sautéed Mushrooms

SERVES 6

Conventional wisdom about cooking mushrooms dictates using a really hot pan and keeping the mushrooms in a single layer, with no crowding, while you watch carefully to make sure they brown without steaming or burning. While it's true that mushrooms will exude water while they cook, it turns out the best—and easiest—way to cook them is to take advantage of all the water they contain. Crowd them and add even more water, and they cook completely as they expel much of the water they contain. Once cooked, boil off the remaining water and they'll brown perfectly, with a concentrated flavor you won't believe. Best of all, you only have to pay attention for a few minutes at the end.

1 pound white button or cremini mushrooms, stems trimmed

2 tablespoons unsalted butter (or olive oil for a vegan dish)

½ teaspoon kosher salt (or ¼ teaspoon fine salt)

¼ cup water

PREP TIME
5 MINUTES

PRESSURE COOK
5 MINUTES, HIGH PRESSURE

RELEASE
QUICK

SEAR/SAUTÉ
5 MINUTES

TOTAL TIME
25 MINUTES

GLUTEN-FREE, VEGAN OPTION, VEGETARIAN, AROUND 30 MINUTES

1. Quarter any medium mushrooms and cut any large mushrooms into eighths. Put the mushrooms, butter or oil (for a vegan option), and salt in the Foodi's™ inner pot. Pour in the water.

2. Lock the Pressure Lid in place, making sure the valve is set to Seal. Select Pressure; adjust the pressure to High and the cook time to 5 minutes. Press Start.

3. After cooking, use a quick pressure release. Carefully unlock and remove the Pressure Lid.

4. Because the mushrooms exuded water as they cooked, there will be more liquid in the pot, and the mushrooms will be smaller than when they started cooking. Select Sear/Sauté and adjust the heat to High. Press Start. Bring to a boil and cook for about 5 minutes or until all the water evaporates. The mushrooms will begin to sizzle in the butter (or oil) that remains. Let them brown for 1 minute or so, then stir to brown the other sides.

Per Serving Calories: 50; Total fat: 4g; Saturated fat: 2g; Cholesterol: 10mg; Sodium: 198mg; Carbohydrates: 2g; Fiber: 1g; Protein: 2g

CUSTOMIZATION TIP: To turn these mushrooms into an easy, delicious topping for steak or a side for roasted chicken, when the mushrooms finish browning, add 1 or 2 sliced shallots and cook for about 2 minutes, stirring, or until the shallots soften and start to brown. Pour in ¼ cup dry sherry or red or white wine to deglaze the pan. Scrape up the browned bits from the bottom of the pan and cook until most of the wine evaporates. Season to taste with salt and pepper.

MAKE-AHEAD TIP: The mushrooms can be made ahead and refrigerated for up to 1 week or frozen for up to 1 month.

Caramelized Onions

MAKES ABOUT 1 CUP

While onions caramelized in the pressure cooker don't turn as dark as those cooked by conventional methods, the cook time is cut substantially, and the flavor is still delicious.

2 tablespoons unsalted butter

3 very large onions, sliced (about 5 cups)

2 tablespoons water

1 teaspoon kosher salt (or ½ teaspoon fine salt)

1. On your Foodi™ select Sear/Sauté and adjust to Medium to preheat the inner pot. Press Start. Allow the pot to preheat for 5 minutes. Add the butter to melt. Add the onions, water, and salt. Stir to combine.

2. Lock the Pressure Lid into place, making sure the valve is set to Seal. Select Pressure; adjust the pressure to High and the cook time to 30 minutes. Press Start.

3. After cooking, let the pressure release naturally for 5 minutes, then quick release any remaining pressure.

4. Carefully unlock and remove the Pressure Lid. The onions should be very soft and light tan in color. There will be quite a lot of liquid in the pressure cooker. Select Sear/Sauté and adjust to Medium-High. Press Start. Simmer until most of the liquid is gone and the onions hold together and darken slightly, about 15 minutes.

Per Serving (¾ cup) Calories: 110; Total fat: 6g; Saturated fat: 4g; Cholesterol: 15mg; Sodium: 588mg; Carbohydrates: 14g; Fiber: 3g; Protein: 2g

PREP TIME
10 MINUTES

SEAR/SAUTÉ
2 MINUTES PLUS 15 MINUTES

PRESSURE COOK
30 MINUTES, HIGH PRESSURE

RELEASE
NATURAL FOR 5 MINUTES, THEN QUICK

TOTAL TIME
1 HOUR 5 MINUTES

GLUTEN-FREE, VEGETARIAN

MAKE-AHEAD TIP: The onions can be refrigerated for several days or frozen for up to 1 month. I divide them into ½-cup portions before freezing.

Cajun Seasoning Mix

MAKES ABOUT ½ CUP

This spice blend is inspired by a mixture in one of Emeril Lagasse's books. It's essential for gumbo, jambalaya, and étouffée, and it adds a New Orleans accent to chicken, shrimp, rice, or pasta.

2 tablespoons paprika

2 tablespoons granulated garlic

1 tablespoon granulated onion

1 tablespoon freshly ground black pepper

1 tablespoon dried thyme leaves

2 teaspoons ground white pepper

2 teaspoons cayenne pepper, or more to taste

1 teaspoon dried basil

TOTAL TIME
5 MINUTES

DAIRY-FREE, GLUTEN-FREE, VEGAN, VEGETARIAN

CUSTOMIZATION TIP: I prefer to make my seasoning mixes without salt, but if you prefer a mix with salt, add 2 teaspoons of kosher salt (or 1 teaspoon of fine salt).

In a small bowl, stir together the paprika, granulated garlic, granulated onion, black pepper, thyme, white pepper, cayenne, and basil. Pour into a jar with a tight-fitting lid. Seal the jar and store in a cool dark place. Use within 3 months.

Per Serving (1 tablespoon) Calories: 18; Total fat: 0g; Saturated fat: 0g; Cholesterol: 0mg; Sodium: 2mg; Carbohydrates: 4g; Fiber: 1g; Protein: 1g

Mexican/Southwestern Seasoning Mix

MAKES ABOUT ¾ CUP

There are many commercial "taco" or "fajita" seasoning blends available, and there's nothing wrong with using them in a pinch. I like to make my own, partly because I prefer a blend that's salt-free (not that I don't like salt; I just prefer to add it separately). Also, this is better than any commercial blend I've found. It's based very loosely on a blend from the Chevys & Rio Bravo cookbook.

3 tablespoons paprika

3 tablespoons ancho chile powder

2 tablespoons freshly ground black pepper

2 tablespoons dried oregano leaves

1 tablespoon granulated garlic

1 tablespoon granulated onion

2 teaspoons cayenne pepper

2 teaspoons ground cumin

TOTAL TIME
5 MINUTES

DAIRY-FREE, GLUTEN-FREE, VEGAN, VEGETARIAN

INGREDIENT TIP: Ancho chile powder is simply ground toasted ancho chiles, without anything else added. It's available from spice purveyors like Penzeys and in some grocery stores under the McCormick Gourmet label. If you can't find it, substitute chili powder, but those blends usually contain salt and other spices, so you may need to adjust your final seasoning.

In a small bowl, stir together the paprika, chile powder, black pepper, oregano, granulated garlic, granulated onion, cayenne, and cumin. Pour into a jar with a tight-fitting lid. Seal the jar and store in a cool dark place. Use within 3 months.

Per Serving (1 tablespoon) Calories: 19; Total fat: 1g; Saturated fat: 0g; Cholesterol: 0mg; Sodium: 21mg; Carbohydrates: 4g; Fiber: 2g; Protein: 1g

Teriyaki Sauce

MAKES ABOUT 1 CUP

If you're familiar with only commercial teriyaki sauce, you'll be surprised at how easy it is to make your own, and you'll go wild over the improved taste. It's great on fish, chicken, or pork. For a gluten-free option, choose a soy sauce without added wheat.

½ **cup soy sauce**

3 **tablespoons honey**

1 **tablespoon rice vinegar**

1 **tablespoon rice wine or dry sherry**

2 **teaspoons minced peeled fresh ginger**

2 **garlic cloves, minced or pressed**

PREP TIME
10 MINUTES

SEAR/SAUTÉ
10 MINUTES (OPTIONAL)

TOTAL TIME
10 TO 20 MINUTES

DAIRY-FREE, GLUTEN-FREE OPTION, VEGETARIAN, AROUND 30 MINUTES

CUSTOMIZATION TIP: For a spicy teriyaki sauce, add 1 to 2 teaspoons Asian chile-garlic sauce.

In a small bowl, combine the soy sauce, honey, vinegar, wine, ginger, and garlic. Whisk until thoroughly combined. Use as is, or, for a thicker sauce or glaze, transfer to the Foodi's™ inner pot. Select Sear/Sauté and adjust to Medium. Press Start. Bring to a simmer and cook for about 10 minutes or until it reaches the desired consistency. The sauce is best used right away, but it can be refrigerated overnight (or for up to 1 week if simmered).

Per Serving (2 tablespoons) Calories: 37; Total fat: 0g; Saturated fat: 0g; Cholesterol: 0mg; Sodium: 1006mg; Carbohydrates: 8g; Fiber: 0g; Protein: 2g

Barbecue Sauce

MAKES ABOUT 2 CUPS

I'm not a big fan of commercial barbecue sauces, because they're always way too sweet for my taste. I make mine a bit spicy, with a good balance of acid and sugar. Use it in Sloppy Joes (page 156) or as a glaze for Meatloaf and Mashed Potatoes (page 139). It's also great on ribs or chicken wings.

1½ cups strained tomatoes

2 garlic cloves, peeled

1 small onion, cut into eighths

2 tablespoons packed brown sugar

1 tablespoon ancho chile powder

1 teaspoon kosher salt (or ½ teaspoon fine salt)

1 teaspoon smoked paprika

1 teaspoon dry mustard

1 teaspoon chipotle purée (see Pantry Staples, page 11)

½ teaspoon freshly ground black pepper

1 tablespoon molasses

1 tablespoon apple cider vinegar

1 teaspoon Worcestershire sauce

PREP TIME
10 MINUTES

PRESSURE COOK
6 MINUTES, HIGH PRESSURE

RELEASE
NATURAL FOR 5 MINUTES, THEN QUICK

TOTAL TIME
25 MINUTES

DAIRY-FREE, GLUTEN-FREE, VEGETARIAN, AROUND 30 MINUTES

SUBSTITUTION TIP: If you don't have molasses on hand, omit it and add 1 extra tablespoon of brown sugar (dark brown sugar is best).

1. Pour the tomatoes into the Foodi's™ inner pot. Add the garlic, onion, brown sugar, chile powder, salt, paprika, dry mustard, chipotle purée, pepper, molasses, vinegar, and Worcestershire sauce.

2. Lock the Pressure Lid into place, making sure the valve is set to Seal. Select Pressure; adjust the pressure to High and the cook time to 6 minutes. Press Start.

3. After cooking, let the pressure release naturally for 5 minutes, then quick release the remaining pressure.

4. Carefully unlock and remove the Pressure Lid. Using an immersion blender, purée the sauce until smooth. Let cool. Keep refrigerated for up to 1 week.

Per Serving (2 tablespoons) Calories: 21; Total fat: 0g; Saturated fat: 0g; Cholesterol: 0mg; Sodium: 204mg; Carbohydrates: 5g; Fiber: 1g; Protein: 0g

Mustard Sauce

MAKES ABOUT 2 CUPS

A little spicy, a little sweet, this mustard sauce is similar to South Carolina's traditional barbecue sauce. My version substitutes Dijon mustard for part of the more typical yellow mustard, making it a little more complex. It's great on pork or beef ribs, or spread over chicken before broiling.

½ cup prepared yellow mustard

½ cup Dijon-style mustard

¼ cup honey

¼ cup apple cider vinegar

2 tablespoons unsalted butter

1 tablespoon ketchup

2 teaspoons Worcestershire sauce

1 teaspoon kosher salt (or ½ teaspoon fine salt)

1 teaspoon freshly ground black pepper

¼ teaspoon hot pepper sauce, such as Tabasco or Crystal

PREP TIME
5 MINUTES

PRESSURE COOK
5 MINUTES, HIGH PRESSURE

RELEASE
NATURAL FOR 5 MINUTES, THEN QUICK

TOTAL TIME
20 MINUTES

DAIRY-FREE OPTION, GLUTEN-FREE, AROUND 30 MINUTES

SUBSTITUTION TIP: For a dairy-free version, use vegetable oil in place of the butter.

1. In the Foodi's™ inner pot, combine the yellow and Dijon mustards, honey, vinegar, butter, ketchup, Worcestershire sauce, salt, pepper, and hot sauce.

2. Lock the Pressure Lid into place, making sure the valve is set to Seal. Select Pressure; adjust the pressure to High and the cook time to 5 minutes. Press Start.

3. After cooking, let the pressure release naturally for 5 minutes, then quick release any remaining pressure.

4. Carefully unlock and remove the Pressure Lid. Cool the sauce, then refrigerate. The sauce will keep for 10 days in the refrigerator.

Per Serving (2 tablespoons) Calories: 41; Total fat: 2g; Saturated fat: 1g; Cholesterol: 4mg; Sodium: 340mg; Carbohydrates: 6g; Fiber: 1g; Protein: 1g

Marinara Sauce

MAKES 4 CUPS

Marinara sauce is so easy to make that once you learn how, you'll never use a jar again. Because there are so few ingredients, it's important to use the best-quality tomatoes your budget allows. San Marzano tomatoes are a classic ingredient for marinara recipes. Use this sauce with any pasta shapes or in the Sausage and Pepper Calzones (page 132) or Mushroom Lasagna (page 68).

1 (28- to 32-ounce) can whole tomatoes

¼ cup olive oil

1 small onion, chopped (about ¾ cup)

2 tablespoons very coarsely chopped garlic

½ teaspoon dried oregano leaves

¼ teaspoon red pepper flakes

1 teaspoon kosher salt (or ½ teaspoon fine salt)

PREP TIME
10 MINUTES

SEAR/SAUTÉ
5 MINUTES

PRESSURE COOK
10 MINUTES, HIGH PRESSURE

RELEASE
NATURAL FOR 5 MINUTES, THEN QUICK

TOTAL TIME
35 MINUTES

DAIRY-FREE, GLUTEN FREE, VEGAN, AROUND 30 MINUTES

CUSTOMIZATION TIP: It's easy to turn this into meat sauce by adding ground beef or Italian sausage. Or transform it into puttanesca with 1 teaspoon of anchovy paste, 1 tablespoon of capers, and a doubling of the red pepper flakes.

MAKE-AHEAD TIP: The sauce can be frozen for up to 1 month. I suggest you pour it into 1-cup containers before freezing so you can pull out just what you need.

1. Pour the tomatoes into a large bowl and use your hands, a large fork, or a potato masher to break them up. You can use an immersion blender, but go easy if you do; you want chunks of tomatoes, not a purée.

2. On your Foodi,™ select Sear/Sauté and adjust to Medium to preheat the inner pot. Press Start. Allow the pot to preheat for 5 minutes. Add the olive oil and heat until shimmering. Add the onion and garlic. Cook for 5 minutes, stirring occasionally, or until the onion and garlic are fragrant and just beginning to brown.

3. Stir in the tomatoes, oregano, red pepper flakes, and salt.

4. Lock the Pressure Lid into place, making sure the valve is set to Seal. Select Pressure; adjust the pressure to High and the cook time to 10 minutes. Press Start.

5. After cooking, let the pressure release naturally for 5 minutes, then quick release any remaining pressure.

6. Carefully unlock and remove the Pressure Lid. If the sauce is too thin, select Sear/Sauté and adjust to Medium-High. Press Start. Bring to a simmer and cook until thickened. If not using immediately, let cool, then refrigerate.

Per Serving (½ cup) Calories: 113; Total fat: 7g; Saturated fat: 1g; Cholesterol: 0mg; Sodium: 611mg; Carbohydrates: 13g; Fiber: 2g; Protein: 2g

NINJA® FOODI™ COOKING TIME CHARTS

PRESSURE COOK

PRESSURE COOKING GRAINS

GRAIN	AMOUNT	WATER	PRESSURE	COOK TIME	RELEASE
For best results, rinse rice in a fine mesh strainer under cold water before cooking.					
Arborio rice	1 cup	3 cups	High	7 mins	Natural
Basmati rice	1 cup	1 cup	High	2 mins	Natural (10 mins) then Quick
Brown rice, short/ medium or long grain	1 cup	1¼ cups	High	15 mins	Natural (10 mins) then Quick
Coarse grits/polenta*	1 cup	3½ cups	High	4 mins	Natural (10 mins) then Quick
Farro	1 cup	2 cups	High	10 mins	Natural (10 mins) then Quick
Jasmine rice	1 cup	1 cup	High	2–3 mins	Natural (10 mins) then Quick
Kamut	1 cup	2 cups	High	30 mins	Natural (10 mins) then Quick
Millet	1 cup	2 cups	High	6 mins	Natural (10 mins) then Quick
Pearl barley	1 cup	2 cups	High	22 mins	Natural (10 mins) then Quick
Quinoa	1 cup	1½ cups	High	2 mins	Natural (10 mins) then Quick
Quinoa, red	1 cup	1½ cups	High	2 mins	Natural (10 mins) then Quick
Spelt	1 cup	2½ cups	High	25 mins	Natural (10 mins) then Quick
Steel-cut oats*	1 cup	3 cups	High	11 mins	Natural (10 mins) then Quick
Sushi rice	1 cup	1½ cups	High	3 mins	Quick
Texmati® rice, brown	1 cup	1¼ cups	High	5 mins	Natural (10 mins) then Quick ➤

*After releasing pressure, stir for 30 seconds to 1 minute, then let sit for 5 minutes.

GRAIN	AMOUNT	WATER	PRESSURE	COOK TIME	RELEASE
Texmati® rice, light brown	1 cup	1¼ cups	High	2 mins	Natural (10 mins) then Quick
Texmati® rice, white	1 cup	1 cup	High	2 mins	Natural (10 mins) then Quick
Wheat berries	1 cup	3 cups	High	15 mins	Natural (10 mins) then Quick
White rice, long grain	1 cup	1 cup	High	2 mins	Natural (10 mins) then Quick
White rice, medium grain	1 cup	1 cup	High	3 mins	Natural (10 mins) then Quick
Wild rice	1 cup	1 cup	High	22 mins	Natural (10 mins) then Quick

PRESSURE COOKING LEGUMES

LEGUME	AMOUNT	WATER	PRESSURE	COOK TIME	RELEASE
For best results, soak beans 8–24 hours before cooking.					
Black beans	1 lb	6 cups	Low	5 mins	Natural (10 mins) then Quick
Black-eyed peas	1 lb	6 cups	Low	5 mins	Natural (10 mins) then Quick
Cannellini beans	1 lb	6 cups	Low	3 mins	Natural (10 mins) then Quick
Cranberry beans	1 lb	6 cups	Low	3 mins	Natural (10 mins) then Quick
Garbanzo beans (chickpeas)	1 lb	6 cups	Low	3 mins	Natural (10 mins) then Quick
Great northern beans	1 lb	6 cups	Low	1 min	Natural (10 mins) then Quick
Lentils (green or brown)	1 cup dry	2 cups	Low	5 mins	Natural (10 mins) then Quick
Lima Beans	1 lb	6 cups	Low	1 min	Natural (10 mins) then Quick
Navy beans	1 lb	6 cups	Low	3 mins	Natural (10 mins) then Quick
Pinto beans	1 lb	6 cups	Low	3 mins	Natural (10 mins) then Quick
Red kidney beans	1 lb	6 cups	Low	3 mins	Natural (10 mins) then Quick

PRESSURE COOKING VEGETABLES

VEGETABLE	AMOUNT	DIRECTIONS	WATER	ACCESSORY	PRESSURE	COOK TIME	RELEASE
Beets	8 small or 4 large	Rinsed well, tops & ends trimmed; cool & peel after cooking	½ cup	N/A	High	15–20 mins	Quick
Broccoli	1 head or 4 cups	Cut in florets, stem removed	½ cup	Reversible Rack in steam position	Low	1 mins	Quick
Brussels sprouts	1 lb	Cut in half	½ cup	Reversible Rack in steam position	Low	1 mins	Quick
Butternut squash (cubed for side dish or salad)	20 oz	Peeled, cut in 1-inch pieces, seeds removed	½ cup	N/A	Low	2 mins	Quick
Butternut squash (for mashed, puree, or soup)	20 oz	Peeled, cut in 1-inch pieces, seeds removed	½ cup	Reversible Rack in steam position	High	5 mins	Quick
Cabbage (braised)	1 head	Cut in half, then cut in ½-inch strips	½ cup	N/A	Low	3 mins	Quick
Cabbage (crisp)	1 head	Cut in half, then cut in ½-inch strips	½ cup	Reversible Rack in steam position	Low	2 mins	Quick
Carrots	1 lb	Peeled, cut in ½-inch pieces	½ cup	N/A	High	2–3 mins	Quick
Cauliflower	1 head	Cut in florets, stem removed	½ cup	N/A	Low	1 mins	Quick
Collard greens	2 bunches or 1 bag (16 oz)	Stems removed, leaves chopped	½ cup	N/A	Low	6 mins	Quick
Green Beans	1 bag (12 oz)	Whole	½ cup	Reversible Rack in steam position	Low	0 mins	Quick ➤

PRESSURE COOKING VEGETABLES continued

VEGETABLE	AMOUNT	DIRECTIONS	WATER	ACCESSORY	PRESSURE	COOK TIME	RELEASE
Kale leaves/greens	2 bunches or 1 bag (16 oz)	Stems removed, leaves chopped	½ cup	N/A	Low	3 mins	Quick
Potatoes, red (cubed for side dish or salad)	2 lbs	Scrubbed, cut in 1-inch cubes	½ cup	N/A	High	1–2 mins	Quick
Potatoes, red (for mashed)	2 lbs	Scrubbed, left whole	½ cup	N/A	High	15–20 mins	Quick
Potatoes, Russet or Yukon (cubed for side dish or salad)	2 lbs	Peeled, cut in 1-inch cubes	½ cup	N/A	High	1–2 mins	Quick
Potatoes, Russet or Yukon (for mashed)	2 lbs	Peeled, cut in 1-inch thick slices	½ cup	N/A	High	6 mins	Quick
Potatoes, sweet (cubed for side dish or salad)	1 lb	Peeled, cut in 1-inch cubes	½ cup	N/A	High	1–2 mins	Quick
Potatoes, sweet (for mashed)	1 lb	Peeled, cut in 1-inch thick slices	½ cup	N/A	High	6 mins	Quick

PRESSURE COOKING MEATS

MEAT	WEIGHT	PREP	WATER	ACCESSORY	PRESSURE	COOK TIME	RELEASE
Poultry							
Chicken breasts	2 lbs	Bone in	1 cup	N/A	High	15 mins	Quick
	4 breasts (6–8 oz each)	Boneless	1 cup	N/A	High	8–10 mins	Quick
	Frozen, 4 large	Boneless	1 cup	N/A	High	25 mins	Quick
Chicken thighs	8 thighs (4 lbs)	Bone in, skin on	1 cup	N/A	High	20 mins	Quick
	8 thighs (4 lbs)	Boneless	1 cup	N/A	High	20 mins	Quick

MEAT	WEIGHT	PREP	WATER	ACCESSORY	PRESSURE	COOK TIME	RELEASE
Chicken, whole	5–6 lbs	Bone in	1 cup	Cook & Crisp™ Basket	High	25–30 mins	Quick
Turkey breast	1 breast (6–8 lbs)	Bone in	1 cup	N/A	High	40–50 mins	Quick
Ground Meat							
Ground beef, pork, or turkey	1–2 lbs	Out of the package	½ cup	N/A	High	5 mins	Quick
Ground beef, pork, or turkey, frozen	1–2 lbs	Frozen ground, not in patties	½ cup	N/A	HIgh	20–25 mins	Quick
Ribs							
Pork baby back ribs	2½–3½ lbs	Cut in thirds	1 cup	N/A	High	20 mins	Quick
Roasts							
Beef brisket	3–4 lbs	Whole	1 cup	N/A	High	1½ hrs	Quick
Boneless beef chuck-eye roast	3–4 lbs	Whole	1 cup	N/A	High	1½ hrs	Quick
Boneless pork butt	4 lbs	Seasoned	1 cup	N/A	High	1½ hrs	Quick
Pork tenderloin	2 tenderloins (1–1½ lbs each)	Seasoned	1 cup	N/A	High	3–4 mins	Quick
Stew Meat							
Boneless beef short ribs	6 ribs (3 lbs)	Whole	1 cup	N/A	High	25 mins	Quick
Boneless leg of lamb	3 lbs	Cut in 1-inch pieces	1 cup	N/A	High	30 mins	Quick
Boneless pork butt	3 lbs	Cut in 1-inch cubes	1 cup	N/A	High	30 mins	Quick
Chuck roast, for stew	2 lbs	Cut in 1-inch cubes	1 cup	N/A	High	25 mins	Quick

AIR CRISP

6.5 QUART

INGREDIENT	AMOUNT	PREP	OIL	TEMP	COOK TIME	TOSS CONTENTS IN BASKET
Vegetables						
Asparagus	1 bunch	Whole, stems trimmed	2 tsp	390°F	8–10 mins	Halfway through cooking
Beets	6 small or 4 large (about 2 lbs)	Whole	None	390°F	45–60 mins	N/A
Bell peppers (for roasting)	4 peppers	Whole	None	400°F	25–30 mins	Halfway through cooking
Broccoli	1 head	Cut into florets	1 tbsp	390°F	10–13 mins	Halfway through cooking
Brussels sprouts	1 lb	Cut in half,	1 tbsp	390°F	15–18 mins	Halfway through cooking
Butternut squash	1–1½ lbs	Cut into 1- to 2-inch pieces	1 tbsp	390°F	20–25 mins	Halfway through cooking
Carrots	1 lb	Peeled, cut into ½-inch pieces	1 tbsp	390°F	15 mins	Halfway through cooking
Cauliflower	1 head	Cut into florets	2 tbsp	390°F	15–20 mins	Halfway through cooking
Corn on the cob	4 ears	Whole ears, husks removed	1 tbsp	390°F	12–15 mins	Halfway through cooking
Green beans	1 bag (12 oz)	Trimmed	1 tbsp	390°F	7–10 mins	Halfway through cooking
Kale (for chips)	6 cups, packed	Torn in pieces, stems removed	None	300°F	10 mins	Halfway through cooking
Mushrooms	8 oz	Cut into ⅛-inch slices	1 tbsp	390°F	7–8 mins	Halfway through cooking
Potatoes, Yukon gold and russet	1½ lbs	Cut into 1-inch wedges	1 tbsp	390°F	20–25 mins	Halfway through cooking
	1 lb	Hand-cut, thin	½–3 tbsp	390°F	20–25 mins	Halfway through cooking
	1 lb	Hand-cut, thick	½–3 tbsp	390°F	25 mins	Halfway through cooking
	4 whole (6–8 oz each)	Pierced with fork 3 times	None	390°F	35–40 mins	N/A

INGREDIENT	AMOUNT	PREP	OIL	TEMP	COOK TIME	TOSS CONTENTS IN BASKET
Potatoes, sweet	2 lbs	Cut into 1-inch chunks	1 tbsp	390°F	15–20 mins	Halfway through cooking
	4 whole (6–8 oz each)	Pierced with fork 3 times	None	390°F	35–40 mins	N/A
Zucchini	1 lb	Cut length-wise into quarters, then cut into 1-inch pieces	1 tbsp	390°F	15–20 mins	Halfway through cooking
Poultry						
Chicken breasts	2 breasts (¾–1½ lbs each)	Bone in	Brushed with oil	375°F	25–35 mins	N/A
	2 breasts (½–¾ lb each)	Boneless	Brushed with oil	375°F	22–25 mins	N/A
Chicken thighs	4 thighs (6–10 oz each)	Bone in	Brushed with oil	390°F	22–28 mins	N/A
	4 thighs (4–8 oz each)	Boneless	Brushed with oil	390°F	18–22 mins	N/A
Chicken wings	2 lbs	Drumettes & flats	1 tbsp	390°F	24–28 mins	Halfway through cooking
Chicken, whole	1 chicken (3–5 lbs)	Trussed	Brushed with oil	375°F	55–75 mins	N/A
Beef						
Burgers	4 patties (¼ lb each)	1 inch thick	None	375°F	10–12 mins	Halfway through cooking
Steaks	2 steaks (8 oz each)	Whole	None	390°F	10–20 mins	N/A
Pork & Lamb						
Bacon	Up to 1 lb	Lay strips over basket	None	325°F	13–16 mins (no preheat)	N/A
Pork chops	2 chops (10–12 oz each)	Thick cut, bone in	Brushed with oil	375°F	15–17 mins	Halfway through cooking
	4 chops (6–8 oz each)	Boneless	Brushed with oil	375°F	15–18 mins	Halfway through cooking ➤

INGREDIENT	AMOUNT	PREP	OIL	TEMP	COOK TIME	TOSS CONTENTS IN BASKET
Pork tenderloins	2 tenderloins (1–1½ lbs each)	Whole	Brushed with oil	375°F	25–35 mins	Halfway through cooking
Sausages	4	Whole	None	390°F	8–10 mins	Turn/flip halfway through cooking
Fish & Seafood						
Crab cakes	2 cakes (6–8 oz each)	None	Brushed with oil	350°F	8–12 mins	N/A
Lobster tails	4 tails (3–4 oz each)	Whole	None	375°F	7–10 mins	N/A
Salmon fillets	2 fillets (4 oz each)	None	Brushed with oil	390°F	10–13 mins	N/A
Shrimp	16 large	Whole, peeled, tails on	1 tbsp	390°F	7–10 mins	N/A
Frozen Foods						
Chicken nuggets	1 box (12 oz)	None	None	390°F	12 mins	Halfway through cooking
Fish fillets	1 box (6 fillets)	None	None	390°F	14 mins	Halfway through cooking
Fish sticks	1 box (14.8 oz)	None	None	390°F	10 mins	Halfway through cooking
French fries	1 lb	None	None	360°F	19 mins	Halfway through cooking
	2 lbs	None	None	360°F	30 mins	
Mozzarella sticks	1 box (11 oz)	None	None	375°F	8 mins	Halfway through cooking
Pot stickers	1 bag (10 count)	None	Toss with 1 tsp oil	390°F	11–14 mins	Halfway through cooking
Pizza rolls	1 bag (20 oz, 40 count)	None	None	390°F	12–15 mins	Halfway through cooking
Popcorn shrimp	1 box (16 oz)	None	None	390°F	9 mins	Halfway through cooking
Tater Tots	1 lb	None	None	360°F	20 mins	Halfway through cooking

AIR CRISP: 8 QUART

INGREDIENT	AMOUNT	PREP	OIL	TEMP	COOK TIME	TOSS CONTENTS IN BASKET
Vegetables						
Asparagus	1 bunch	Whole, stems trimmed	2 tsp	390°F	5–10 mins	Halfway through cooking
Beets	6 small or 4 large (about 2 lbs)	Whole	None	390°F	45–60 mins	N/A
Bell peppers (for roasting)	4 peppers	Whole	None	400°F	25–30 mins	Halfway through cooking
Broccoli	1 head	Cut into florets	1 tbsp	390°F	7–10 mins	Halfway through cooking
Brussels sprouts	1 lb	Cut in half, stems removed	1 tbsp	390°F	12–15 mins	Halfway through cooking
Butternut squash	1–1½ lbs	Cut into 1- to 2-inch pieces	1 tbsp	390°F	20–25 mins	Halfway through cooking
Carrots	1 lb	Peeled, cut into ½-inch pieces	1 tbsp	390°F	14–16 mins	Halfway through cooking
Cauliflower	1 head	Cut into florets	2 tbsp	390°F	15–20 mins	Halfway through cooking
Corn on the cob	4 ears	Whole ears, husks removed	1 tbsp	390°F	12–15 mins	Halfway through cooking
Green beans	1 bag (12 oz)	Trimmed	1 tbsp	390°F	5–6 mins	Halfway through cooking
Kale (for chips)	6 cups, packed	Torn into pieces, stems removed	None	300°F	8–11 mins	Halfway through cooking
Mushrooms	8 oz	Cut into ⅛-inch slices	1 tbsp	390°F	5–7 mins	Halfway through cooking
Potatoes, Yukon gold and russet	1½ lbs	Cut into 1-inch wedges	1 tbsp	390°F	15 mins	Halfway through cooking
	2 lbs	Hand-cut, thin	2 tbsp	390°F	28 mins	Halfway through cooking
	2 lbs	Hand-cut, thick	2 tbsp	390°F	30 mins	Halfway through cooking
	4 whole (6–8 oz each)	Pierced with fork 3 times	None	390°F	30–35 mins	N/A ➤

INGREDIENT	AMOUNT	PREP	OIL	TEMP	COOK TIME	TOSS CONTENTS IN BASKET
Potatoes, sweet	2 lbs	Cut into 1-inch chunks	1 tbsp	325°F	15–20 mins	Halfway through cooking
	4 whole (6–8 oz each)	Pierced with fork 3 times	None	390°F	30–35 mins	N/A
Zucchini	1 lb	Cut lengthwise into quarters, then cut into 1-inch pieces	1 tbsp	390°F	15–20 mins	Halfway through cooking
Poultry						
Chicken breasts	2 breasts (¾–1½ lb. each)	Bone in	Brushed with oil	375°F	25–35 mins	N/A
	2 breasts (½–¾ lb each)	Boneless	Brushed with oil	375°F	12–17 mins	N/A
Chicken thighs	4 thighs (6–10 oz each)	Bone in	Brushed with oil	390°F	22–28 mins	N/A
	4 thighs (4–8 oz each)	Boneless	Brushed with oil	390°F	18–22 mins	N/A
Chicken wings	2 lbs	Drumettes & flats	1 tbsp	390°F	25–30 mins	Halfway through cooking
Chicken, whole	1 chicken (3–5 lbs)	Trussed	Brushed with oil	375°F	55–75 mins	Halfway through cooking
Beef						
Burgers	4 patties (¼ lb each)	1 inch thick	None	375°F	8–10 mins	Halfway through cooking
Steaks	2 steaks (8 oz each)	Whole	None	390°F	10–20 mins	N/A
Pork & Lamb						
Bacon	10 strips	Drape over Roasting Rack insert	None	375°F	10–15 mins	N/A
Lamb loin chops	5 chops (¼ lb each)	1 inch thick	Brushed with oil	390°F	8–12 mins	N/A

INGREDIENT	AMOUNT	PREP	OIL	TEMP	COOK TIME	TOSS CONTENTS IN BASKET
Pork chops	2 chops (10–12 oz each)	Thick cut, bone in	Brushed with oil	375°F	15–17 mins	Halfway through cooking
	4 chops (¼ lb each)	Thinly sliced, boneless	Brushed with oil	375°F	7–12 mins	Halfway through cooking
Pork tenderloins	2 tender-loins (1–1½ lbs each)	Whole	Brushed with oil	375°F	25–35 mins	Halfway through cooking
Sausages	4 sausages	Whole	None	390°F	8–10 mins	Turn/flip halfway through cooking

Fish & Seafood

INGREDIENT	AMOUNT	PREP	OIL	TEMP	COOK TIME	TOSS CONTENTS IN BASKET
Crab cakes	2 cakes (6–8 oz each)	None	Brushed with oil	350°F	10–15 mins	N/A
Lobster tails	4 tails (3–4 oz each)	Whole	None	375°F	5–7 mins	N/A
Salmon fillets	2 fillets (4 oz each)	None	Brushed with oil	390°F	6–10 mins	N/A
Shrimp	16 large	Whole, peeled, tails on	1 tbsp	390°F	5–7 mins	N/A

Frozen Foods

INGREDIENT	AMOUNT	PREP	OIL	TEMP	COOK TIME	TOSS CONTENTS IN BASKET
Chicken nuggets	1 box (12 oz)	None	None	390°F	12 mins	Halfway through cooking
Egg rolls	4 egg rolls	None	None	390°F	12 mins	N/A
Fish fillets	1 box (6 fillets)	None	None	390°F	14 mins	Halfway through cooking
Fish sticks	1 box (14.8 oz)	None	None	390°F	10 mins	Halfway through cooking
French fries	1 lb	None	None	360°F	19 mins	Halfway through cooking
Mozzarella sticks	1 box (11 oz)	None	None	375°F	8 mins	Halfway through cooking
Onion rings	1 bag (16 oz)	None	None	390°F	8 mins	Halfway through cooking ➤

INGREDIENT	AMOUNT	PREP	OIL	TEMP	COOK TIME	TOSS CONTENTS IN BASKET
Pot stickers	1 bag (24 oz, 20 count)	None	None	390°F	12–14 mins	Halfway through cooking
Pizza rolls	1 bag (20 oz, 40 count)	None	None	390°F	12 mins	Halfway through cooking
Shrimp, breaded	1 box (9 oz, 12 count)	None	None	390°F	9 mins	Halfway through cooking

STEAM

INGREDIENT	AMOUNT	PREP	LIQUID	COOK TIME
Vegetables				
Asparagus	1 bunch	Whole spears	2 cups	7–15 mins
Broccoli	1 crown or 1 (12-oz) bag	Cut into florets	2 cups	5–9 mins
Green beans	1 (12-oz) bag	Whole	2 cups	6–12 mins
Brussels sprouts	1 lb	Whole, trimmed	2 cups	8–17 mins
Carrots	1 lb	Cut into 1-inch pieces	2 cups	7–12 mins
Cabbage	1 head	Cut into wedges	2 cups	6–12 mins
Cauliflower	1 head	Cut into florets	2 cups	5–10 mins
Corn on the cob	4	Whole, husks removed	2 cups	4–9 mins
Kale	1 (16-oz) bag	Trimmed	2 cups	7–10 mins
Sugar snap peas	1 lb	Whole pods, trimmed	2 cups	5–8 mins
Potatoes	1 lb	Peeled and cut into 1-inch pieces	2 cups	12–17 mins
Spinach	1 (16-oz) bag	Whole leaves	2 cups	3–7 mins
Butternut squash	24 oz	Peeled, cut into 1-inch cubes	2 cups	10–15 mins
Sweet potatoes	1 lb	Cut into ½-inch cubes	2 cups	8–14 mins
Zucchini or summer squash	1 lb	Cut into 1-inch slices	2 cups	5–10 mins
Eggs				
Poached eggs	4	In ramekin or silicone cup	1 cup	3–6 mins

DEHYDRATE

FOOD LOAD	PREP	TEMP	DEHYDRATE TIME
Fruits & Vegetables			
Apple chips	Core removed, sliced ⅛ inch thick, rinsed in lemon water	135°F	7–8 hrs
Asparagus	Washed and cut into 1-inch pieces; blanched	135°F	6–8 hrs
Bananas	Peeled, cut into ⅜-inch pieces	135°F	8–10 hrs
Beet chips	Peeled, cut into ⅛-inch pieces	135°F	7–8 hrs
Eggplant	Peeled, sliced ¼ inch thick; blanched	135°F	6–8 hrs
Fresh herbs	Rinsed, patted dry, stems removed	135°F	4–6 hrs
Gingerroot	Cut into ⅜-inch pieces	135°F	6 hrs
Mangos	Peeled, cut into ⅜-inch pieces	135°F	6–8 hrs
Mushrooms	Cleaned with soft brush—do not wash	135°F	6–8 hrs
Pineapple	Cored, peeled, and sliced ⅜ inch to ½ inch thick	135°F	6–8 hrs
Strawberries	Halved or sliced ½ inch thick	135°F	6–8 hrs
Tomatoes	Washed and sliced ⅜ inch thick or grated. Steam if you plan to rehydrate.	135°F	6–8 hrs
Meats			
All jerky (not salmon)	Cut into ¼-inch slices, follow jerky recipe in the Inspiration Guide that came with your Foodi™	150°F	5–7 hrs
Salmon jerky	Cut into ¼-inch slices, follow jerky recipe in the Inspiration Guide that came with your Foodi™	165°F	5–8 hrs

MEASUREMENT CONVERSIONS

VOLUME EQUIVALENTS (LIQUID)

US STANDARD	US STANDARD (OUNCES)	METRIC (APPROXIMATE)
2 tablespoons	1 fl. oz.	30 mL
¼ cup	2 fl. oz.	60 mL
½ cup	4 fl. oz.	120 mL
1 cup	8 fl. oz.	240 mL
1½ cups	12 fl. oz.	355 mL
2 cups or 1 pint	16 fl. oz.	475 mL
4 cups or 1 quart	32 fl. oz.	1 L
1 gallon	128 fl. oz.	4 L

VOLUME EQUIVALENTS (DRY)

US STANDARD	METRIC (APPROXIMATE)
⅛ teaspoon	0.5 mL
¼ teaspoon	1 mL
½ teaspoon	2 mL
¾ teaspoon	4 mL
1 teaspoon	5 mL
1 tablespoon	15 mL
¼ cup	59 mL
⅓ cup	79 mL
½ cup	118 mL
⅔ cup	156 mL
¾ cup	177 mL
1 cup	235 mL
2 cups or 1 pint	475 mL
3 cups	700 mL
4 cups or 1 quart	1 L

OVEN TEMPERATURES

FAHRENHEIT (F)	CELSIUS (C) (APPROXIMATE)
250°	120°
300°	150°
325°	165°
350°	180°
375°	190°
400°	200°
425°	220°
450°	230°

WEIGHT EQUIVALENTS

US STANDARD	METRIC (APPROXIMATE)
½ ounce	15 g
1 ounce	30 g
2 ounces	60 g
4 ounces	115 g
8 ounces	225 g
12 ounces	340 g
16 ounces or 1 pound	455 g

THE DIRTY DOZEN™ AND THE CLEAN FIFTEEN™

A nonprofit environmental watchdog organization called Environmental Working Group (EWG) looks at data supplied by the U.S. Department of Agriculture (USDA) and the Food and Drug Administration (FDA) about pesticide residues. Each year it compiles a list of the best and worst pesticide loads found in commercial crops. You can use these lists to decide which fruits and vegetables to buy organic to minimize your exposure to pesticides and which produce is considered safe enough to buy conventionally. This does not mean they are pesticide-free, though, so wash these fruits and vegetables thoroughly.

DIRTY DOZEN

apples
celery
cherries
grapes
nectarines
peaches
pears
potatoes
spinach
strawberries
sweet bell peppers
tomatoes

*Additionally, nearly three-quarters of **hot pepper** samples contained pesticide residues.

CLEAN FIFTEEN

asparagus
avocados
broccoli
cabbages
cantaloupes
cauliflower
eggplants
honeydew melons
kiwis
mangoes
onions
papayas
pineapples
sweet corn
sweet peas (frozen)

INDEX

A

Air Crisp function, 4, 236–242
Apples
    Apple Turnovers, 36–37
    dehydrating chart, 243
    Tarte Tatin, 207
    Turkey and Wild Rice
        Salad, 112–113
Around 30 minutes
    Artichoke and Red Pepper
        Frittata, 32–33
    Barbecue Sauce, 226
    Beef Satay with Peanut
        Sauce, 145–147
    Bow Tie Pasta with Shrimp
        and Arugula, 160–161
    Cheesy Tuna Noodle
        Casserole, 186–187
    Chicken Shawarma with
        Garlic-Yogurt Sauce, 98–99
    Chicken Stroganoff, 110–111
    Creamy Pasta
        Primavera, 62–63
    Creamy Steel-Cut Oats with
        Toasted Almonds, 40–41
    Crème Brûlée, 202–203
    Easy Chicken Cordon Bleu
        with Green Beans, 102–103
    Egg Muffin Breakfast
        Sandwich, 30–31
    French Cinnamon
        Toast, 26–27
    Italian Beef Sandwiches,
        148–149
    Japanese Pork Cutlets
        (Tonkatsu) with
        Ramen, 143–144
    Kielbasa with Braised Cabbage
        and Noodles,
        124–125
    Kung Pao Tofu and
        Peppers, 64–65
    Marinara Sauce, 228–229
    Masoor Dal (Indian Red
        Lentils), 60–61
    Mediterranean White Bean
        Salad, 50–51

    Minestrone with Garlic Cheese
        Toasts and Pesto, 56–57
    Mocha Pots de Crème, 213
    Mustard Sauce, 227
    Peach Cobbler, 198–199
    Penne with Mushrooms and
        Gruyère, 46–47
    Pork Lo Mein with Vegetables,
        137–138
    Pork Tenderloin with
        Peppers and Roasted
        Potatoes, 154–155
    Potato-Crusted Cod with
        Succotash, 188–189
    Quinoa Pilaf with Smoked
        Trout and Corn, 190–191
    Risotto with Chard,
        Caramelized Onions, and
        Mushrooms, 66–67
    Roasted Red Pepper Soup and
        Grilled Cheese, 70–71
    Sautéed Mushrooms,
        220–221
    Savory Custards with Bacon
        and Cheese, 28–29
    Sesame-Garlic Chicken
        Wings, 76–77
    Shakshuka, 38–39
    Simple Potato Gratin with
        Ham and Peas, 135–136
    Sloppy Joes, 156–157
    "Spanish" Rice and
        Beans, 54–55
    Spiced Poached Pears,
        214–215
    Spicy Air-Crisped Chicken and
        Potatoes, 80–81
    Tarte Tatin, 207
    Teriyaki Salmon and
        Vegetables, 166–167
    Teriyaki Sauce, 225
    Thai Fish Curry, 175–176
    Tilapia Veracruz, 184–185
    Trout Florentine, 192–193
    Vegetable Korma, 58–59
    Warm Potato and Green Bean
        Salad with Tuna, 164–165

Artichoke hearts
    Artichoke and Red Pepper
        Frittata, 32–33
    Braised Chicken Thighs
        with Mushrooms and
        Artichokes, 84–85
Arugula
    Bow Tie Pasta with Shrimp
        and Arugula, 160–161
Asparagus
    air crisping charts, 236, 239
    Crab and Roasted Asparagus
        Risotto, 173–174
    Creamy Pasta
        Primavera, 62–63
    dehydrating chart, 243
    steam chart, 242

B

Bacon
    Chicken Fajitas with
        Refritos, 82–83
    Clam Chowder with
        Parmesan
        Crackers, 171–172
    Coq au Vin, 106–107
    Kielbasa with Braised Cabbage
        and Noodles,
        124–125
    Quick Cassoulet, 78–79
    Savory Custards with Bacon
        and Cheese, 28–29
    Trout Florentine, 192–193
Bake/Roast function, 4
Basil
    Creamy Pasta Primavera,
        62–63
    Thai Fish Curry, 175–176
Beans. *See also* Chickpeas;
        Green beans
    Chicken Fajitas with
        Refritos, 82–83
    Italian Wedding Soup with
        Turkey Sausage,
        108–109
    Jerk Pork, 141–142

Beans *(continued)*

    Mediterranean White Bean
      Salad, 50–51

    Minestrone with Garlic Cheese
      Toasts and Pesto, 56–57

    Potato-Crusted Cod with
      Succotash, 188–189

    pressure cooking chart, 232

    Quick Cassoulet, 78–79

    "Spanish" Rice and
      Beans, 54–55

Beef

    air crisping charts, 237, 240

    Beef Satay with Peanut
      Sauce, 145–147

    Beefy Onion Soup with Cheese
      Croutons, 122–123

    Carbonnade Flamande,
      152–153

    dehydrating chart, 243

    Italian Beef Sandwiches,
      148–149

    pressure cooking chart,
      235

    Sloppy Joes, 156–157

    Southwestern Shepherd's
      Pie, 130–131

    Sunday Pot Roast and
      Biscuits, 120–121

Bell peppers. *See also* Roasted
    red peppers

    air crisping charts, 236, 239

    Artichoke and Red Pepper
      Frittata, 32–33

    Chicken Fajitas with
      Refritos, 82–83

    Chorizo-Stuffed Peppers,
      128–129

    Italian Beef Sandwiches,
      148–149

    Kung Pao Tofu and
      Peppers, 64–65

    Mediterranean White Bean
      Salad, 50–51

    Pork Lo Mein with
      Vegetables, 137–138

    Pork Tenderloin with
      Peppers and Roasted
      Potatoes, 154–155

    Salmon Cakes, 179–181

    Sausage and Pepper Calzones,
      132–134

    Shakshuka, 38–39

    Shrimp and Sausage
      Gumbo, 182–183

    Sloppy Joes, 156–157

    Teriyaki Salmon and
      Vegetables,
      166–167

    Thai Fish Curry, 175–176

Berries

    Blueberry Cream
      Tart, 208–210

    dehydrating chart, 243

    Mixed Berry Crisp, 196–197

Bread dough

    Monkey Bread, 20–21

    Sausage and Pepper Calzones,
      132–134

Broccoli

    air crisping charts, 236, 239

    Creamy Pasta Primavera,
      62–63

    steam chart, 242

Broil function, 4

C

Cabbage

    Kielbasa with Braised Cabbage
      and Noodles, 124–125

    Shrimp and Vegetable Egg
      Rolls, 168–170

    steam chart, 242

Caramel sauce

    Caramel-Pecan Brownies,
      211–212

Carrots

    air crisping charts, 236, 239

    Cajun Chicken and
      Dumplings, 88–89

    Japanese Pork Cutlets
      (Tonkatsu) with
      Ramen, 143–144

    Minestrone with Garlic Cheese
      Toasts and Pesto, 56–57

    Pork Lo Mein with
      Vegetables, 137–138

    Pork Ragu with Penne,
      126–127

    Quick Cassoulet, 78–79

    Roasted Vegetable Stock, 219

    Shrimp and Vegetable Egg
      Rolls, 168–170

    steam chart, 242

    Sunday Pot Roast and
      Biscuits, 120–121

    Vegetable Korma, 58–59

Cauliflower

    air crisping charts, 236, 239

    steam chart, 242

    Vegetable Korma, 58–59

Celery

    Cajun Chicken and
      Dumplings, 88–89

    Cheesy Tuna Noodle
      Casserole, 186–187

    Clam Chowder with Parmesan
      Crackers, 171–172

    Italian Wedding Soup with
      Turkey Sausage,
      108–109

    Mediterranean White Bean
      Salad, 50–51

    Minestrone with Garlic Cheese
      Toasts and Pesto, 56–57

    Pork Ragu with Penne,
      126–127

    Salmon Cakes, 179–181

    Shrimp and Sausage
      Gumbo, 182–183

    Turkey and Wild Rice
      Salad, 112–113

Chard

    Risotto with Chard,
      Caramelized Onions, and
      Mushrooms, 66–67

Cheddar cheese

    Cajun Twice-Baked
      Potatoes, 52–53

    Cheesy Tuna Noodle
      Casserole, 186–187

    Egg Muffin Breakfast
      Sandwich, 30–31

    Roasted Red Pepper Soup and
      Grilled Cheese, 70–71

    Sausage-Mushroom
      Strata, 34–35

    Simple Potato Gratin with
      Ham and Peas, 135–136

Cheese. *See specific*

Cherries

    Breakfast Clafoutis, 42–43

Chicken

    air crisping charts,
      237, 240–241

    Braised Chicken Thighs
      with Mushrooms and
      Artichokes, 84–85

    Cajun Chicken and
      Dumplings, 88–89

Chicken and Spinach
Quesadillas, 86–87
Chicken Caesar Salad, 90–92
Chicken Chili Verde with
Nachos, 104–105
Chicken Fajitas with
Refritos, 82–83
Chicken Shawarma
with Garlic-Yogurt
Sauce, 98–99
Chicken Stock, 218
Chicken Stroganoff, 110–111
Chicken Tikka Masala with
Rice, 93–95
Coq au Vin, 106–107
Easy Chicken Cordon
Bleu with Green
Beans, 102–103
pressure cooking chart, 234–235
Quick Cassoulet, 78–79
Sesame-Garlic Chicken
Wings, 76–77
Spicy Air-Crisped Chicken and
Potatoes, 80–81
Tandoori Chicken and
Coconut Rice, 96–97
Chickpeas
pressure cooking chart, 232
Tunisian Chickpea
Soup, 72–73
Chocolate. *See also* Cocoa
powder
Caramel-Pecan Brownies,
211–212
Chocolate Marble Cheesecake,
200–201
Cilantro
Chicken Chili Verde with
Nachos, 104–105
Chicken Tikka Masala with
Rice, 93–95
Masoor Dal (Indian Red
Lentils), 60–61
"Spanish" Rice and
Beans, 54–55
Tandoori Chicken and
Coconut Rice, 96–97
Vegetable Korma, 58–59
Clams
Clam Chowder with Parmesan
Crackers, 171–172
Cocoa powder
Mocha Pots de Crème, 213

Coconut milk
Beef Satay with Peanut
Sauce, 145–147
Tandoori Chicken and
Coconut Rice, 96–97
Thai Fish Curry, 175–176
Vegetable Korma, 58–59
Cook & Crisp™ Basket, 5, 6
Corn
air crisping charts, 236, 239
Potato-Crusted Cod with
Succotash, 188–189
Quinoa Pilaf with Smoked
Trout and Corn, 190–191
Southwestern Shepherd's
Pie, 130–131
steam chart, 242
Crabmeat
Crab and Roasted Asparagus
Risotto, 173–174
Cream
Blueberry Cream
Tart, 208–210
Braised Chicken Thighs
with Mushrooms and
Artichokes, 84–85
Breakfast Clafoutis, 42–43
Cajun Chicken and
Dumplings, 88–89
Cajun Roasted Turkey
Breast with Sweet
Potatoes, 100–101
Cajun Twice-Baked
Potatoes, 52–53
Chicken Tikka Masala with
Rice, 93–95
Chocolate Marble Cheesecake,
200–201
Creamy Pasta Primavera,
62–63
Crème Brûlée, 202–203
French Cinnamon
Toast, 26–27
Lax Pudding, 162–163
Meatloaf and Mashed
Potatoes, 139–140
Mocha Pots de Crème, 213
Peach Cobbler, 198–199
Roasted Red Pepper Soup and
Grilled Cheese, 70–71
Savory Custards with Bacon
and Cheese, 28–29
Simple Potato Gratin with
Ham and Peas, 135–136

Tarte Tatin, 207
Tex-Mex Breakfast Casserole,
22–23
Trout Florentine, 192–193
Cream cheese
Blueberry Cream
Tart, 208–210
Chicken and Spinach
Quesadillas,
86–87
Chocolate Marble Cheesecake,
200–201
Savory Custards with Bacon
and Cheese, 28–29
Crisping Lid, 4, 6
Cucumbers
Beef Satay with Peanut
Sauce, 145–147
Chicken Shawarma
with Garlic-Yogurt
Sauce, 98–99
Mediterranean White Bean
Salad, 50–51

D

Dairy-free/dairy-free option
Barbecue Sauce, 226
Beef Satay with Peanut
Sauce, 145–147
Bow Tie Pasta with Shrimp
and Arugula, 160–161
Braised Chicken Thighs
with Mushrooms and
Artichokes, 84–85
Cajun Seasoning Mix, 223
Carbonnade Flamande,
152–153
Chicken Fajitas with
Refritos, 82–83
Chicken Stock, 218
Coq au Vin, 106–107
Deviled Short Ribs with
Noodles, 150–151
Honey-Mustard Spare
Ribs, 116–117
Italian Beef Sandwiches,
148–149
Japanese Pork Cutlets
(Tonkatsu) with
Ramen, 143–144
Jerk Pork, 141–142

Dairy-free/dairy-free option
(continued)

Kielbasa with Braised Cabbage
and Noodles, 124–125
Kung Pao Tofu and
Peppers, 64–65
Marinara Sauce, 228–229
Masoor Dal (Indian Red
Lentils), 60–61
Mediterranean White Bean
Salad, 50–51
Mexican/Southwestern
Seasoning Mix, 224
Mustard Sauce, 227
Pork Lo Mein with Vegetables,
137–138
Potato-Crusted Cod with
Succotash, 188–189
Quick Cassoulet, 78–79
Quinoa Pilaf with Smoked
Trout and Corn, 190–191
Roasted Vegetable Stock, 219
Sesame-Garlic Chicken
Wings, 76–77
Shakshuka, 38–39
Shrimp and Sausage
Gumbo, 182–183
Shrimp and Vegetable Egg
Rolls, 168–170
Sloppy Joes, 156–157
"Spanish" Rice and
Beans, 54–55
Spiced Poached Pears,
214–215
Sunday Pot Roast and
Biscuits, 120–121
Teriyaki Salmon and
Vegetables, 166–167
Teriyaki Sauce, 225
Thai Fish Curry, 175–176
Tilapia Veracruz, 184–185
Tunisian Chickpea
Soup, 72–73
Turkey and Wild Rice
Salad, 112–113
Vegetable Korma, 58–59
Warm Potato and Green Bean
Salad with Tuna, 164–165
Dehydrating chart, 243
Dill
Chicken Stroganoff, 110–111
Lax Pudding, 162–163

E

Egg noodles
Cheesy Tuna Noodle
Casserole, 186–187
Chicken Stroganoff, 110–111
Deviled Short Ribs with
Noodles, 150–151
Kielbasa with Braised Cabbage
and Noodles, 124–125
Eggplants
dehydrating chart, 243
Easy Eggplant Parmesan,
48–49
Eggs
Artichoke and Red Pepper
Frittata, 32–33
Breakfast Clafoutis, 42–43
Cajun Chicken and
Dumplings, 88–89
Caramel-Pecan Brownies,
211–212
Chocolate Marble Cheesecake,
200–201
Crème Brûlée, 202–203
Egg Muffin Breakfast
Sandwich, 30–31
French Cinnamon
Toast, 26–27
Japanese Pork Cutlets
(Tonkatsu) with
Ramen, 143–144
Lax Pudding, 162–163
Lemon Bars, 204–206
Meatloaf and Mashed
Potatoes, 139–140
Mocha Pots de Crème, 213
Mushroom Lasagna, 68–69
Penne with Mushrooms and
Gruyère, 46–47
Salmon Cakes, 179–181
Sausage-Mushroom
Strata, 34–35
Savory Custards with Bacon
and Cheese, 28–29
Scotch Eggs, 24–25
Shakshuka, 38–39
Southwestern Shepherd's
Pie, 130–131
steam chart, 242
Tex-Mex Breakfast Casserole,
22–23
Espresso powder
Mocha Pots de Crème, 213

F

Feta cheese
Mediterranean White Bean
Salad, 50–51
Shakshuka, 38–39
Warm Potato and Green Bean
Salad with Tuna, 164–165
Fish
air crisping charts, 238, 241
Blackened Salmon with
Creamy Grits,
177–178
Cheesy Tuna Noodle
Casserole, 186–187
Lax Pudding, 162–163
Potato-Crusted Cod with
Succotash, 188–189
Quinoa Pilaf with Smoked
Trout and Corn, 190–191
Salmon Cakes, 179–181
Teriyaki Salmon and
Vegetables,
166–167
Thai Fish Curry, 175–176
Tilapia Veracruz, 184–185
Trout Florentine, 192–193
Warm Potato and Green Bean
Salad with Tuna, 164–165
Freezer staples, 11
Frozen foods, 8, 238, 241–242

G

Ginger
Chicken Tikka Masala with
Rice, 93–95
dehydrating chart, 243
Jerk Pork, 141–142
Kung Pao Tofu and
Peppers, 64–65
Shrimp and Vegetable Egg
Rolls, 168–170
Teriyaki Sauce, 225
Gluten-free/gluten-free option
Artichoke and Red Pepper
Frittata, 32–33
Barbecue Sauce, 226
Blackened Salmon with
Creamy Grits,
177–178
Braised Chicken Thighs
with Mushrooms and
Artichokes, 84–85

Cajun Roasted Turkey
Breast with Sweet
Potatoes, 100–101
Cajun Seasoning Mix, 223
Cajun Twice-Baked
Potatoes, 52–53
Caramelized Onions, 222
Carnitas, 118–119
Chicken Chili Verde with
Nachos, 104–105
Chicken Fajitas with
Refritos, 82–83
Chicken Stock, 218
Chicken Tikka Masala with
Rice, 93–95
Chocolate Marble Cheesecake,
200–201
Coq au Vin, 106–107
Crab and Roasted Asparagus
Risotto, 173–174
Creamy Steel-Cut Oats with
Toasted Almonds, 40–41
Crème Brûlée, 202–203
Honey-Mustard Spare
Ribs, 116–117
Jerk Pork, 141–142
Kielbasa with Braised Cabbage
and Noodles, 124–125
Lax Pudding, 162–163
Marinara Sauce, 228–229
Masoor Dal (Indian Red
Lentils), 60–61
Mediterranean White Bean
Salad, 50–51
Mexican/Southwestern
Seasoning Mix, 224
Mixed Berry Crisp, 196–197
Mocha Pots de Crème, 213
Mustard Sauce, 227
Pork Tenderloin with
Peppers and Roasted
Potatoes, 154–155
Potato-Crusted Cod with
Succotash, 188–189
Quinoa Pilaf with Smoked
Trout and Corn, 190–191
Risotto with Chard,
Caramelized Onions, and
Mushrooms, 66–67
Roasted Vegetable Stock, 219
Salmon Cakes, 179–181
Sautéed Mushrooms, 220–221
Savory Custards with Bacon
and Cheese, 28–29

Scotch Eggs, 24–25
Sesame-Garlic Chicken
Wings, 76–77
Shakshuka, 38–39
Simple Potato Gratin with
Ham and Peas, 135–136
"Spanish" Rice and
Beans, 54–55
Spiced Poached Pears,
214–215
Spicy Air-Crisped Chicken and
Potatoes, 80–81
Tandoori Chicken and
Coconut Rice, 96–97
Teriyaki Sauce, 225
Tex-Mex Breakfast Casserole,
22–23
Thai Fish Curry, 175–176
Tilapia Veracruz, 184–185
Turkey and Wild Rice
Salad, 112–113
Vegetable Korma, 58–59
Warm Potato and Green Bean
Salad with Tuna, 164–165
Greek yogurt
Chicken Shawarma
with Garlic-Yogurt
Sauce, 98–99
Tunisian Chickpea
Soup, 72–73
Green beans
air crisping charts, 236, 239
Easy Chicken Cordon
Bleu with Green
Beans, 102–103
steam chart, 242
Warm Potato and Green Bean
Salad with Tuna, 164–165
Grits
Blackened Salmon with
Creamy Grits,
177–178
Gruyère cheese
Beefy Onion Soup with Cheese
Croutons, 122–123
Easy Chicken Cordon
Bleu with Green
Beans, 102–103
Penne with Mushrooms and
Gruyère, 46–47
Savory Custards with Bacon
and Cheese, 28–29

H
Habanero chiles
Jerk Pork, 141–142
Ham
Easy Chicken Cordon
Bleu with Green
Beans, 102–103
Egg Muffin Breakfast
Sandwich, 30–31
Simple Potato Gratin with
Ham and Peas, 135–136

J
Jalapeño peppers
Chicken and Spinach
Quesadillas, 86–87
Chicken Chili Verde with
Nachos, 104–105
Chicken Fajitas with
Refritos, 82–83
Masoor Dal (Indian Red
Lentils), 60–61
Potato-Crusted Cod with
Succotash, 188–189
Shakshuka, 38–39
Shrimp and Sausage
Gumbo, 182–183
"Spanish" Rice and
Beans, 54–55
Tilapia Veracruz, 184–185
Vegetable Korma, 58–59

K
Kale
air crisping charts, 236, 239
Italian Wedding Soup with
Turkey Sausage,
108–109
steam chart, 242
Kitchen equipment, 7

L
Lemons
Blueberry Cream
Tart, 208–210
Bow Tie Pasta with Shrimp
and Arugula, 160–161

Lemons *(continued)*

  Chicken Shawarma
    with Garlic-Yogurt
    Sauce, 98–99
  Lemon Bars, 204–206
  Mediterranean White Bean
    Salad, 50–51
  Mixed Berry Crisp, 196–197
  Spiced Poached Pears,
    214–215
  Tunisian Chickpea
    Soup, 72–73
Lentils
  Masoor Dal (Indian Red
    Lentils), 60–61
  pressure cooking chart, 232
Lettuce
  Chicken Caesar Salad, 90–92
Lima beans
  Potato-Crusted Cod with
    Succotash, 188–189
  pressure cooking chart, 232
Limes
  Beef Satay with Peanut
    Sauce, 145–147
  Carnitas, 118–119
  Chicken Chili Verde with
    Nachos, 104–105
  Thai Fish Curry, 175–176

M

Meats, 12. *See also specific*
  air crisping charts,
    237–238, 240–241
  cooking charts, 234–235
  dehydrating chart, 243
Milk. *See also* Cream
  Artichoke and Red Pepper
    Frittata, 32–33
  Blackened Salmon with
    Creamy Grits,
    177–178
  Breakfast Clafoutis, 42–43
  Cheesy Tuna Noodle
    Casserole, 186–187
  Creamy Steel-Cut Oats with
    Toasted Almonds, 40–41
  French Cinnamon
    Toast, 26–27
  Lax Pudding, 162–163

Meatloaf and Mashed
  Potatoes, 139–140
Mocha Pots de Crème, 213
Penne with Mushrooms and
  Gruyère, 46–47
Sausage-Mushroom
  Strata, 34–35
Southwestern Shepherd's Pie,
  130–131
Tex-Mex Breakfast Casserole,
  22–23
Mint
  Mediterranean White Bean
    Salad, 50–51
Monterey Jack cheese
  Chicken and Spinach
    Quesadillas,
    86–87
  Chicken Chili Verde with
    Nachos, 104–105
  Chorizo-Stuffed Peppers,
    128–129
Mozzarella cheese
  Artichoke and Red Pepper
    Frittata, 32–33
  Easy Eggplant Parmesan,
    48–49
  Mushroom Lasagna, 68–69
  Sausage and Pepper Calzones,
    132–134
Mushrooms
  air crisping charts, 236, 239
  Braised Chicken Thighs
    with Mushrooms and
    Artichokes, 84–85
  Chicken Stroganoff, 110–111
  Coq au Vin, 106–107
  dehydrating chart, 243
  Mushroom Lasagna, 68–69
  Penne with Mushrooms and
    Gruyère, 46–47
  Pork Lo Mein with Vegetables,
    137–138
  Risotto with Chard,
    Caramelized Onions, and
    Mushrooms, 66–67
  Roasted Vegetable Stock, 219
  Sausage-Mushroom
    Strata, 34–35
  Sautéed Mushrooms, 220–221

Shrimp and Vegetable Egg
  Rolls, 168–170
Teriyaki Salmon and
  Vegetables,
  166–167

N

Ninja® Foodi™
  accessories, 5–7
  air crisping charts, 236–242
  benefits of, 7–8
  Crisping Lid and functions, 4
  dehydrating chart, 243
  frequently asked
    questions, 13–14
  parts, 6
  pressure cooking
    charts, 231–235
  Pressure Lid and
    functions, 2–3
  safety, 7
  steam chart, 242
  TenderCrisp™ Technology, 2, 7
Nuts
  Caramel-Pecan Brownies,
    211–212
  Creamy Steel-Cut Oats with
    Toasted Almonds, 40–41
  Kung Pao Tofu and
    Peppers, 64–65
  Mixed Berry Crisp, 196–197
  Quinoa Pilaf with Smoked
    Trout and Corn, 190–191
  Thai Fish Curry, 175–176
  Turkey and Wild Rice
    Salad, 112–113
  Vegetable Korma, 58–59

O

Oats
  Creamy Steel-Cut Oats with
    Toasted Almonds, 40–41
  Mixed Berry Crisp, 196–197
  pressure cooking chart, 231
Olives
  Tilapia Veracruz, 184–185
  Warm Potato and Green Bean
    Salad with Tuna, 164–165
Onions. *See also* Scallions
  Artichoke and Red Pepper
    Frittata, 32–33

Barbecue Sauce, 226

Beef Satay with Peanut Sauce, 145–147

Beefy Onion Soup with Cheese Croutons, 122–123

Braised Chicken Thighs with Mushrooms and Artichokes, 84–85

Cajun Chicken and Dumplings, 88–89

Caramelized Onions, 222

Carbonnade Flamande, 152–153

Carnitas, 118–119

Cheesy Tuna Noodle Casserole, 186–187

Chicken and Spinach Quesadillas, 86–87

Chicken Chili Verde with Nachos, 104–105

Chicken Fajitas with Refritos, 82–83

Chicken Stroganoff, 110–111

Chicken Tikka Masala with Rice, 93–95

Chorizo-Stuffed Peppers, 128–129

Clam Chowder with Parmesan Crackers, 171–172

Coq au Vin, 106–107

Crab and Roasted Asparagus Risotto, 173–174

Italian Wedding Soup with Turkey Sausage, 108–109

Kielbasa with Braised Cabbage and Noodles, 124–125

Marinara Sauce, 228–229

Masoor Dal (Indian Red Lentils), 60–61

Meatloaf and Mashed Potatoes, 139–140

Minestrone with Garlic Cheese Toasts and Pesto, 56–57

Pork Ragu with Penne, 126–127

Potato-Crusted Cod with Succotash, 188–189

Quick Cassoulet, 78–79

Risotto with Chard, Caramelized Onions, and Mushrooms, 66–67

Roasted Red Pepper Soup and Grilled Cheese, 70–71

Roasted Vegetable Stock, 219

Salmon Cakes, 179–181

Savory Custards with Bacon and Cheese, 28–29

Shakshuka, 38–39

Shrimp and Sausage Gumbo, 182–183

Sloppy Joes, 156–157

Southwestern Shepherd's Pie, 130–131

"Spanish" Rice and Beans, 54–55

Sunday Pot Roast and Biscuits, 120–121

Thai Fish Curry, 175–176

Tilapia Veracruz, 184–185

Trout Florentine, 192–193

Tunisian Chickpea Soup, 72–73

Vegetable Korma, 58–59

Oranges

Carnitas, 118–119

P

Pantry staples, 10–11

Parmesan cheese

Artichoke and Red Pepper Frittata, 32–33

Cajun Twice-Baked Potatoes, 52–53

Chicken and Spinach Quesadillas, 86–87

Chicken Caesar Salad, 90–92

Clam Chowder with Parmesan Crackers, 171–172

Crab and Roasted Asparagus Risotto, 173–174

Creamy Pasta Primavera, 62–63

Easy Chicken Cordon Bleu with Green Beans, 102–103

Easy Eggplant Parmesan, 48–49

Italian Wedding Soup with Turkey Sausage, 108–109

Minestrone with Garlic Cheese Toasts and Pesto, 56–57

Mushroom Lasagna, 68–69

Penne with Mushrooms and Gruyère, 46–47

Pork Ragu with Penne, 126–127

Risotto with Chard, Caramelized Onions, and Mushrooms, 66–67

Simple Potato Gratin with Ham and Peas, 135–136

Parsley

Carbonnade Flamande, 152–153

Chicken Shawarma with Garlic-Yogurt Sauce, 98–99

Chicken Stroganoff, 110–111

Clam Chowder with Parmesan Crackers, 171–172

Creamy Pasta Primavera, 62–63

Meatloaf and Mashed Potatoes, 139–140

Mediterranean White Bean Salad, 50–51

Penne with Mushrooms and Gruyère, 46–47

Potato-Crusted Cod with Succotash, 188–189

Shakshuka, 38–39

Tilapia Veracruz, 184–185

Trout Florentine, 192–193

Warm Potato and Green Bean Salad with Tuna, 164–165

Pasta

Bow Tie Pasta with Shrimp and Arugula, 160–161

Creamy Pasta Primavera, 62–63

Minestrone with Garlic Cheese Toasts and Pesto, 56–57

Mushroom Lasagna, 68–69

Penne with Mushrooms and Gruyère, 46–47

Pork Ragu with Penne, 126–127

Peaches

Peach Cobbler, 198–199

Peanut butter

Beef Satay with Peanut Sauce, 145–147

Pears

Spiced Poached Pears, 214–215

Peas

Cajun Chicken and Dumplings, 88–89

Cheesy Tuna Noodle Casserole, 186–187

Peas *(continued)*

    Japanese Pork Cutlets
      (Tonkatsu) with
      Ramen, 143–144

    Pork Lo Mein with Vegetables,
      137–138

    Simple Potato Gratin with
      Ham and Peas, 135–136

    steam chart, 242

    Tandoori Chicken and
      Coconut Rice, 96–97

    Teriyaki Salmon and
      Vegetables,
      166–167

    Vegetable Korma, 58–59

Pepper Jack cheese

    Tex-Mex Breakfast Casserole,
      22–23

Pesto

    Minestrone with Garlic Cheese
      Toasts and Pesto, 56–57

Piecrust

    Blueberry Cream
      Tart, 208–210

    Tarte Tatin, 207

Pizza dough

    Monkey Bread, 20–21

    Sausage and Pepper Calzones,
      132–134

Poblano chiles

    Chicken Chili Verde with
      Nachos, 104–105

    Southwestern Shepherd's
      Pie, 130–131

Pork. *See also* Bacon;
    Ham; Sausage

    air crisping charts,
      237–248, 240–241

    Carnitas, 118–119

    dehydrating chart, 243

    Deviled Short Ribs with
      Noodles, 150–151

    Honey-Mustard Spare
      Ribs, 116–117

    Japanese Pork Cutlets
      (Tonkatsu) with
      Ramen, 143–144

    Jerk Pork, 141–142

    Pork Lo Mein with Vegetables,
      137–138

    Pork Ragu with Penne,
      126–127

Pork Tenderloin with
    Peppers and Roasted
    Potatoes, 154–155

    pressure cooking chart, 235

Potatoes. *See also* Sweet
    potatoes

    air crisping charts, 236, 239

    Cajun Twice-Baked
      Potatoes, 52–53

    Clam Chowder with Parmesan
      Crackers, 171–172

    Lax Pudding, 162–163

    Meatloaf and Mashed
      Potatoes, 139–140

    Pork Tenderloin with
      Peppers and Roasted
      Potatoes, 154–155

    Simple Potato Gratin with
      Ham and Peas, 135–136

    Spicy Air-Crisped Chicken and
      Potatoes, 80–81

    Sunday Pot Roast and
      Biscuits, 120–121

    Vegetable Korma, 58–59

    Warm Potato and Green Bean
      Salad with Tuna, 164–165

Poultry, 12. *See also*
    Chicken; Turkey

    air crisping charts, 237, 240

    cooking charts, 234–235

Pressure cooking, 3

Pressure function, 2, 231–235

Pressure Lid, 2, 6

Puff pastry

    Apple Turnovers, 36–37

Q

Quinoa

    Quinoa Pilaf with Smoked
      Trout and Corn, 190–191

R

Ramen noodles

    Japanese Pork Cutlets
      (Tonkatsu) with
      Ramen, 143–144

    Pork Lo Mein with Vegetables,
      137–138

Recipes

    about, 14–16

    combining, 9

Refrigerator staples, 11

Reversible Rack, 5, 6

Rice

    Chicken Tikka Masala with
      Rice, 93–95

    Chorizo-Stuffed Peppers,
      128–129

    Crab and Roasted Asparagus
      Risotto, 173–174

    Jerk Pork, 141–142

    pressure cooking
      chart, 231–232

    Risotto with Chard,
      Caramelized Onions, and
      Mushrooms, 66–67

    Shrimp and Sausage
      Gumbo, 182–183

    "Spanish" Rice and
      Beans, 54–55

    Tandoori Chicken and
      Coconut Rice, 96–97

    Turkey and Wild Rice
      Salad, 112–113

Ricotta cheese

    Mushroom Lasagna, 68–69

Roasted red peppers

    Cajun Twice-Baked
      Potatoes, 52–53

    Roasted Red Pepper Soup and
      Grilled Cheese, 70–71

    Warm Potato and Green Bean
      Salad with Tuna, 164–165

S

Safety, 7

Salads

    Chicken Caesar Salad, 90–92

    Mediterranean White Bean
      Salad, 50–51

    Turkey and Wild Rice
      Salad, 112–113

    Warm Potato and Green Bean
      Salad with Tuna, 164–165

Salmon

    air crisping charts, 238, 241

    Blackened Salmon with
      Creamy Grits,
      177–178

    dehydrating chart, 243

Lax Pudding, 162–163
Salmon Cakes, 179–181
Teriyaki Salmon and
   Vegetables,
   166–167
Sauces
   Barbecue Sauce, 226
   Marinara Sauce, 228
   Mustard Sauce, 227
   Teriyaki Sauce, 225
Sausage
   Chorizo-Stuffed Peppers,
      128–129
   Italian Wedding Soup with
      Turkey Sausage, 108
   Kielbasa with Braised Cabbage
      and Noodles, 124–125
   Pork Ragu with Penne,
      126–127
   Quick Cassoulet, 78–79
   Sausage and Pepper Calzones,
      132–134
   Sausage-Mushroom
      Strata, 34–35
   Scotch Eggs, 24–25
   Shrimp and Sausage
      Gumbo, 182–183
Scallions
   Cajun Twice-Baked
      Potatoes, 52–53
   Japanese Pork Cutlets
      (Tonkatsu) with
      Ramen, 143–144
   Kung Pao Tofu and
      Peppers, 64–65
   Mediterranean White Bean
      Salad, 50–51
   Pork Lo Mein with Vegetables,
      137–138
   Quinoa Pilaf with Smoked
      Trout and Corn, 190–191
   Shrimp and Sausage
      Gumbo, 182–183
   Shrimp and Vegetable Egg
      Rolls, 168–170
   Simple Potato Gratin with
      Ham and Peas, 135–136
   Teriyaki Salmon and
      Vegetables,
      166–167

Seafood, 12–13. *See also* Fish
   air crisping charts, 238, 241
   Bow Tie Pasta with Shrimp
      and Arugula, 160–161
   Clam Chowder with Parmesan
      Crackers, 171–172
   Crab and Roasted Asparagus
      Risotto, 173–174
   Shrimp and Sausage
      Gumbo, 182–183
   Shrimp and Vegetable Egg
      Rolls, 168–170
Sear/Sauté function, 3
Seasoning mixes
   Cajun Seasoning Mix, 223
   Mexican/Southwestern
      Seasoning Mix, 224
Shrimp
   air crisping charts, 238, 241
   Bow Tie Pasta with Shrimp
      and Arugula, 160–161
   Shrimp and Sausage
      Gumbo, 182–183
   Shrimp and Vegetable Egg
      Rolls, 168–170
Slow Cook function, 3
Soups and stews
   Beefy Onion Soup with Cheese
      Croutons, 122–123
   Clam Chowder with Parmesan
      Crackers, 171–172
   Italian Wedding Soup with
      Turkey Sausage,
      108–109
   Minestrone with Garlic Cheese
      Toasts and Pesto, 56–57
   Roasted Red Pepper Soup and
      Grilled Cheese, 70–71
   Shrimp and Sausage
      Gumbo, 182–183
   Tunisian Chickpea
      Soup, 72–73
Sour cream
   Cajun Twice-Baked
      Potatoes, 52–53
   Chicken Stroganoff, 110–111
   Chocolate Marble Cheesecake,
      200–201
   Penne with Mushrooms and
      Gruyère, 46–47
Spinach
   Chicken and Spinach
      Quesadillas, 86–87
   steam chart, 242

Thai Fish Curry, 175–176
Trout Florentine, 192–193
Steam function, 2–3, 242
Stocks
   Chicken Stock, 218
   Roasted Vegetable Stock, 219
Sweet potatoes
   Cajun Roasted Turkey
      Breast with Sweet
      Potatoes, 100–101
   steam chart, 242

T
TenderCrisp™ Technology, 2, 7
Tofu
   Kung Pao Tofu and
      Peppers, 64–65
Tomatillos
   Chicken Chili Verde with
      Nachos, 104–105
Tomatoes
   Barbecue Sauce, 226
   Chicken Shawarma
      with Garlic-Yogurt
      Sauce, 98–99
   Chicken Tikka Masala with
      Rice, 93–95
   Chorizo-Stuffed Peppers,
      128–129
   Creamy Pasta Primavera,
      62–63
   dehydrating chart, 243
   Marinara Sauce, 228–229
   Masoor Dal (Indian Red
      Lentils), 60–61
   Mediterranean White Bean
      Salad, 50–51
   Minestrone with Garlic Cheese
      Toasts and Pesto, 56–57
   Pork Ragu with Penne,
      126–127
   Potato-Crusted Cod with
      Succotash, 188–189
   Quinoa Pilaf with Smoked
      Trout and Corn, 190–191
   Shakshuka, 38–39
   Southwestern Shepherd's
      Pie, 130–131
   Thai Fish Curry, 175–176
   Tilapia Veracruz, 184–185
   Vegetable Korma, 58–59

Tortilla chips
    Chicken Chili Verde with
        Nachos, 104–105
    Tex-Mex Breakfast Casserole,
        22–23
Trout
    Quinoa Pilaf with Smoked
        Trout and Corn, 190–191
    Trout Florentine, 192–193
Tuna
    Cheesy Tuna Noodle
        Casserole, 186–187
    Warm Potato and Green Bean
        Salad with Tuna, 164–165
Turkey
    Cajun Roasted Turkey
        Breast with Sweet
        Potatoes, 100–101
    Italian Wedding Soup with
        Turkey Sausage,
        108–109
    pressure cooking chart, 235
    Turkey and Wild Rice
        Salad, 112–113

U

Under 60 minutes
    Apple Turnovers, 36–37
    Blackened Salmon with
        Creamy Grits,
        177–178
    Blueberry Cream
        Tart, 208–210
    Braised Chicken Thighs
        with Mushrooms and
        Artichokes, 84–85
    Breakfast Clafoutis, 42–43
    Cajun Chicken and
        Dumplings, 88–89
    Cajun Twice-Baked
        Potatoes, 52–53
    Carnitas, 118–119
    Chicken and Spinach
        Quesadillas,
        86–87
    Chicken Caesar Salad, 90–92
    Chicken Chili Verde with
        Nachos, 104–105
    Chicken Fajitas with
        Refritos, 82–83

Chicken Tikka Masala with
    Rice, 93–95
Chorizo-Stuffed Peppers,
    128–129
Clam Chowder with Parmesan
    Crackers, 171–172
Crab and Roasted Asparagus
    Risotto, 173–174
Easy Eggplant Parmesan,
    48–49
Honey-Mustard Spare
    Ribs, 116–117
Italian Wedding Soup with
    Turkey Sausage,
    108–109
Jerk Pork, 141–142
Lax Pudding, 162–163
Meatloaf and Mashed
    Potatoes, 139–140
Mixed Berry Crisp, 196–197
Mushroom Lasagna, 68–69
Quick Cassoulet, 78–79
Salmon Cakes, 179–181
Sausage and Pepper Calzones,
    132–134
Sausage-Mushroom
    Strata, 34–35
Scotch Eggs, 24–25
Shrimp and Sausage
    Gumbo, 182–183
Shrimp and Vegetable Egg
    Rolls, 168–170
Tandoori Chicken and
    Coconut Rice, 96–97
Tex-Mex Breakfast Casserole,
    22–23
Tunisian Chickpea
    Soup, 72–73

V

Vegan/vegan option
    Cajun Seasoning Mix, 223
    Kung Pao Tofu and
        Peppers, 64–65
    Marinara Sauce, 228–229
    Masoor Dal (Indian Red
        Lentils), 60–61
    Mediterranean White Bean
        Salad, 50–51
    Mexican/Southwestern
        Seasoning Mix, 224

Roasted Vegetable Stock, 219
Sautéed Mushrooms, 220–221
"Spanish" Rice and
    Beans, 54–55
Spiced Poached Pears,
    214–215
Tunisian Chickpea
    Soup, 72–73
Vegetable Korma, 58–59
Vegetarian
    Apple Turnovers, 36–37
    Barbecue Sauce, 226
    Blueberry Cream
        Tart, 208–210
    Breakfast Clafoutis, 42–43
    Cajun Seasoning Mix, 223
    Cajun Twice-Baked
        Potatoes, 52–53
    Caramelized Onions, 222
    Caramel-Pecan Brownies,
        211–212
    Chocolate Marble Cheesecake,
        200–201
    Creamy Pasta Primavera,
        62–63
    Creamy Steel-Cut Oats with
        Toasted Almonds, 40–41
    Crème Brûlée, 202–203
    Easy Eggplant Parmesan,
        48–49
    French Cinnamon
        Toast, 26–27
    Lemon Bars, 204–206
    Masoor Dal (Indian Red
        Lentils), 60–61
    Mediterranean White Bean
        Salad, 50–51
    Mexican/Southwestern
        Seasoning Mix, 224
    Minestrone with Garlic Cheese
        Toasts and Pesto, 56–57
    Mixed Berry Crisp, 196–197
    Mocha Pots de Crème, 213
    Monkey Bread, 20–21
    Mushroom Lasagna, 68–69
    Peach Cobbler, 198–199
    Penne with Mushrooms and
        Gruyère, 46–47
    Risotto with Chard,
        Caramelized Onions, and
        Mushrooms, 66–67

Roasted Red Pepper Soup and Grilled Cheese, 70–71
Roasted Vegetable Stock, 219
Sautéed Mushrooms, 220–221
Shakshuka, 38–39
"Spanish" Rice and Beans, 54–55
Spiced Poached Pears, 214–215
Tarte Tatin, 207
Teriyaki Sauce, 225
Tex-Mex Breakfast Casserole, 22–23
Tunisian Chickpea Soup, 72–73
Vegetable Korma, 58–59

Y

Yogurt. *See also* Greek yogurt
Chicken Tikka Masala with Rice, 93–95
Tandoori Chicken and Coconut Rice, 96–97

Z

Zucchini
air crisping charts, 237, 240
Minestrone with Garlic Cheese Toasts and Pesto, 56–57
steam chart, 242
Thai Fish Curry, 175–176

ACKNOWLEDGMENTS

Thanks to Talia Platz and Kim Suarez from Callisto Media, who provided me with the opportunity to write this book, and especially to Mary Cassells, who checked all my recipes and corrected my errors.

Thanks to Kenzie Swanhart and Sam Ferguson at Ninja, who answered my many questions with patience.

Finally, thanks to Caitlin, Zach, and Sean for trying my recipes without complaining and Dave for helping with my kitchen experiments—and cleaning up after them.

ABOUT THE AUTHOR

 **Janet A. Zimmerman** is the author of four previous cookbooks. For almost 20 years, she has taught culinary classes and written about food. She lives in Atlanta with her partner Dave, and they have an ever-expanding collection of kitchen equipment

Also available in the Official
Ninja® Foodi™ Companion Book Series